Creamy & Crunchy

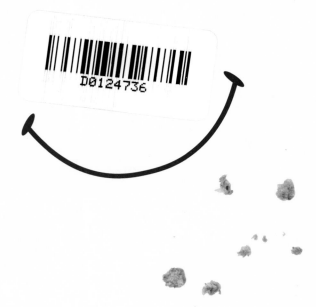

ARTS AND TRADITIONS OF THE TABLE

PERSPECTIVES ON CULINARY HISTORY

JON KRAMPNER

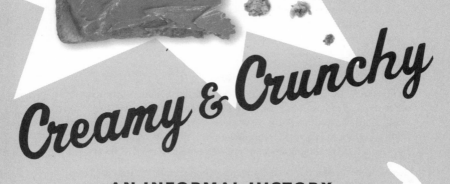

Creamy & Crunchy

AN INFORMAL HISTORY OF PEANUT BUTTER, THE ALL-AMERICAN FOOD

COLUMBIA UNIVERSITY PRESS / NEW YORK

Columbia University Press
Publishers Since 1893
New York Chichester, West Sussex
cup.columbia.edu

Library of Congress Cataloging-in-Publication Data
Krampner, Jon, 1952–
Creamy and crunchy : an informal history of peanut butter, the all-American food / Jon Krampner.
p. cm.—(Arts and traditions of the table)
Includes bibliographical references and index.
ISBN 978-0-231-16232-6 (cloth : alk. paper)
ISBN 978-0-231-53093-4 (e-book)
1. Peanut butter—United States—History. I. Title.
TX803.P35K73 2013
641.3'56596—dc23 2012008529

Columbia University Press books are printed on permanent and durable acid-free paper.

This book is printed on paper with recycled content.
Printed in the United States of America

c 10 9 8 7 6 5 4 3 2 1

Cover image: Alamy Cover design: Lisa Hamm

To the Center for Constitutional Rights,

whose dedication to truth, justice, and the American way

ain't just peanuts

And to Veronica,

a friend of animals and the environment

Several workmen are opening their lunches at a construction site.

One cries out, "Oh, no! Peanut butter and jelly sandwiches again. I hate peanut butter and jelly sandwiches!"

Another worker says, "Why don't you ask your wife to fix you something else?"

"You don't understand," the worker replies. "I make my own lunch."

★ ★ ★ ★ ★

CONTENTS

PREFACE

By temperament and inclination, I'm a biographer. My first two books were biographies of people; this is the biography of a product.

Live-television-drama producer Fred Coe and postwar Broadway star Kim Stanley, the heroes of those first two books, were tormented geniuses who lapsed into obscurity because of drinking problems. I wanted to write about something more cheerful this time. Peanut butter may make you fat, but it won't give you cirrhosis of the liver.

Although my memory may be playing tricks with me, I remember eating only two foods as a child: peanut butter and hamburgers. When I went away to college, I stopped eating peanut butter to see what else the world held gastronomically. In the early 1980s, though, after a bad romance ended, I self-medicated with large jars of Skippy. My weight climbed to the point that it took a good nutritionist and visits to the gym to get it back under control. I gave up peanut butter again, and it wasn't until I began working on this book that I resumed eating it on a regular basis (purely for research purposes, you understand).

I thought that writing a history of peanut butter in the manner of Mark Kurlansky's *Cod*, John McPhee's *Oranges*, or Steve Almond's *Candyfreak* would be less research intensive than biography. Boy, was I wrong.

In addition to delving into the production and history of peanut butter, I had to learn about agriculture, botany, nutrition, geology, organic chemistry, food contamination, allergies, patents and trademarks, antitrust law, the history of the American South, advertising, industrial design, statistics, and the federal rule-making process. And I still had to do biographical profiles anyway.

A few recommendations for further research: While corporations in general are reluctant to yield their secrets, Peter Pan and its various owners easily proved the most opaque, even after I hired someone I consider the Willie Mays of business researchers to help me look into it. More writing about Peter Pan, especially its early days, remains to be done. Also, historians of peanut butter have yet to settle whether St. Louis food manufacturer George Bayle, in 1894 or earlier, was making peanut butter before John Harvey Kellogg, who many regard as the founding father of peanut butter.

Although it's not just for children, peanut butter is a staple of childhood, and it's a comfort food. In times of economic distress and emotional uncertainty (like the present), Americans turn to it. But remarkably, given its widespread popularity, there hasn't been a book about peanut butter on the burgeoning shelf of pop food histories. Now there is.

ACKNOWLEDGMENTS

Herb Dow got me started, and Stanley Pittman, to whom Herb introduced me, was the best possible guide to peanut country.

At Columbia University Press, Jennifer Crewe acquired the manuscript and ably edited it, while Anne McCoy was (and is) the congenial managing editor. Asya Graf and Kathryn Schell assisted Jennifer and me, and Irene Pavitt turned her eagle eye on the manuscript. Thanks also to publicist Peter Barrett and art director Julia Kushnirsky, and to John Donohue at Westchester Publishing Services.

At the various peanut industry trade organizations, thanks to Don Koehler of the Georgia Peanut Commission; Patrick Archer, Cindy Stickles, and Louise McKerchar of the American Peanut Council; Leslie Wagner of the Southern Peanut Growers; John Powell of the American Peanut Shellers Association; and Pat Kearney of the Peanut Institute.

Andrew F. Smith and Noel Riley Fitch served as my mentors. Anthony Prillaman of the National Agricultural Statistics Service fielded my endless e-mails as I tried to make sense of peanut-butter statistics.

Frank Delfino is a genuine original and living museum of Skippy peanut butter. Rick Rosefield provided several helpful interviews about the peanut butter his grandfather developed. I also received help with the Skippy story from Larry Shearon, Carl "Rocky" Bleier, Thomas Fuller, Bert Gannon, James Hirchak, George Mackin, and Earl Spady.

Help with the Jif story came from Paul Kiely, Neil Kreisberg, William Covington, John Gretz, David Guin, Rita Keys, Don Taylor, William T. Young Jr., Ted Woehrle, Hunter Yager, and Edward Meyer.

Background on Deaf Smith and the New Mexico peanut and peanut butter industries came from the late Frank Ford, and from Boyd Foster, George Speck, Herb Marchman, Jimmy Shearer, James Glueck, and Verla Brown.

Lavina Wilson helped me with the story of Beech-Nut peanut butter.

The honor roll of librarians includes Duncan McCluskey at the Coastal Plain Experiment Station in Tifton, Georgia; Karen Weis of the National Agricultural Library in Beltsville, Maryland; Karin Lundstrom of the Alameda Free Library; Jean E. Meeh Gosebrink of the special collections department of the St. Louis Public Library; Sheryn Morris and Judy Ostrander of the Los Angeles Public Library; Denise Shanks of the Kentucky Room at the Lexington Public Library; Chris Tonjes of the District of Columbia Public Library; Diane Wagner and Nicole LaFlamme of the Procter & Gamble Corporate Archives and Heritage Center; Edie Carmichael of the Wilson Historical Room of the Portsmouth, Virginia, Public Library; Mary Braswell at the *Albany Herald* (Albany, Ga.); George Livingston of the Willard Memorial Library in Battle Creek, Michigan; Holly Fiedler and Sally Rappa of the Canojaharie, New York, Public Library; Michelle Carver at the Center for Research Libraries; and Helene Mochedlover of the Los Angeles Public Library (ret.).

Thanks to Walt Albritton for his tour of Tara Foods in Albany, Georgia, and to Gregg Grimsley for his tour of the Birdsong shelling plant in Sylvester, Georgia.

Gregg Brandow allowed me to hitchhike on his faculty borrowing privileges. Ruth Elwell provided the index.

My research staff included Teri Jurgens Lefever and Veldean Petri in Cripple Creek, Colorado, and Matthew Gilmore of the Department of Consumer and Regulatory Affairs for the District of Columbia.

In the groves of academe, thanks to Chris Craney, Dan Gorbet, Richard Hazlett, Donald Prothero, and Barry Tillman. Thanks also to Janet Miller of the Hinsdale, Illinois, Historical Society, and Jamie Millard of the Lexington History Museum.

Helpful interviews were provided by John Beasley, Suzanne Corbett, Frank Ford, Boyd Foster, Brian Giunta, Ned Groth, Ben Houston, the late

Dave Hovet, Suzanne Junod, Paul Kiely, Jeff Koeze, Gary List, Charles Perry, Martha Pierce, Jeffery Pittman, Roy Pittman, Stoy Proctor, Tim Sanders, Dr. Scott Sicherer, Christopher Weiss, Wendell Williams, Mary Ellen Young of Information Resources Inc. (IRI), and Lee Zalben.

Christie Haynes labored mightily to get me a photo of the peanut statue.

Keith Briggman helped me grow my own peanut patch.

Karl Schneider of the National Agricultural Library of the U.S. Department of Agriculture provided the book's epigraph.

I also want to thank Michael Larsen and Elizabeth Pomada, even though things didn't work out exactly as we expected.

Chapter readers included Ann (Breitkopf) Webb and Diane (DeeDee) Taub (both of whom ate peanut butter on hike day at Camp Farrington), Stanley Pittman, Dan Gorbet, Chris Craney, Tim Sanders, Gary List, Barry Levenson and his law students at the University of Wisconsin, Scott Sicherer, Ned Groth, Chris Weiss, Mark and Mardi Manary, Andrew F. Smith, Tim Sanders, Gary List, Frank Delfino, Larry Shearon, Paul Kiely, Hunter Yager, Boyd Foster, George Speck, Noel Riley Fitch, Herb Dow, and Bill Marler.

Anita Fore and Michael Gross of the Authors Guild provided solid advice on contract negotiations. Jonathan Kirsch provided helpful legal advice. Carol Eisner was the publicist with the mostest.

The genial Mark Glubke helped me overcome a ferocious case of writer's block.

Iris Berl gets her standing credit.

David Drum provided moral support during advisory sessions at Señor Fish.

Finally, thanks to Dick Davis, who kept asking me if I'd finished it already and for whom I didn't finish it on time.

Creamy & Crunchy

PEANUTS 101

About 80 million years ago, the Coastal Plain began to form along the southeastern and Gulf coasts of what's now the United States. The sandy loam it left behind, along with the warm southern climate, would prove ideal for growing peanuts.

Sandy loam is loose and soft; it looks a little like beach sand but is more nutritious for plants and is found as far inland as the Fall Line, a twenty-mile-wide zone separating the soft sediments of the Coastal Plain from the denser clay soils of the Appalachian foothills. The Fall Line got its name because the junction of Coastal Plain sediments with the crystalline rocks of the foothills gave rise to rapids and waterfalls, as streams unable to erode Piedmont rock easily cut away the softer coastal sediments. In Georgia, the Fall Line runs through Columbus, Macon, Milledgeville, and Augusta, all of which became commercial centers in the nineteenth century because of their position at the upstream limit of navigation.[1]

In the clays of the Piedmont, shoots from peanut plants that burrow underground to become peanuts find it hard to penetrate the soil. Even if they're successful, peanuts break off at the stem when harvesters try to pull them from the ground. Just as peanuts aren't adapted to clay soils, they can't tolerate excessively sandy soils either, and in Florida, few peanuts are grown south of the Panhandle.

But for all the importance of peanuts to American foodways in general and peanut butter in particular, they aren't native to the United States. They originated in South America and arrived here obliquely.

The scientific name of the peanut is *Arachis hypogaea*, bestowed by eighteenth-century Swedish botanist Carl Linnaeus based on the Greek *Arachis* (weed) and *hypogaea* (underground chamber). As inelegant as it may sound, the Latin name for peanut means "weed whose fruit grows underground." The genus *Arachis* consists of about seventy species of annual and perennial flowering plants in the pea family, with the peanut the most prominent.

Despite their name, peanuts aren't nuts. They're legumes, more closely related botanically to peas, beans, clover, and alfalfa than to walnuts and almonds, which have hard shells and grow on trees. "Peanuts are not nuts," an article in *Consumer Bulletin* once noted, "and peanut butter is not butter."[2]

Plants in the genus *Arachis* originated in the Gran Pantanal, the world's largest wetland, occupying between 50,000 and 75,000 square miles in parts of tropical Brazil, Bolivia, and Paraguay. According to Argentine botanist Antonio Krapovickas, cultivated peanuts likely originated in Bolivia,[3] at the base of the Andes or in the Andean foothills; a wide variety of peanut plants are found in this area.

It's difficult to pick an epicenter for the origin of the cultivated peanut with any precision, although a good candidate might be Bolivia's Amboro National Park, where three different ecosystems intersect: the foothills of the Andes, the northern expanse of the Gran Chaco (the hot, semi-arid lowlands surrounding the Rio de la Plata), and the Amazon Basin. The diversity of uses for peanuts in Bolivia indicates they've been part of the local culture for a long time: they're used in *chichi de mani*, a nonalcoholic drink; soap is produced from them in the province of Santa Cruz de la Sierra; and in the woodland zone of northern Bolivia, natives eat the entire peanut, shell and all, at the stage when the shell is still juicy.[4]

Runners and Virginias, the two most common types of peanuts grown in the United States, are almost identical and have the same botanical name, *Arachis hypogaea hypogaea*. The two other kinds of peanuts grown in the United States, Spanish and Valencia, are from the *fastigiata* branch of the family.

The greatest number of varieties of Spanish peanuts has been found in Paraguay and the adjoining provinces of Brazil, and Krapovickas believes that Spanish peanuts originated in Brazil.[5] They were introduced into the United States in 1871, shipped out of Málaga, Spain,[6] and arrived just in time to find useful employment in the production of peanut butter, which began in the 1890s. In combination with Virginias, Spanish would be the primary peanut used in making peanut butter for more than seventy years.[7] Valencias also originated in Paraguay and central Brazil, and were dispersed later, arriving in the United States via Spain around 1910.[8]

Although Virginia peanuts are similar to runners, they have a slightly different shape and oil chemistry. A point of origin for them in South America has not been determined. The area where the greatest variability of wild Virginias has been found is in Zimbabwe,[9] which is intriguing, as no modern botanist has suggested that any variety of peanut originated in Africa.

How long have peanuts been cultivated? They were found at a 3,800-year-old archaeological site in Peru,[10] and domesticated peanuts are known from Peruvian excavations of 3000 to 2000 B.C.E.,[11] although cultivation probably began much earlier. The Incas used peanuts—food historian Andrew F. Smith notes that by 500 to 100 B.C.E., peanuts were so common on the coast of Peru that archaeologists say some sites from this period look like poorly swept baseball stadiums with peanut shells scattered about.[12]

Although peanut butter got its start in the American Midwest in the 1890s, it has venerable ancestors. Almost 3,000 years ago, South American Indians ground peanuts into a sticky paste.[13] It was not as spreadable as modern peanut butter and was mixed with cocoa. Peanuts have been part of West African cuisine for 500 years, and when writer David Grunwald lived in Sierra Leone in the mid-1960s, his steward ground roasted peanuts with a roller until they achieved a grainy consistency like the filling in peanut butter cups, then mixed in honey and red pepper.[14] And in the American South in 1865 and earlier, shelled and roasted peanuts were chopped, ground, or beaten into a paste in a cloth bag and eaten with salt.[15] During the Civil War, Confederate soldiers dined on "peanut porridge."[16]

In pre-Columbian times, peanuts may have been introduced to the Caribbean by the Arawak Indians of South America; they also moved up the Pacific Coast from Peru to Mexico.[17] Spanish and Portuguese explorers brought peanuts back to Europe in the early sixteenth century,[18] although, even after 500 years, they've never really caught on there; as Smith notes, if a European candy contains a nut, it's most likely an almond,[19] and the most popular nut spread on the Continent is Nutella, made from chocolate and hazelnuts.

Heading westward, the Spanish took peanuts across the Pacific on galleons that regularly sailed between Acapulco and Manila from 1565 to 1815.[20] They were introduced to the Malayan Archipelago in the sixteenth century and reached China by 1608.[21] Heading eastward, the Portuguese carried peanuts from Brazil to Africa and then India in the sixteenth century.[22] (In India, the original name for peanuts was Mozambique beans.) From Africa, peanuts made their way back to the Americas on slave ships landing in the eastern United States in the seventeenth century.

The peanut industry is understandably vague about how its mainstay got here. *USA Peanuts*, a pamphlet published by the American Peanut Council, says, "The peanut made its way . . . to North America on sailing ships in the 1700's."[23] Because the slave trade was under way by the seventeenth century, the euphemism "sailing ships" is a bit jarring, as if its passengers were participating in a regatta rather than being shipped here as human cargo so they and generations of their descendants could work as slaves under conditions of unimaginable brutality.

By the eighteenth century, peanuts were found in temperate regions around the world.

★★★

Like most legumes, peanuts replenish rather than deplete the soil, adding the nitrogen many plants remove. What makes peanuts unusual botanically is the way they reproduce. Cultivated peanuts are annuals, and the peanut, planted two inches underground, is the seed. Out of it grows the peanut plant, whose twinned pairs of gray-green, clamshell-shaped leaves sparkle slightly in the morning sun and fold up against each other at night, as is the custom among legumes. About thirty days after planting, small and delicate flowers appear close to the ground. Yellow with red and

FIGURE 1.1 PEANUT PLANT

Unique in the plant world, the peanut plant flowers aboveground but fruits belowground. It has small yellow flowers and twinned pairs of gray-green leaves that fold up against each other at night and grows best in sandy loam soil. (Courtesy of Wayne P. Armstrong)

orange highlights, like small orchids, they live for a day, then wither and fall off. In their place a shoot develops; called a peg, it turns downward and burrows into the ground. The tip of the peg becomes the peanut (figure 1.1). The only other plant to flower aboveground but fruit below is the bambarra groundnut of West Africa.

Owing to their high oil content, roasted and salted peanuts are about 50 percent fat and provide 585 calories per 100 grams.[24] So long as one doesn't overindulge in peanuts—which can be a challenge—that fat is mostly beneficial: half is monounsaturated and about a third is polyunsaturated. About 15 percent is saturated, though,[25] which is not so good, as saturated fat has been associated with heart disease and some cancers. Peanuts are 26 percent protein, making them popular among vegetarians as a protein substitute for meat, and contain a moderate amount of carbohydrates (just under 20 percent). They're 2 to 3 percent fiber[26] and so are a good source of this nutrient as well. They provide vitamins and minerals such as phosphorus, sodium, potassium, and magnesium, as well as thiamine (B1), niacine (B3), folic acid (B9), and vitamin E.[27] Nutritionally, peanuts are also valuable for what they don't contain: cholesterol.

The two main fatty acids in peanut oil are oleic and linoleic. Linoleic acid, which is polyunsaturated, is important in human nutrition. But it oxidizes, or becomes rancid, ten times more quickly than oleic acid, which is monounsaturated.[28] This is why peanut breeders concentrate on developing high-oleic varieties of peanuts; the peanut butter made from them deteriorates more slowly and has a longer shelf life.

Roasted peanuts rival blackberries and strawberries in their antioxidant content and are richer in antioxidants than apples, carrots, or beets.[29] In particular, peanuts are a significant source of resveratrol, which has been studied for its potential anti-aging effects and associated with reduced cardiovascular disease and reduced cancer risk.

"[The peanut] is a concentrated food: pound for pound, peanuts have more protein, minerals, and vitamins than beef liver, more fat than heavy cream, and more food energy or calories than sugar," the *Encyclopedia Britannica* notes.[30] Not everyone will regard these attributes as virtues, of course.

For all their benefits, peanuts can hold perils for the consumer. There's all that fat, of course, even if much of it is unsaturated. Peanuts can also cause allergic reactions, sometimes severe and even fatal, in a growing percent of the population: as many as 6 of every 1,000 Americans may suffer from peanut allergies.[31] Andrew F. Smith, a historian of food in general and peanuts in particular, advised his daughter not to give peanuts or peanut butter to his grandchildren until they were five years old.[32]

The flavor of roasted peanuts is the flavor of peanut butter, and roasted peanuts have a kind of flavor found in no other food. According to William Cobb and Bobby Johnson of the food science department at North Carolina State University, "The roasted aroma and flavor of peanuts is unique among all foods. Nowhere is this character reproduced, although the chemical makeup of the flavors of potato chips, coffee, and cocoa have been found to be somewhat similar."[33] Roasted peanut flavor is created by the Maillard reaction, a chemical interaction between amino acids and sugars in peanuts when they're roasted.[34] The process is similar to caramelization and is what makes the crust of bread brown, as well as producing the flavors of maple syrup, malt whiskey, roasted meat, and condensed milk.

The peanut heart—which is the germ of the peanut—and skin are bitter. Peanut butters that contain one or both are appreciated by the same kind of people who prefer bittersweet to milk chocolate. Ben Houston managed the now-closed Sessions Company of Enterprise, Alabama, which made peanut butter under various labels. "Some peanut butter companies take the hearts out; some don't," he told me in 2006. "We used to take them out, but we don't now. It does affect the flavor: they're a little more bitter but provide more of a peanutty flavor."[35] Supposedly, they turn rancid more quickly than the rest of the peanut, which is why many major manufacturers remove them.

Peanuts are versatile not only as a food; they have many nonfood uses. The whole peanut can be used to make facial creams, soaps, shampoo, and lamp oil. Peanut oil is used in paints, varnishes, lubricating oils, furniture polishes, insecticides, and even nitroglycerin. Peanut solids are used in textile fiber, and peanut skins in making paper. The shells help make fuel, mucilage, fire logs, cat litter, and wallboard, while the peanut plant can be made into hay or animal feed or used to fertilize the soil.[36]

The best-known nickname for peanuts is "Goobers." That's also the name of the chocolate-covered peanut candy I ate as a boy growing up in Brooklyn's Park Slope in the early 1960s. The word is testimony to the peanut's importance in Africa: from *nguba*, the word for "peanut" in the Kimbundu language of Angola, it is one of the few words in American English with an African derivation. In South Carolina, peanuts are sometimes called pindars or pinders—from another African word, *mpinda*, which means "peanut" in the Kongo language used in Angola, Zaire, and the Congo.[37]

In Latin America and the Caribbean (except for Mexico and northern Central America), peanuts are known as *mani*.[38] The word was spread by Spanish explorers, who ran across it in the Antilles.[39] The word is still current in Spain—in the summer of 2007, when I was traveling there, the only brand of peanut butter I could find was Capitan Mani. *Cacahuete* and *cacahuate*, used in Mexico and Guatemala, are derived from *tlalcacauatl*, a word in Nahuatl (the language of the Aztecs) that means either "chocolate

Nani's Groundnut Stew

Peanuts arrived in the United States aboard slave ships from Africa; this recipe celebrates the heritage of those who unwillingly made the Middle Passage to the Americas.

2 tablespoons peanut or vegetable oil
4 chicken breast halves, cut into pieces, or 1 broiler or fryer chicken, cut into serving pieces
2 cloves garlic, minced
3 tablespoons chopped dried shrimp
1 6-ounce can tomato paste
2 cups water
½ teaspoon cayenne pepper, or to taste
½ teaspoon curry powder
½ teaspoon dried thyme
⅔ cup chunky-style peanut butter

In heavy-bottomed Dutch oven or large iron skillet, heat oil; add chicken, browning on all sides, about 7 minutes.

Remove chicken; pour off and discard all but 2 tablespoons fat.

Add garlic and shrimp; sauté until garlic is golden, about 2 minutes.

Stir in tomato paste and water; cook 1 minute.

Stir in cayenne, curry, and thyme; simmer 5 minutes.

In medium-size bowl, thin peanut butter with a little hot tomato liquid; gradually add to pot, blending well.

Return chicken to oven or skillet; over medium-low heat, simmer until chicken is done and of desired tenderness, about 15 minutes (for white meat) and up to 40 (for dark meat).

This stew can be served with brown rice, broccoli or green beans, carrots, and fried plantain.

★★★

Yield: 4 to 6 servings.

COURTESY OF NANCY J. FAIRLEY, PROFESSOR OF ANTHROPOLOGY, DAVIDSON COLLEGE. IT APPEARED IN *ESSENCE*, FEBRUARY 1991.

bean that grows underground"[40] or "cacao seed from the earth."[41] In Honduras, peanuts are still called *cacao*.

Of the four kinds of peanuts grown in the United States, runners predominate—they're about 80 percent of the U.S. crop,[42] grown mainly in Georgia (where they're 99 percent of the crop),[43] Alabama, northern Florida, Texas, and Oklahoma. They're small (although not as small as Spanish peanuts); a little bland, some would say; and used in most peanut butter. Virginias are about 15 percent of the U.S. crop. They have a distinctive, subtle flavor and are the largest of the four market types of U.S. peanuts. They're sold as in-shell peanuts in supermarkets and baseball stadiums, and used in kung-pao chicken. They're grown mainly in the Carolinas and Virginia, but also in West Texas (figure 1.2).

Although Virginias used to be common in peanut butter, they've been supplanted by runners, and now it's hard to find a peanut butter that uses Virginias. The only ones I know of are the Koeze Company of Grand Rapids, Michigan, which makes the Cream-Nut brand, and the Peanut Shop of Williamsburg, Virginia. With some interruptions, Koeze (pronounced Cousy, like the Boston Celtics basketball great) has been making peanut butter with Virginias since 1925. Why has the company persisted? "If you were buying peanuts in the 1920s, you were buying Virginias," owner Jeff Koeze says. "We just kept doing it because we like them."[44]

Spanish peanuts, once as common in peanut butter as buffalo on the Great Plains, are now only 4 percent of the U.S. peanut crop. They have reddish-brown skins and a high oil content, with a somewhat sweeter taste. Ordinarily sold as canned cocktail peanuts and used in peanut candy, they're mainly grown in West Texas and adjoining parts of Oklahoma. Their former status as ruler of the peanut butter roost was noted by the *Consumers' Research Bulletin* in 1945: "The best peanut butter is considered by the trade to be made from No. 1 Virginia-type peanuts and No. 1 Spanish-type nuts."[45] (Whole peanuts are No. 1s, split kernels are No. 2s, and off-quality peanuts, broken, immature or shriveled, are No. 3s. No. 3s are not considered fit to eat and are crushed to make peanut oil.)

As is the case with Virginias, Spanish peanuts are rarely used today in peanut butter, as runners are less expensive, easier to grow and harvest, and produce higher yields. One brand that still uses them exclusively is the Krema Nut Company of Columbus, Ohio (there are actually two peanut-butter-making Kremas in Columbus, the other being the larger

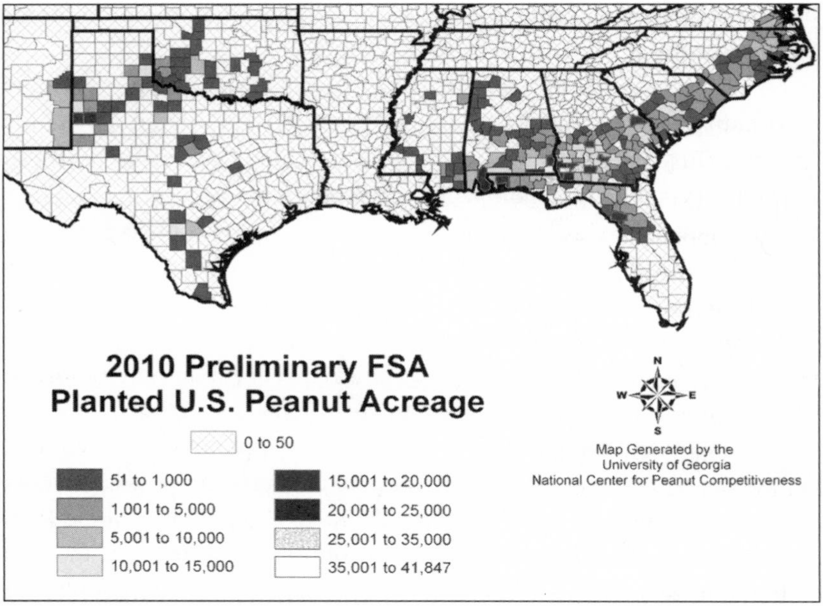

FIGURE 1.2 PEANUT ACREAGE MAP

In the United States, peanuts are grown mainly on the Coastal Plain, whose sandy loam soil ends at the Fall Line, visible as it stretches from Virginia through Georgia. In Georgia, Alabama, and Florida, farmers grow runners almost exclusively; most Virginias are planted in southern Virginia and North Carolina. Spanish peanuts are grown in west Texas and southwestern Oklahoma, while growers in southeastern New Mexico and adjacent Texas counties plant Valencias. (Courtesy of National Center for Peanut Competitiveness, University of Georgia)

and more wholesale-oriented Krema Products). Krema has been making natural peanut butter since 1908 and is the oldest manufacturer of peanut butter in the United States.

The Krema Nut Company is a small operation. When I called Krema one day, I didn't get a boiler-room operative in India, but Brian Giunta, son of owner Mike Giunta. I told him I'd bought a few jars recently, and he said, "Oh, yeah. I just shipped an order out to California."[46] Giunta calls No. 1 Spanish the Maserati of peanuts. Mike Kubicek, executive secretary of the Oklahoma Peanut Commission, feels the same way. "The peanut that's the nuttiest of all is the Spanish," he says. "It was the primary peanut butter peanut for so long because of its flavor."[47]

Valencias are only 1 or 2 percent of all peanuts grown in the United States. With bright red skins, they are the naturally sweetest variety, and the only one to have three or more peanuts to a shell. Because they are limited in supply and require the most care and attention to farm, they are the most expensive type of U.S. peanut, and are mostly grown commercially in southeastern New Mexico and the adjoining counties of the Texas Panhandle. They're either sold in the shell or used in peanut butter, or in the South, sometimes harvested while immature and boiled in brine; the result is a unique and distinctive southern delicacy that is at best an acquired taste. Unlike the other three kinds of American peanuts, Valencias do not have a long-standing pedigree in peanut butter; they've been used only since the 1970s. But they've carved out a niche for themselves: brands that use Valencias include Arrowhead Mills, Sunland, Trader Joe's, Kirkland (Costco's house brand), Once Again, and Joseph's Sugar-Free.[48]

Runners and Virginias grow on low, spreading vines and form peanuts anywhere along the plant's root system, while Valencia and Spanish plants are more upright and bushy with peanuts clustering around the central taproot. For this reason, yields of Spanish and Valencias are lower than runners and Virginias.

Another reason why farmers have turned away from Spanish and Valencia peanuts is their lack of what's known as fresh-seed dormancy. "When runners and Virginias are mature, they can't sprout right away and produce a plant," says Dan Gorbet, a retired peanut breeder from the University of Florida. "With Valencias and Spanish, if you have the right conditions, they will sprout in the ground and you can lose the whole crop if your harvest is delayed. There's much more risk, and that's a factor in the Southeast, where we can have hurricanes come in or weather patterns that delay the harvest."[49]

Although it's now the main peanut in peanut butter, the runner lacks the romance of other peanuts. This may be because its name evokes no sense of place, either in its point of departure (Spanish, Valencia) or arrival (Virginia). Although it has the same botanical name as Virginias (*Arachis hypogaea hypogaea*), it's the underappreciated kid brother—by comparison, Virginias are larger and more elegant. To critics, runners lack the distinctive flavor of other peanuts. Frank Delfino, a former engineer and plant manager for Skippy, says they taste like straw.[50] George Speck, active in the New Mexico Valencia industry, says of the runner, "For some reason, it stays the same level of blandness all the time."[51] Mike Kubicek of the Oklahoma Peanut Commission adds, "The runner peanut is a bland, cardboardy-type peanut—manufacturers can tweak the flavor to their own [formula] by adding sugar or other ingredients. Consumers like to have consistency, with every jar tasting the same. You can do that with runners. With Spanish, the flavor may change depending on the maturity of the crop and the amount of oil, because the flavor comes from roasting the oil. If you did blindfolded taste tests around the United States, the runner would be last."[52]

But peanut breeders such as Dan Gorbet have worked to develop better-tasting runner varieties. And the runner has its defenders in the industry. John Gretz, who used to work in engineering at the Jif plant in Lexington, Kentucky, says, "When I was in the business and used to grab a handful out of the roaster, I definitely had a preference for runners."[53] The runner lends itself to mechanized harvesting in a way the more idiosyncratic Valencia doesn't. Because the runner is so prolific, it provides greater profits to farmers. It's cheaper than other varieties, helping peanut butter manufacturers keep their costs down. Because runners all tend to be about the same size, they roast evenly, making them ideal for peanut butter. The runner, by virtue of its blandness, conformity, and amenability to large-scale industrial production, is the very essence of a corporate peanut.

Some food experts feel that prolific crops such as runner peanuts (current varieties produce at least 25 percent more per acre than their predecessors) also overtax the soil. In *The Taste of America*, John and Karen Hess say:

> French peasants believe that a hectare of ground has only so much taste to impart to a crop, so that, all other things being equal, the bigger the crop, the smaller the flavor in a bushel—*c'est mathematique*, they say. This principle is so well established that any region allowed to market its wine under an *appellation controlée* or local label must limit the production per hectare in order to maintain quality; the volume is

> from one sixth to one third of what may be obtained by growers of *vin ordinaire*.[54]

From this point of view, runners are *vin ordinaire*. But Stanley Pittman, a retired farmer in Jackson County, Florida, disagrees. "The taste comes from the variety, from the seed itself," he says. "The taste is all in the genetics, and it doesn't change, unless you don't get enough rain on them, or too much, or unless something else changes. But the taste doesn't change."[55]

THE SOCIAL RISE OF THE PEANUT

Peanuts are uniquely evocative of the South. In early October 2008, as the U.S. and world economies were collapsing, I was in Tifton, Georgia, the heart of the peanut belt. On a cool bright morning, as I walked out of my motel along Interstate 75, the musty, fragrant scent of peanuts lying in windrows outside the city wafted through the air, discernable over the diesel exhalations of big rigs heading north on the interstate. In Southwest Georgia, peanuts are a harbinger of autumn, much as pumpkins are in the Midwest or iridescent leaves are in New England. "Fall is my favorite season," says Don Koehler, executive director of the Georgia Peanut Commission, "and peanuts make fall what it is."[1]

In late October, Dothan, Alabama, holds the National Peanut Festival. Earlier in the month, Wilson County, Texas, holds the Floresville Peanut Festival, presided over by King Reboog ("goober" spelled backward). In his youth, John Connally served as King Reboog. The governor of Texas for much of the 1960s, he was in the car with President Kennedy when he was assassinated on November 22, 1963. In November, well after the peanuts have been harvested, Grand Saline, Texas, holds the Great American Peanut Butter Festival. And Suffolk, Virginia, hosts the Suffolk Peanut Festival, featuring the world's only sculpture contest in which a prize is awarded for the person who can make a sculpture entirely out of peanut butter.

The South's fondness for the peanut is also displayed in monuments.[2] In Dothan, "Peanuts Around Town" is a series of colorful, four-foot-high peanuts in public places by artists in the spirit of "Cows on Parade" in Chicago and the "Community of Angels" project in Los Angeles. In Blakely, Georgia, there's a statue paying homage to the peanut on the grounds of the county courthouse (figure 2.1), while just off Courthouse

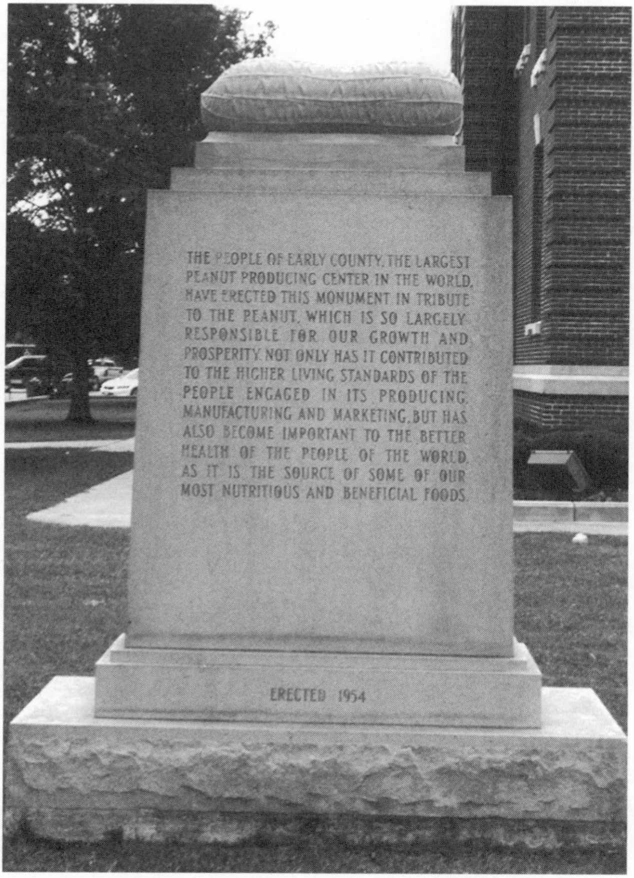

FIGURE 2.1 PEANUT STATUE

In front of the Early County Courthouse in Blakely, Georgia, this statue thanks the peanut for bringing agricultural prosperity to the area. Statues honoring the peanut can be found across the southern peanut belt. (Courtesy of Billy Fleming)

Square is the Birdsong mural, with a long-ago farmer harvesting peanuts by mule-driven plow (Birdsong is one of the largest peanut-shelling companies in the United States). But the most august tribute to the peanut (and perhaps the weirdest) is the Boll Weevil Monument in Enterprise, Alabama (figure 2.2). Probably the only Greek Revival–style statue in the United States dedicated to a pestilential insect, it was built by the citizens of Enterprise in 1919 to thank the boll weevil for laying waste to southern cotton so the peanut could come to the fore as a cash crop. George Washington Carver was scheduled to speak at its dedication, but heavy rains made local roads impassable, and he was forced to forgo the honor.[3]

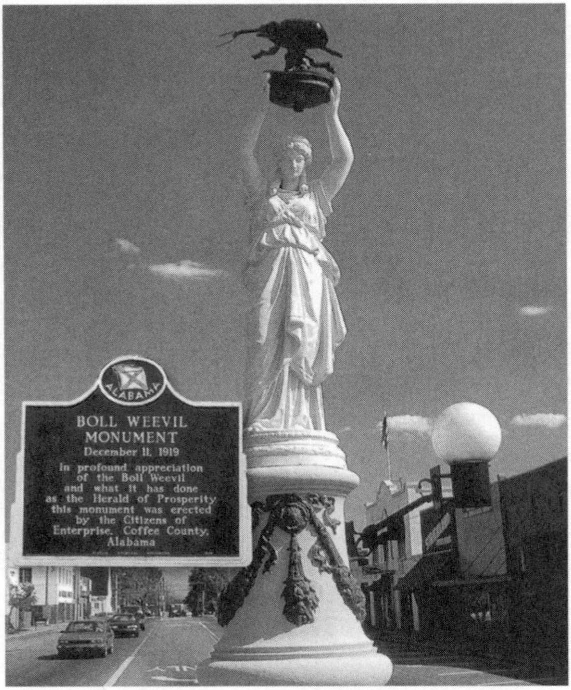

FIGURE 2.2 BOLL WEEVIL MONUMENT

Perhaps the only Greek Revival–style monument in the United States dedicated to a pestilential insect, the Boll Weevil Monument stands in downtown Enterprise, Alabama. When it destroyed southern cotton in the early twentieth century, the boll weevil paved the way for the growth of the peanut as a cash crop. (Courtesy of Tristar Sales, Inc. Photo: Bob Reardon)

Georgia is the number-one peanut-growing state, with 47 percent of the U.S. crop, followed by Alabama and Texas (14 percent each), Florida (10 percent), North Carolina (6 percent), South Carolina (4 percent), Mississippi (2 percent), and Virginia, Oklahoma, and New Mexico (1 percent each).[4] Around the world, 75 percent of all peanuts are produced by (in this order) India, China, Nigeria, the United States, and Senegal.[5]

The United States uses peanuts differently from most countries. About half our crop is turned into peanut butter, a quarter is used to make snack nuts, and a quarter winds up in peanut candies.[6] In other countries where peanuts are grown, especially China and India, they're used primarily for peanut oil. When refined, it's a good-quality cooking oil that can be heated to high temperatures without smoking, and it doesn't absorb the flavors of food or transfer them from one food to another. The United States and Europe started importing peanuts from Gambia in the 1830s, but while Europeans used them to make cooking oil, even then Americans were abidingly fond of the taste of roasted peanuts.[7]

★★★

Jackson County, in the central Florida panhandle, borders Georgia and Alabama and is one of the most prolific peanut-growing counties in the United States. It's mostly rural, with a population density of about 50 people per square mile.[8] (Manhattan's population density is about 70,000 per square mile.)[9] In 2000, the village of Bascom, where retired farmer Stanley Pittman lives, had a population of 106, and it doesn't look like it's gotten any bigger. According to the 2000 census, the racial makeup of the town was 100 percent white. Wendell Williams, a black farmer Pittman introduced me to, lives down the road, so he must be in the next town over. The people of Jackson County are friendly and hospitable, and the county's rolling meadows and endless woods are a tonic for anyone who spends too much time in the big city.

When Pittman graduated from high school in 1957, he and his father plowed with mules, stacking peanuts against stackpoles in the fields for weeks to dry, then hauling them to stationary, gasoline-driven peanut-picking machines to separate the peanuts from the vines. He's grown many crops in his career but retains a particular fondness for peanuts and peanut butter. "I love peanut butter and we eat it quite a bit," he says.

"If I was president of a country and had to choose one product to feed my country with, it would be peanuts. That would get old, I'm sure, but the peanut would do it."[10]

Now that he's easing into retirement, most of what was Stanley's farm is worked and run by his thirty-seven-year-old second cousin, Jeffery Pittman, whom Stanley proudly describes as a fine young farmer. Jeffery faces a host of problems unique to growing peanuts. Farmers harvest peanuts when most of them are mature, but that isn't always easy to determine: even on an individual plant, peanuts mature at different times. And they're underground, making Jeffery's decision about when to plow more difficult. To pick the right time to harvest he has to inspect peanuts from several plants in each of his fields every three or four days near the end of the growing season. If it's rained and the soil is too wet, it's hard to separate the peanuts from the soil. If it's been dry and the soil is hard, digger blades from the harvester, instead of going under the peanuts and scooping them up, ride up into the peanut zone, slashing the peanuts and causing extensive crop loss.

All kinds of foreign materials may pass through Jeffery's harvester and combine, including dirt, sticks, peanut plant leaves and stems, weeds, and metal from the harvester or combine themselves. And that's not all. "Peanuts are an agricultural product," says Walt Albritton, technical services manager at Tara Foods in Albany, Georgia, which makes peanut butter and other foods. "They're dug out of a field. The field's got rocks and stones. People ride by and throw a beer bottle out in the poor old farmer's field. They have dove shoots in peanut fields. Shotgun shells all over the field."[11]

If he chooses to—and if he can afford it—Jeffery Pittman has access to peanut-farming equipment that Stanley Pittman couldn't have dreamed of in 1957. There are sophisticated planting tractors guided by global-positioning satellites to make sure farmers plant their peanuts in straight rows. When it's time to harvest, tractors towing digger-shaker-inverters are driven through the peanut fields. An attachment with special blades loosens the soil and cuts the taproot of the plants, lifts them up, shakes the dirt off them, turns them upside down, and deposits them on the ground, where they sit until the light of two or three noonday suns has hit them (figure 2.3). Peanuts dry better when sunlight and air can reach the top of the inverted plant than they would resting on the ground.

FIGURE 2.3 HARVESTING PEANUTS

Modern peanut farming is highly mechanized. Tractors tow digger-shaker-inverters (shown here) through as many as six rows of peanut plants at a time. The peanut plants sit in the fields in windrows for two or three days before combines separate the peanuts from the plants, the first step in the process of making peanut butter. (Courtesy of American Peanut Council)

A few days later, the farmer and his assistants ride through the field again on their tractors, now towing a combine, which separates the peanuts from the rest of the plant. The peanuts are taken from the combines by small trucks called dump wagons, which deposit the peanuts in trailers that have heat vents at the bottom to further dry the peanuts. The leaves and stems of the peanut plant are thrown back onto the field, where they're either plowed under to fertilize the field or baled into protein-rich peanut hay. (Cows love peanut hay and produce thick, creamy milk when they eat it.) Large harvesters can pick six rows at a time, and combines can pick the peanuts off six pairs of windrows at once. But these machines are expensive: Stanley and I watched Jeffery and his hired hands picking peanuts from windrows one afternoon. Three combines were going through the field. "You're looking at three-quarters of a million dollars' worth of equipment," Stanley told me.[12]

Once peanuts are harvested, farmers take them to buying points to have their size and quality assessed and their price determined. Buying points are privately owned, but the workers who analyze and grade the peanuts are federal and state employees who also examine them for insect damage and carcinogenic aflatoxin, produced by *Aspergillus flavus*, a mold that grows on peanut shells. For all the mechanization of modern farming, I'm reminded how difficult a life it is when I meet a young farmer and his wife who have brought their peanuts in to a buying point. Their peanuts are good—one of their loads is 77 percent good-quality peanuts (it's impossible to have higher than 80 percent, as peanuts are about 20 percent shells) with low moisture. As the farmer shows me the chart explaining how much they'll be paid for their peanuts, I can't help but notice his hands—large, rough, sun-reddened, with several scars. (I also notice that most of those who work indoors at the buying point are white; most of those who work outside are black.)

Given all the challenges farmers face, Ben Houston, who used to manage the Sessions Company peanut butter plant in Enterprise, Alabama, says "Farmers are the biggest gamblers in the world."[13] Wendell Williams, one of the few remaining black farmers in Jackson County, agrees. "They are," he laughs. "It's worse than sitting at the poker table."[14]

At the time Stanley Pittman introduced me to him in the fall of 2008, Williams was fifty-nine years old and farmed 700 acres, growing peanuts, cotton, corn, wheat, and oats. He was understated, laconic, and not given to complaining, although he had much to complain about, including the death of his wife from cancer a few years earlier. Farming, he said, is an especially tough row to hoe for black farmers. "Things are so high now—fertilizer, diesel fuel, stuff like that—it's gettin' where you can't hardly go. It's rough when you payin' $3.61 a gallon for fuel goin' in that tractor and it burns 100 gallons a day."[15]

Black farmers tend to have less desirable land than their white counterparts, and less of it. I asked Williams how the peanut crop had done that year, and he said peanuts on irrigated land did well, while those on land that wasn't irrigated didn't.

"What percentage of your land is irrigated?" I asked.

"All of mine are dry land," he answered. "All of mine are dry land."

"Are there any young black farmers coming up through the ranks?"

"I don't know of any other than Dexter Gilbert—he's probably in his mid-forties," Williams said. "That's the only guy under my age I know of."

After Jeffery Pittman and Wendell Williams have their peanuts graded at a buying point, those that aren't going to be sold in the shell go to shelling plants. Along with the Golden Peanut Company, Birdsong Peanuts is one of the largest shellers in the United States, with four plants in Georgia, one in Virginia, and one in Texas. Its four Georgia plants shell 25 percent of the U.S. peanut crop. One of its Georgia plants is in Sylvester, the home of Peter Pan, and up to 75 percent of the peanuts shelled at Birdsong-Sylvester wind up in Peter Pan.[16]

Birdsong analyzes peanuts even more thoroughly than federal and state inspectors at buying points, performing a chemical analysis to check for aflatoxin rather than just a visual inspection. "When it's determined on a visual basis, it's sort of hit and miss," says Gregg Grimsley of the Sylvester plant. "When you do it on a chemical basis, you're much more precise. So we catch a lot of aflatoxin that's missed by federal and state inspectors."[17]

But sometimes Birdsong misses things as well: in the fall of 2009, the Occupational Safety and Health Administration of the U.S. Department of Labor identified forty-one safety and health violations at Birdsong's plants in Sylvester and Blakely, Georgia, following an incident in which a worker at the Blakely plant died after being caught in a conveyor belt.[18]

While peanuts are important, they're peanuts compared with corn, soybeans, and cotton. There are about 80 million acres each of corn and soybeans in the United States,[19] about 15 million acres of cotton,[20] and perhaps 1 to 2 million acres of peanuts. For that reason, new peanut varieties are not developed by for-profit corporations. Rather, they come from breeding programs at public universities in the South and Southwest, and from U.S. Department of Agriculture labs in Georgia and Texas.[21] Among other things, these programs work on improving the yield and disease resistance of peanuts, as well as tinkering with their flavor and chemistry to produce a higher ratio of oleic to linoleic oil, thus making a peanut butter with a longer shelf life.

The first peanuts to arrive in the United States weren't so carefully crafted. Apparently garden-variety runners, peanuts originally grown in the Southeast, were small and had a spreading growth habit, with vines low to the ground. Before the Civil War, the most important peanut-growing region in the United States was around Cape Fear in North Carolina, where peanuts were being grown commercially by 1818.[22] The first commercial crop of peanuts in Virginia was supposedly grown near Waverly in Sussex County in 1842.[23] Before the Civil War, peanuts were regarded as a southern regional food.

During the Civil War, the Northern naval blockade of the South forced the Confederacy to use peanut oil as a substitute for whale oil to lubricate machinery, and southern housewives used peanut oil instead of lard as a shortening in bread and pastry and as a salad dressing, instead of olive

Frozen Peanut Butter Brandy Alexander

Nothing says social elegance, in a peanut butter kind of way, like this drink.

½ cup ice
1 cup vanilla ice cream
3 tablespoons (1½ ounces) brandy
3 tablespoons (1½ ounces) white crème de cacao
3 tablespoons creamy standard peanut butter
¼ teaspoon vanilla extract
Pinch of grated nutmeg

Place the ingredients in the order listed in a large blender; blend until smooth, making sure the ice cream and ice are thoroughly incorporated into the drink. Pour into two martini glasses and serve at once.

★★★

Yield: 2 martini-style drinks.

FROM BRUCE WEINSTEIN AND MARK SCARBROUGH, *THE ULTIMATE PEANUT BUTTER* BOOK (NEW YORK: HARPERCOLLINS, 2005), © 2005. REPRINTED WITH PERMISSION FROM HARPERCOLLINS PUBLISHERS.

oil.[24] The importance of peanuts in Confederate soldiers' rations is evoked in the song "Goober Peas." Northern soldiers, who saw peanut plants for the first time when they marched past southern peanut fields, ate them as well. All those soldiers gobbling goobers led to the first major spike in U.S. peanut consumption.

It took a long time for peanuts to become a major commercial crop because of their labor-intensiveness: they had to be planted and dug up by hand, stacked in the field for weeks against stackpoles to dry out, and separated from the plants by hand. Around the turn of the twentieth century, machinery was invented that made harvesting them more efficient; only then did they become a viable, large-scale cash crop.

Peanuts had been grown by slaves and fed to hogs, so they were not regarded as haute cuisine. The peanut was associated with the peanut gallery, the uppermost section of a theater farthest from the stage, where seats were cheapest and patrons rowdiest. But peanuts steadily became more commercially significant. Only 150,000 bushels of peanuts were produced in the United States in 1860;[25] by 1895 that figure had risen to 8 million.[26] Peanut producers were determined to clean up the peanut's image, and by the turn of the twentieth century, they had largely succeeded. The *Richmond Dispatch* wrote that peanuts were no longer considered vulgar,[27] while a 1902 *Good Housekeeping* issue featured an article on "The Social Rise of the Peanut," accompanied by an illustration of a peanut wearing a top hat, monocle, gloves, and spats and carrying a cane,[28] looking like an early prototype of Planters' Mr. Peanut. And it was just before the turn of the century that a new food was created from the social-climbing peanut.

THE BIRTH OF PEANUT BUTTER

In 1891, following the Battle of Wounded Knee in South Dakota, the Sioux surrendered to the U.S. Army, marking the end of the Indian wars and the closing of the American frontier. Seven years later, the era of American imperialism began with the Spanish-American War. The doings of society's upper crust in the Gay Nineties were chronicled by Edith Wharton and Henry James, although things weren't always so gay for ordinary people: the Panic of 1893 led to an economic depression that lasted four years. If they had a little money, though, Americans could try several new comfort foods: the hamburger, the hot dog, the ice cream cone, and, in its modern incarnation, peanut butter.

With its rich roasted-peanut flavor and aroma, caramel hue, and gooey, consoling texture, peanut butter has been an American favorite from the start. But it's gone through five major changes: first, in the type of peanut used to make it. Originally, peanut butter was made from a combination of Spanish (whose high percentage of oil makes it especially flavorful) and Virginia peanuts (whose lower oil content counterbalances the Spanish, producing a better consistency in the butter).[1] Now, it's mostly runners, prized by large companies for their lower cost and tendency to roast uniformly.

The second change is in how it's prepared. In the 1890s, there was no hydrogenation; all peanut butter was natural, or old-fashioned. The popularity of stabilized peanut butter grew following its introduction in the 1920s, until by the 1960s it was hard to find natural peanut butter. But since the early 1970s, natural has enjoyed a resurgence.

In the pre-stabilization era, nothing was taken from peanuts except the skins and the heart (or germ); nothing was added except salt. Although the formula was simpler, it was more difficult to make, as peanut oils and solids separate; keeping them together required constant agitation. As a result, early peanut butter makers were faced with the dilemma confronted today by manufacturers of natural peanut butter: If you grind the peanuts more finely, the butter is smoother and more digestible, but more oil is released and pools on top. If, in order to minimize separation, you don't grind it as finely, the butter is coarser and a little harder to digest, especially for adults.

Does hydrogenation improve the flavor of peanut butter? Jerome Rosefield, the son of Skippy founder Joseph Rosefield and a consummate salesman, insisted it does. "I still recall a statement [my father] made one day," he told U.S. Food and Drug Administration hearings in 1966. "In the plant, he tasted some peanut butter coming out of . . . the machine and said, 'Gee, if we could just get a product to the consumer that tasted as this does right here!' "[2] But a food-industry trade magazine article from the 1940s differed: "It is recommended . . . that wherever possible, means other than hydrogenation be used to prevent oil separation since hydrogenated oil tends to dilute the flavor."[3]

A third difference between peanut butter then and now is in the kinds of textures available. Now there are creamy (which is a majority of the market)[4] and crunchy. But at the start, there was no crunchy or chunky, which debuted in 1935.[5] From the outset, there was another texture, though: regular or standard, which had a coarse or grainy quality. Once popular, it's now rare.

A 1919 article in the trade journal *The Peanut Promoter* noted, "The product . . . ground by a mill properly constructed is of a uniform texture and preferably of slightly granular consistency."[6] The author of the article was A. P. Grohens, president of the Lambert Machine Company, a pioneer in the manufacture of peanut-butter-making machinery. He added, "Attempts to prove that quality depends on . . . smooth . . . or paste-like consistency . . . have met with disappointment, and today the best known and most popular brands are found to be of . . . granular texture." In

1957, *Consumer Reports* noted that peanut butter still came in these three textures: regular, or standard; creamy; and chunky.[7]

Although no longer a common item of trade, coarse or grainy peanut butter still exists. The Cream-Nut brand, made from Virginia peanuts by the Koeze Company in Grand Rapids, Michigan, is still coarse-ground. "My own judgment is that modern, high-speed mills create a really soupy kind of liquid that separates quickly," says Jeff Koeze, whose peanut butter is made on World War II–era drum roasters that are similar to coffee roasters. "So it's a matter of taste. I think it's nice to have it kind of sticky and crunchy."[8] The Somis Nut House in Southern California also manufactures a coarse or grainy peanut butter from unblanched Spanish peanuts.

The fourth change involves the container. Originally, peanut butter was dispensed from large open vats in grocery stores; then, until World War II, it was sold in tins. When the war gave the military first claim on metal, the industry switched to glass jars. Now plastic is standard. These changes did not occur as a purely linear progression. From its start in 1909, Heinz peanut butter was sold in glass jars.[9] Similarly, early ads for Beech-Nut peanut butter proclaimed "never sold in bulk, always in glass jars with all the freshness, moistness and fragrance protected by airless sealing."[10]

The fifth change involves distribution: originally distributed locally and regionally, peanut butter now has national and even international distribution, thanks to stabilizers.

Peanut butter began as an upper-class food: guests at turn-of-the-twentieth-century health sanitariums helped establish its popularity among the well-to-do. Food historian Andrew F. Smith notes, "Dainty tearooms and high-class restaurants proudly announced that their salads, sandwiches, and soups were made with peanut butter."[11] Paradoxically, peanut butter became an upper-class food at a time when peanuts had barely shaken off their image as a food of the lower class, the denizens of the peanut gallery. But then peanut butter itself moved down the class ladder. "It was a delicacy in tea rooms in New York City and Boston until the price dropped," Smith says. "When that happened and anyone could buy it, it went out of the upper class and into the lower class."[12]

As a result of Americans' fondness for the taste of roasted peanuts, the spread of this spread from the 1890s to the early 1900s was rapid. "You're talking ten years from the time it was invented until the time it's

Beech-Nut Peanut Butter and Nasturtium Sandwich

As Beech-Nut was the first national brand to sell peanut butter, it was featured in early recipes, such as this one from Alma B. Cosey of the Cosey Tea Shop, 19 East Thirty-third Street, in New York City.

★★★

Cut thin slices of bread in circle sandwiches to fit the small leaves of the nasturtium.

Mix Beech-Nut peanut butter with a few drops of French dressing, spread between the slices of bread, then place on the leaves.

Dress with a few petals of the flower.

FROM *BEECH-NUT PEANUT BUTTER: THE GREAT TEA AND LUNCHEON DELICACY AS SERVED IN NEW YORK TEA ROOMS* (1914), IN ANDREW F. SMITH, *PEANUTS: THE ILLUSTRIOUS HISTORY OF THE GOOBER PEA* (URBANA: UNIVERSITY OF ILLINOIS PRESS, 2002).

in virtually every city in America," Smith says. "That's an incredible adoption rate."[13]

Not only were there new foods in the 1890s, there were new ways to eat them. In *Peanuts: The Illustrious History of the Goober Pea,* Smith says sandwiches become popular in the United States toward the end of the nineteenth century, just as peanut butter appeared.[14] An 1896 article in *Good Housekeeping* encouraged housewives to use a meat grinder on peanuts and spread them on bread. That year, recipes for peanut butter sandwiches appeared for what may have been the first time in cookbooks. The first reference Smith has found to the peanut butter and jelly sandwich dates to 1901, when it was mentioned by Julia Davis Chandler in the *Boston Cooking-School Magazine.*

Not just a sandwich, the PBJ meets the commonly accepted definition of a meal: a form of protein, one or more fruits or vegetables, and a serving of starch.[15] As of 1998, jelly made from native Concord grapes was the most popular in the United States.[16] You could call a PBJ an Appomattox, as it represents the peaceful coming together of peanuts, grown in the states of the old Confederacy, and grapes, grown in such Yankee precincts as the Northeast, Midwest, and Washington State.[17]

One of the first places peanut butter was made was the Western Health Reform Institute in Battle Creek, Michigan, run by the Kellogg brothers of cereal fame. Both the institute and the food owed their origins to the Seventh-Day Adventist Church, of which John Harvey Kellogg and his brother, Will, were members. The church was formally organized in 1863, with headquarters in Battle Creek.[18] In the late nineteenth century, as the church was coalescing, there was a widespread health reform movement in the United States, and the church's thinking both influenced and was influenced by that movement.

One of the Adventists' fundamental beliefs is that people are God's stewards, entrusted by him with the blessings of the earth and its resources and responsible to him for their proper use.[19] This stewardship is commonly interpreted by church members as calling for a healthy diet and taking care of the body God has given us. Adventists are often vegetarians, and Andrew F. Smith jokingly calls the early popularization of peanut butter "a vegetarian conspiracy."[20]

Ellen G. White, a founding figure in the Seventh-Day Adventist movement, encouraged the use of nuts as a substitute for meats.[21] White called for the church to establish a sanitarium,[22] and one was founded in 1866 as the Western Health Reform Institute;[23] the name was changed to the Battle Creek Sanitarium in 1902.[24] Its purpose was to treat the sick and disseminate information about health to the public.[25]

John Harvey Kellogg, who was a physician, became superintendent of the institute in 1876 (figure 3.1).[26] There are two versions of how he became a peanut butter pioneer: in the possibly apocryphal version, Kellogg reprimanded an employee for roasting peanuts in a sanitarium oven. Furious, the employee went home and smashed the peanuts with a hammer.[27] The likelier version is that shortly after 1890, Kellogg started grinding roasted peanuts into a paste for patients who had difficulty chewing or digesting them properly; he switched to steaming them after he decided

FIGURE 3.1 JOHN HARVEY KELLOGG

John Harvey Kellogg, who with his brother, Will, developed corn flakes as a breakfast cereal, is regarded by some as the inventor of peanut butter. His 1895 patent called for boiling peanuts rather than roasting them before turning them into a paste. (Courtesy of Ellen G. White Estate, Inc.)

that roasting caused peanut oil to decompose and that the decomposed oil irritated the digestive organs.[28] The many talks he gave about this new food helped popularize it.

On November 4, 1895, John Harvey Kellogg filed a patent application for a "Food compound" that is generally regarded as the first effort to patent peanut butter.[29] The filing spoke of passing nuts—not necessarily peanuts, but peanuts or almonds—between rollers, separating them into two different substances, one a relatively dry, almost white, pasty nutmeal, the other a moist, pasty, brown, and adhesive substance "which for distinction is termed 'butter' or 'paste.'" Although most writers say Kellogg steamed his peanuts, his application indicates that the nuts were to be boiled in water for four to six hours, which would produce a substance that was nothing like contemporary peanut butter in consistency or flavor. Kellogg subsequently filed two more patent applications for early forms of peanut butter: one, in 1897, for a "Process of preparing nutmeal," and another in 1898, for a "Process of producing alimentary products."[30] Oddly and inaccurately, Kellogg said in 1899 that he didn't think patenting peanut butter was a good idea, so he hadn't done it. Instead, he wrote, "It was a thing the world ought to have; let everybody that wants it have it, and make the best use of it."[31]

As a Seventh-Day Adventist, Kellogg was ahead of his time in realizing the superiority of a plant- and grain-based diet over a meat-based one. But he has his critics. In T. C. Boyle's satirical novel *The Road to Wellville*, Kellogg is portrayed as a humanitarian who adopted fifty-two children, many of whom became successful doctors and lawyers. But Boyle also depicts him as a flake and an unethical doctor who deliberately misinformed his patients and used circus tricks to demonstrate that eating meat supposedly made one violent.[32] In *The Omnivore's Dilemma*, food writer Michael Pollan notes that Kellogg's sanitarium featured all-grape diets and almost hourly enemas.[33] Some of the ominous-sounding techniques used at the Western Health Reform Institute under Kellogg's supervision included cold-mitten friction, wet-sheet rubs, and salt glows.[34] When Pollan calls the sanitarium "legendarily nutty," he doesn't appear to be referring to peanuts, adding that this period marked the first golden age of American food faddism.[35]

Still, Kellogg was highly regarded in his day: his diverse roster of clients included President Warren G. Harding, abolitionist and women's rights activist Sojourner Truth, aviator Amelia Earhart, actor Johnny Weissmuller, and auto magnate Henry Ford.[36] And some people were even more "out there" than the Kelloggs. The thirty years leading up to the turn of the twentieth century were a less medically sophisticated time; among the patent medicines then popular was Lydia E. Pinkham's Vegetable Compound, which purported to relieve women's menstrual and menopausal pains with a formula that included 18 percent alcohol.[37]

Peanut butter's vegetarian roots are also evident in Dr. Schindler's Peanut Butter. Schindler's Peanut Products was started before the turn of the twentieth century by Dr. Schindler, a German-American physician (we don't know his first name). The company's original name was the Vegetarian Food and Nut Company.[38] Schindler made peanut butter from raw peanuts and supposedly fed it to his constipated patients,[39] which seems medically counterintuitive, as nuts are not generally known for their laxative qualities.[40]

Dr. Schindler's was made in Baltimore and Washington, D.C.; its District of Columbia plant was across the street from what is now the Washington Nationals baseball stadium.[41] Although presumably no longer focusing on constipated patients, Dr. Schindler's was still in business in the mid-1950s, when Willard Scott, then a weatherman for Washington NBC affiliate WRC-TV, appeared in its commercials with Jim Henson and an early version of the Muppets. Kermit the Frog would open his mouth, Scott would give him a big spoonful of Dr. Schindler's, and Kermit would say "Ahh."[42]

For vegetarians, peanut butter was a health food. For others, though, it was considered a snack food. Paul Fine, a psychological consultant to major food companies, once decried the diet of the American mainstream as "Oreos, peanut butter, Crisco, TV dinners, cake mix, macaroni and cheese, Pepsi and Coke, pizzas, Jell-O, hamburgers, Rice-a-Roni, Spaghetti-O's, pork and beans, Heinz ketchup, and instant coffee."[43] If John Harvey Kellogg represents peanut butter as a vegetarian health food, the peanut butter pioneer who represents it as a popular snack food is George Bayle.

Born in Philadelphia in 1850, Bayle moved to Alton, Illinois, and became a traveling salesman for the Kendall Cracker Company.[44] For ten years he called on clients and potential customers along the Mississippi River and rose in the company, which later became the Kendall-Bayle Cracker Company, and moved its factory to St. Louis. There, in 1888, Bayle started the George A. Bayle Company, which made pretzels, Saratoga chip potatoes, and other snack foods. According to one account, he was the first to sell horseradish sauce and was one of the earliest salters of peanuts.[45] He is also credited by many with another innovation—the development of peanut butter, supposedly in concert with a doctor who wanted a high-protein food for his patients with bad teeth who couldn't chew meat.

George A. Bayle Company advertisements in 1921 and 1922 issues of *The Peanut Promoter,* a trade magazine, carry the slogan "Original Manufacturers of Peanut Butter" (figure 3.2).[46] No one wrote in to dispute the

FIGURE 3.2 BAYLE TIN

St. Louis snack-food maker George Bayle is also credited as having invented peanut butter in the mid-1890s. The label on this tin of Bayle's Acorn brand calls the company the "Originators of Peanut Butter," although supporters of John Harvey Kellogg dispute that claim. (Courtesy of Allan Dean Walker)

claim. What is subject to dispute is the claim that Bayle worked with a doctor to develop peanut butter, a legend much loved by writers about peanut butter.[47] But a feature article in the April 1920 issue of *The Peanut Promoter*, possibly by editor M. M. Osborn, tells a different story: In 1894, Bayle, who had a peanut grinder in his office, was making "a brand of cheese put up in small jars," a kind of early-day Cheez Whiz. As *The Peanut Promoter* tells it, "A customer persuaded them to begin the manufacture of 'Cheese-Nut,' cheese flavored with peanut butter or ground nuts. 'Cheese-Nut' did not find favor with the housewives and soon was dropped from the list of products [sold] by this company, but the nut butter itself was found to be in demand."[48]

Before 1894, the article continues, the use of peanut butter had largely been restricted to sanitariums, notably the one at Battle Creek. The Bayle Company claimed it was the first to see its possibilities as a food without regard to any "health doctrines or policies." The Cheese-Nut story is more plausible than Bayle having worked with a doctor: while nutritional science was less advanced in the 1890s than it is now, it seems unlikely that even then a doctor would turn to a junk-food manufacturer to popularize his health-food brainchild.

The earliest evidence I found of Bayle making peanut butter is a 1914 article in which a food scientist analyzed twenty-one brands of peanut butter for sale in Kansas.[49] But it has to be assumed Bayle was making it well before then: it would have made no sense for him to claim primacy in a 1921 ad in the trade publication of a twenty-five-year-old industry if he'd only been in the business for seven.

Nailing down Bayle's claim isn't easy, though. An 1891 St. Louis business directory indicates Bayle made pretzels, potato chips, and crackers but doesn't say anything about peanut butter.[50] St. Louis food historian Suzanne Corbett, who worked on the Bayle Company files, recalls donating them to the National Peanut Council (now the American Peanut Council), which can't account for them. Corbett also interviewed Elva Norman, whose husband worked with George Bayle. Norman purportedly donated her papers to the St. Louis Public Library or the University of Missouri, but I had no luck finding them, either.

Whether he was the grand old man of peanut butter or not, Bayle certainly acted the part. He served as president of the George A. Bayle Company until the fall of 1920 and remained on the board of directors until his death in December 1921.[51] He kept his office at the company's plant at 111 South Second Street in downtown St. Louis, a stone's throw from the Mississippi River. There, he kept an open door to colleagues from the industry who wanted to drop in and discuss the peanut market, peanuts, and peanut butter.[52] His plant, which today would be in the shadow of the St. Louis Gateway Arch, was torn down in the 1940s when St. Louis created the Jefferson National Expansion Memorial Park along the riverfront. One American landmark vanished to make way for another.

Determined to learn more about George Bayle, I decided to do what no writer about peanut butter has done: track down his descendants. The Missouri Historical Society provided me with a 1921 obituary for Bayle, which said his daughter, Hallie, had married James Van Vleck of Chicago. Records from the 1930 Illinois census indicated the Van Vlecks had three children, including sixteen-year-old George, and lived in the Chicago suburb of Downers Grove.

I called the Downers Grove Historical Society, where a staffer told me the 1951 phone book had George living in nearby Hinsdale. Downers Grove and Hinsdale had separate phone books after 1958, so I contacted the Hinsdale Historical Society, which e-mailed me to say George was a local magistrate in the 1960s. That's all we have, though, they said, and that appeared to be that.

But half an hour later, I received another e-mail from Hinsdale: its obituary expert had discovered not one but two obituaries for Van Vleck, and they were attached. Who knew the Hinsdale Historical Society had an obituary expert? Poring over them, I saw George had a daughter, Martha Pierce. A telephone-directory Web site showed two Martha Pierces in the Chicago suburbs. I called the first one, who said it wasn't her. The voice on the answering machine of the second sounded too young—I estimated the right Martha Pierce would be in her sixties or seventies. I left a message anyway.

Later that day, I got a call from Martha Bayle Van Vleck Pierce of Evanston, Illinois. "Yes," she said, "I'm George Bayle's great-granddaughter." The too-young voice on the answering machine had been her daughter's. The family legend, she said, was that Bayle invented peanut butter. Eureka!

"What can you tell me about him?" I asked eagerly.

"Well," she said, "he was a doctor and found that peanut butter was something his elderly patients could digest."

Sigh.

I knew more about him than she did.

Martha was pleasant and inclined to be helpful, but there wasn't much she could tell me beyond the fact that Bayle's daughter, Phoebe, had lived with the Van Vlecks when Martha was young and that her sister, Mary, had gone to college courtesy of the "peanut butter money" her great-aunt Phoebe left when she died.

★★★

So who's the father of modern peanut butter, master promoter John Harvey Kellogg or snack-food salesman George Bayle?

Food historian Andrew F. Smith says John Harvey Kellogg, by virtue of his firsts: he took out the first peanut butter patent and ran the first documented advertisement. In *Peanuts: The Illustrious History of the Goober*

Pea, Smith notes that an 1897 sales catalog carries advertisements for nut butters made by Sanitas, a company established by the Kellogg brothers.[53] Ray Hammons, a research geneticist with the U.S. Department of Agriculture's Agricultural Research Service, investigated Bayle's claim to primacy and wasn't impressed. "The notion is widely held that an unnamed St. Louis physician first popularized peanut butter about 1890 as a nutritious, easily digested food for certain of his patients," he wrote. "I found no critical published evidence to support this claim. Neither the American Medical Association nor the Peanut Butter Manufacturers Association [today the Peanut and Tree Nut Processors Association] have any information concerning this belief."[54] The Kellogg Company lines up behind its namesake. In a 1990 newspaper article, a Kellogg spokeswoman said John Harvey Kellogg developed several foods between 1895 and 1905. "One of the foods invented in 1895 was peanut butter," Kellogg senior communications coordinator Diane Dickey said. "That's what the records show."[55]

But George Bayle has his advocates as well. University of Georgia professor of food science Jasper Woodroof wrote, "Possibly the first attempt to make and use peanut butter or paste other than as a subsistence food in the United States was when a physician in St. Louis, Missouri, was reportedly the first to manufacture peanut butter commercially,"[56] which supports the Bayle-worked-with-a-doctor story. The Southern Peanut Growers (until 2010 known as the Peanut Advisory Board) have said an unknown St. Louis doctor, working with Bayle, deserves the title.[57]

And food historian Suzanne Corbett is adamant on the subject. "George Bayle was the first man to successfully produce and market peanut butter," she says. "John Harvey Kellogg shouldn't get the credit, because the formula is completely different. Kellogg's peanut butter spread was steamed. It didn't resemble the taste or texture of what George Bayle was doing, which was the equivalent of modern peanut butter." Corbett adds that when Kellogg switched from roasting peanuts to steaming them, "it tasted terrible. So they said, 'To heck with that, let's concentrate on cereal.' "[58] Because Kellogg's ground peanut paste probably bore only a cursory similarity to today's peanut butter, I fall into the Bayle camp, assuming the claims of those backing him can be confirmed.

Two early peanut butter makers whose pre-1900 existence can be confirmed are the Atlantic Peanut Refinery of Philadelphia and the Peanolia

Food Company of New Haven, Connecticut.[59] According to Andrew F. Smith, Atlantic received the first trademark for peanut butter and in 1898 became the first company to use the words "peanut butter" on the label. Early peanut-butter-making industrial machinery was smaller and slower than today's equipment, and not as good at screening out defective peanuts and foreign material. Women standing at sorting tables would try to spot defective peanuts just by looking at them and pick them out; today high-speed electronic color sorters do the job more efficiently and quickly. Primordial peanut-butter equipment was also simpler because it did not need a separate step for the addition of stabilizers.

One of the first people to manufacture industrial peanut-butter-making equipment was Joseph Lambert, who had worked at the Western Health Reform Institute under Kellogg. In 1896 he left the institute and began selling nut-based products and small machines for grinding peanuts.[60] As peanut butter became more popular, he developed larger peanut-grinding machines and founded the Lambert Company of Marshall, Michigan, an important early manufacturer of peanut butter mills. Another early equipment maker was Ambrose Straub of Philadelphia. One early testimonial for Straub's Quaker City Peanut Butter Mills came from Joseph Rosefield of the Rosefield Packing Company in Alameda, California. Rosefield, who would later found Skippy, testified in a 1921 Straub ad that "there are many points of superiority in your mills."[61]

In 1904 the World's Fair, also known as the Louisiana Purchase Centennial Exposition, was held in St. Louis (figure 3.3). It marked a milestone in the introduction of peanut butter to the American public. The exposition was one of four world's fairs held in the United States in the first decade of the twentieth century, along with Buffalo in 1901, Hampton Roads, Virginia, in 1907, and Seattle in 1909. Together they stood as an announcement by the United States that it was now a major player on the world stage.

The fair in St. Louis, then the fourth-largest city in the country, was spectacular, drawing millions of visitors and inspiring the song "Meet Me in St. Louis." The third modern Olympic Games, originally awarded to Chicago, were moved to St. Louis to coincide with the fair. (Only six other countries bothered to show up, and the United States won twenty-two of twenty-three track-and-field events.)[62]

One of the last vendors to rent a booth at the fair was C. H. Sumner, apparently the only concessionaire to sell peanut butter. Using Ambrose

FIGURE 3.3 ST. LOUIS WORLD'S FAIR

Many Americans tasted peanut butter for the first time in 1904 at the concession stand of C. H. Sumner at the St. Louis World's Fair. The fair also helped popularize hamburgers, hot dogs, and the ice cream cone. (Keystone-Mast Collection, UCR/California Museum of Photography, University of California, Riverside)

Straub's Quaker City mills,[63] he generated $705 in receipts in 1904 dollars.[64] St. Louis would play one more role in the development of peanut butter's popularity: in the late 1920s, local baker Gustav Papendick developed a process for slicing and wrapping bread.[65] Children could now make their own peanut butter and jelly sandwiches with nothing more dangerous than a butter knife.

To this day, the Midwest remains the U.S. region where people, on average, eat the most peanut butter. Don Koehler, executive director of the Georgia Peanut Commission, says, "For some reason, our largest per-capita consumption is still in the Midwest." He adds that midwesterners like their peanut butter on the salty side, while southerners prefer sweet peanut butter; New Englanders also like it sweet, but not as sweet as southerners.[66]

As important as the 1904 St. Louis World's Fair was, a more important event in peanut butter's rollout occurred that year when the Beech-Nut Packing Company became the first national brand to make peanut butter.[67] Beech-Nut peanut butter was made in the town of Canajoharie in the Mohawk Valley of upstate New York. The town's name came from a local Indian word referring to a nearby lake as "the kettle that washes itself."

Just like the lake, the company was fastidious about cleanliness: from early on, it came in glasses as a quality-control measure. Early Beech-Nut ads proclaimed, "Beech-Nut peanut butter is pure, free from grit,"[68] suggesting that early peanut-butter-making machinery was not thorough in weeding out plant and other field debris (figure 3.4). Beech-Nut peanut butter was made until 1956, when Beech-Nut merged with Life Savers.

Another national brand to enter the peanut butter market was Heinz, in 1909 (figure 3.5).[69] From the start, Heinz peanut butter also came only in glass jars; in 1923 it would become the first stabilized or hydrogenated peanut butter.[70] Beech-Nut and Heinz were still leading brands in the late 1920s and early 1930s; Heinz sold peanut butter until 1950,[71] when, according to Heinz spokesman Michael Mullen, it was driven out of the market by a plethora of competitors, many using artificial flavors and coloring and selling at bargain prices.

Although never a major brand, Krema, based in Columbus, Ohio, began selling peanut butter in 1908.[72] Still in business today, it's the oldest peanut butter company based in the United States. Founder Benton Black's motto was "I refuse to sell outside of Ohio,"[73] which made sense in the pre-stabilized peanut butter era, when there were no interstate highways, jet travel, or overnight delivery.

Just as Krema got started, the boll weevil began its General Sherman–like march through the southern cotton crop, with profound implications for peanuts and peanut butter. A native of Central America, the weevil migrated north through Mexico, reaching the United States around the turn of the twentieth century. It crossed the Rio Grande as early as 1903,[74] when a U.S. Department of Agriculture official traveled to Texas to deal with it; the official reported seeing deserted farms, as well as "a wretched people facing starvation" and "whole towns deserted."[75]

FIGURE 3.4 BEECH-NUT ADVERTISEMENT

In 1904 Beech-Nut became the first national brand to make peanut butter. Quality-control standards at the time were not as high as they are today, and this Beech-Nut ad touted its corps of women who examined peanuts after roasting to check for defective nuts and extraneous material. Today that task is handled by powerful optical-scanning machines. (Courtesy of the Arkell Museum at Canajoharie)

The boll weevil advanced north and east from Texas, decimating cotton harvests, which dropped by almost 90 percent in Pike County, Mississippi, and 96 percent in Hancock County, Georgia.[76] *Southern Living* magazine says the weevil reached Alabama by 1910. Farmers turned to peanuts as an alternative.

According to legend, this is where George Washington Carver rides to the rescue (figure 3.6). A former slave with a lifelong interest in botany and agriculture, Carver was one of the first black Americans to achieve professional success and celebrity at a national level. He supposedly

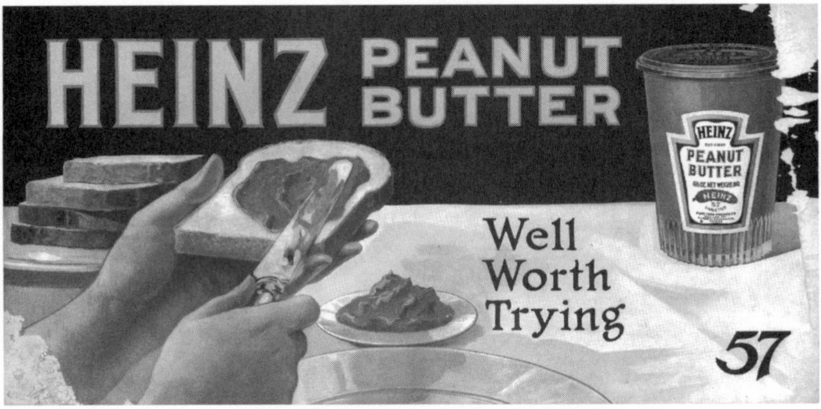

FIGURE 3.5 HEINZ ADVERTISEMENT

Heinz entered the peanut butter market in 1909, and in 1923 its peanut butter became the first one stabilized by hydrogenation. This ad appeared in urban streetcars and trolleys in 1917. (Library and Archives Division, Sen. John Heinz History Center)

created hundreds of uses for the peanut and just as many peanut-based recipes, invented peanut butter, and saved southern agriculture by persuading farmers to switch from cotton to peanuts. Almost none of this is true, but Carver's life and legacy are testimony to the line from *The Man Who Shot Liberty Valance*: "When the legend becomes fact, print the legend."

Among Carver's legitimate accomplishments, he testified before the House Ways and Means Committee in January 1921, possibly the first African American to appear before a committee of Congress. He was beloved by the media. According to a 1923 issue of *Current Opinion*, "Professor Carver took the friendless goober into his laboratory, cracked its shell, and probed deep into the secrets of its nutty meat."[77] When he died in 1943, Congress passed legislation, signed by President Roosevelt, to make his birthplace a national monument. The only two Americans previously so honored were George Washington and Abraham Lincoln.

Carver was recruited by Booker T. Washington in 1896 to head the agricultural program at Alabama's Tuskegee Institute.[78] The pamphlet for which he is best known, *How to Grow the Peanut and 105 Ways of Prepar-*

FIGURE 3.6 GEORGE WASHINGTON CARVER

Although he is credited by some as the inventor of peanut butter and by many as the "Wizard of Tuskegee" who discovered many innovative uses for peanuts, George Washington Carver was neither. While he did introduce black farmers to the principle of crop rotation, much of his reputation is the result of the approval he received from the white Establishment of his day, which admired his adherence to segregation. (The Tuskegee University Archives, Tuskegee University)

ing It for Human Consumption, was published in 1916, well after southern farmers had started switching to peanuts. Remarkably, the pamphlet reveals that Carver didn't understand some peanut basics. He says peanuts are easy to plant (they are), easy to grow (they require a lot of attention), and easy to harvest.[79] That last one is flat-out wrong, especially during Carver's day, when harvesting peanuts was back-breaking, labor-intensive work that included pulling the plants from the ground by hand, leaning them against stackpoles in the fields, and, after they dried out weeks later, dragging them to stationary peanut-picking machines in the field for separation from the vines before taking the peanuts to shelling plants.

And according to *How to Grow the Peanut*, more bushels per acre of peanuts could be grown in stiff, clayey soil than light, sandy soil.[80] But John Beasley, a professor and extension peanut agronomist with the Crop and Soil Sciences Department of the University of Georgia, shoots that one down. "You really hate to disagree with George Washington Carver," he says, "but we produce most of our higher-yielding peanut crops on sandy soils."[81] Elsewhere, Carver made the medically suspect claim that raw peanut butter sandwiches helped to soothe upset stomachs.[82]

Piled on Carver's own inaccurate claims are those made for him. In the conservative journal of opinion *National Review*, William F. Buckley Jr. mistakenly proclaimed, "George Washington Carver invented peanut butter."[83] He had nothing to do with it. After his death, the Carver Museum, which Carver himself helped set up at Tuskegee, claimed he had developed 287 peanut commodities.[84] But there were many redundancies on the list, as well as things that can't plausibly be sourced to him, such as salted peanuts. Of the uses he demonstrated for the peanut, historian Barry Mackintosh notes, "Because most of the non-standard products created by Carver could be made more easily from other substances, they were essentially curiosities." The only patent he was ever granted was for a peanut-based cosmetic.[85]

Although Carver did encourage farmers to rotate to other crops from cotton, this was old news by the time he began to do so. The boll weevil hit the United States soon after the turn of the twentieth century. The U.S. Department of Agriculture noted as early as 1909 that the peanut was becoming an important crop in the South.[86] Carver wasn't prominently associated with peanuts until well after that. His earliest acclaim appears to have come in 1919, when he was invited to speak at the dedication of the Boll Weevil Monument in Enterprise, Alabama.[87]

Where Carver does appear to have done some good is that under his supervision, the Tuskegee Agricultural Experiment Station was staffed by blacks and helped to improve the agricultural practices of black farmers who hadn't had much exposure to modern farming methods.[88]

So why is Dr. Carver such an icon? The historically disagreeable truth is that he was an Uncle Tom—a black who truckled to the white power structure. In *American Heritage*, Barry Mackintosh writes, "White Southerners found Carver's adherence to the rules and customs of segregation exemplary. When two nonconforming white visitors to Tuskegee asked him to join them for dinner, he excused himself. In 1921, *Success Magazine*, which dubbed him 'Columbus of the Soil,' approvingly noted how, when he testified before the House Ways and Means Committee, he 'deferentially remained in the background until all the white men had been heard.' "[89] A 1937 profile of Carver in the *Literary Digest* praises him without reserve, but describes the seventy-two-year-old Carver as "stoop-shouldered," "shuffling down" to join a ceremony at which his Tuskegee colleagues honored him, "listen[ing] meekly" and "scurry[ing] back to his test tubes and peanuts."[90]

The Negro Vanguard noted, "No white scientist with precisely the same achievements would have been called a 'wizard' or 'the greatest industrial chemist in the world.' "[91] At a time when few black Americans gained national recognition, Mackintosh notes, they had an obvious stake in the legend. But, he adds, "The mass media most responsible for Carver's reputation were governed by and directed to white Americans, including those indifferent or hostile to black advancement. . . . By placing a token black on a pedestal, whites of varying persuasions could deny or atone for prejudice against blacks as a class."[92]

With no help from Carver, peanut butter was becoming more popular. John Garwood, a young boy in Carroll, Nebraska, later recalled Roberts' Grocery there as "a mystic alchemy of smells—coffee, fresh bread, soap, spices, fruit, an oiled floor, grains and new leather. And then," he adds, "there was peanut butter. With a heavy spoon, Mr. Roberts would ladle a couple of pounds from the large wooden tub. It wasn't labeled chunky, super-chunky, regular, smooth, free of salt or sugar. There was just the sight and smell of the raw sin of all that peanut butter."[93]

One time at home, Garwood added, "My mother—anxious, I suspect, about our apple snatching in the high branches—called my friend and me down for a surprise. Inside a small box covered with a dish towel was punch, freshly baked bread, and peanut butter. I noticed the misty look in my friend's eyes. As we finished and lay back on the grass, there was a peace that passes all understanding."[94]

But there were holdouts who resisted the growing popularity of peanuts and peanut butter. In 1945 an executive of Peter Pan, interviewed by a reporter for *Sales Management* magazine, cautiously glanced at the writer's silvering hair and asked, "When you were a small boy, your mother never gave you any peanut butter, right?" He was right.[95] And one evening in 1921, well after midnight, Joseph Burstein of Brooklyn's Coney Island came home, woke his wife, and insisted she help him finish a bag of peanuts he'd bought on sale. As *The Peanut Promoter* noted, "She declined to share the succulent goobers." "This seemed to enrage him,"

Mrs. Burstein said, "and he emptied the bag in my face and forced me to swallow some of the nuts. He became abusive and finally ran out, only to return later, when he packed up his belongings and stayed away for three days." Mrs. Burstein filed for divorce.[96]

Her aversion notwithstanding, peanut butter production took off between 1899 and 1919 (figure 3.7). Two million pounds were produced in 1899;[97] by 1907, that had grown to about 34 million pounds.[98] In 1911 production declined to 23 million pounds,[99] possibly because it was an El Niño year, with attendant drought and decreased agricultural production.

But when the United States entered World War I, the government encouraged Americans to eat more peanuts and less wheat, as grain was

FIGURE 3.7 MULTIPLE TINS

Peanut butter often came in tins until World War II, when the metal was needed for the war effort. Pond Brand, first in the top row, was made by Swift and was a precursor of Peter Pan. Luncheon brand, in the middle of the bottom row, was made by the Rosefield Packing Company and was a precursor of Skippy. (Courtesy of Craig Kuziel)

needed by our European allies and the American armed forces.[100] An ad for Beech-Nut peanut butter called it "a new patriotic way to conserve animal fats."[101] There were also practical considerations: Andrew F. Smith has noted, "As transportation space was limited by the war effort and unshelled nuts wasted valuable shipping space, demand grew for peanut products, such as peanut butter, that could be easily transported."[102]

In 1914 some 537,000 acres of peanuts were grown in the South; by 1918 that figure had risen to 4 million acres.[103] In 1919, at the end of World War I, peanut butter production was 158 million pounds,[104] nearly quintuple that of 1907. A 1919 article in *The Peanut Promoter* noted, "The consumption of peanut butter during the last three years more than equals that of all the previous years combined."[105]

But that wasn't enough for some in the peanut butter industry. In 1923, ten years before he founded Skippy, Joseph Rosefield of Alameda, California, was making Luncheon brand, an unstabilized peanut butter. "Peanut butter is only eaten by a small percentage of our population," he wrote in a peanut industry trade publication. "It should now be our effort to bring it to the attention of the general public so that it may, in time to come, be a common article of diet."[106] Peanut butter had now achieved a measure of popularity. But despite the fact that such brands as Beech-Nut and Heinz were marketed nationwide, it was a mostly local and regional phenomenon. It might have remained so if not for Rosefield and an obscure inventor from Pittsburgh named Frank Stockton.

PETER PAN

"IMPROVED BY HYDROGENATION"

In 1906 Upton Sinclair wrote *The Jungle*, an exposé of working conditions at Chicago meatpackers such as Swift & Company. But like the other Chicago packers, Swift was expanding to other foods: two years earlier, it had bought H. C. Derby and its subsidiary E. K. Pond.[1] Originally a tripe and pigs' feet shop, by 1914 Derby was making peanut butter,[2] and in 1920 it introduced the E. K. Pond brand.[3]

Peanut butter lore holds that Peter Pan, introduced in 1928 (or possibly as early as 1927),[4] was born by renaming the E. K. Pond brand and hydrogenating it, but that doesn't appear to be the case. Jerome and Marvin Rosefield were the sons of Joseph Rosefield, who came up with one of the first patents for hydrogenating peanut butter; he later founded Skippy. Testifying in a 1980 court case, Jerome and Marvin said Peter Pan was not the first peanut butter made by Swift using their father's hydrogenation patent.[5] That brand, known either as Dainty or Delicia,[6] was sold in a brick or bar form starting in 1924. When it didn't do well, Swift tried again—putting it in a tin and calling it Peter Pan.

At the beginning of the 1920s, peanut butter was soaring in popularity. "Today, there is hardly a city in the United States of 30,000 population and over which does not have one or more peanut butter factories," A. P. Grohens, president of the Lambert Machine Company, which made equipment for peanut butter factories, wrote in 1919. "And even in many smaller places we find peanut butter plants doing a thriving business. The consumption of peanut butter during the last three years more than equals that of all previous years combined."[7]

The rapid growth of peanut butter at this time may owe a debt to the boll weevil. By the end of the 1910s, the insect had thoroughly decimated cotton crops across the South, leaving southern farmers looking for a new crop. Once they had all those peanuts, they needed a market for them, and peanut butter, with its roasted-peanut flavor, had begun to gain favor with the American public. In 1922 the National Peanut Butter Manufacturers Association (today the Peanut and Tree Nut Processors Association) was formed.

Although the 1920s were the era of Prohibition, alcohol still retained its popularity. In December 1921, a large quantity of liquor was seized from a saloon keeper in Brooklyn, New York, according to *The Peanut Promoter*, an early trade journal for the peanut and peanut butter industries. To get it back from the government, the saloon keeper obtained a license to become a wholesale druggist, then applied for the liquor's return on the grounds it was going to be sold for medicinal purposes. The courts granted his request.[8]

Culturally, the Roaring Twenties were marked by the prominence of jazz, flappers, and art deco. Organized labor increased in strength, but in response to massive immigration, conservative forces sought to seal off the nation's borders. In the business world, chain stores such as A&P, Piggly Wiggly, and Kresge began to take an increasing market share from small, independent "mom-and-pop" stores. The spirit of growing civic and business boosterism was satirized by Sinclair Lewis in books such as *Main Street*. *The Peanut Promoter* sniffed that the problem with *Main Street* was that Lewis only wrote about one side of the street.[9]

★ ★ ★

The 1920s saw progress in the peanut butter industry with the introduction of hydrogenation, perhaps the most significant development in the industry's history. "For the first time, one saw peanut butter stocked in warehouses around the country and sold through wholesale grocery chains that could deal in carloads with economy to the consumer and profit to the manufacturer," said Lee Avera, who started working in the 1920s for

Rosefield Packing Company, which later made Skippy. "[It] allowed peanut butter to be handled as a less perishable item."[10]

Hydrogenation raises the melting point of peanut oil so that it is solid at room temperature, preventing it from separating from the peanut solids. This is why peanut butter with hydrogenated oil doesn't need to be refrigerated: there's no chance for the peanut oil to pool on top, where, exposed to light and air, it can quickly go rancid. Hydrogenation also increases a product's shelf life. Before hydrogenation, peanut butter was a local product or, at best, a regional one. Since manufacturers no longer had to worry about peanut butter going bad during shipping, hydrogenation made the rise of national brands possible.

Nor did people have to worry about their peanut butter going bad at home. Before the 1920s, refrigeration was something of a novelty, and primitive iceboxes were the only way to preserve unstabilized peanut butter. The first refrigerator in common use, the General Electric Monitor Top, was introduced in 1927,[11] but early refrigerators were expensive. Hydrogenation allowed the masses to keep peanut butter sitting safely on their kitchen shelves. Stabilized or hydrogenated peanut butter would not rapidly dethrone old-fashioned peanut butter, however: natural continued to outsell hydrogenated peanut butter until 1941.[12]

Credit for the first patent to hydrogenate peanut butter usually goes to Joseph Rosefield of Alameda, California.[13] On April 5, 1921, under his birth name Joseph Rosenfield, he filed a patent, "Peanut butter and process of manufacturing the same,"[14] which described a process for partial hydrogenation of peanut oil used to stabilize peanut butter. The stabilized oil in Rosefield's process ordinarily had a melting point of 98 degrees, although that temperature could be higher for peanut butter sold in warmer climates. In partial hydrogenation, crystals in hydrogenated peanut oil are divided finely, rather than coarsely, as is the case with full hydrogenation, helping to create a smoother peanut butter. And its low melting point, closer to body temperature, avoids the waxy feeling associated with hardened or fully hydrogenated oil. Rosefield licensed his patent to the E. K. Pond Company, a wholly owned subsidiary of Swift, in 1923 or 1924.[15]

But history has cheated Pittsburgh inventor Frank Stockton, who filed the first patent for hydrogenating peanut butter almost three weeks before Rosefield, on March 17, 1921.[16] His patent was titled simply "Food product." Little is known about Stockton beyond the fact that he filed twenty-one patents in the early twentieth century. Pittsburgh was a creative and industrious place in the 1920s: U.S. Steel and its competitors produced much of the nation's steel. In 1920 KDKA, the nation's first commercial radio station, went on the air. Companies like H. J. Heinz were growing, financed in part by local institutions such as the Mellon Bank.

The Stockton patent was the first to use the words "peanut butter"; the Kellogg patents had referred simply to "nut butter." Stockton used full rather than partial hydrogenation, as in the case of the Rosefield patent. The molecules in peanut oil are primarily chains of carbon, many of which have hydrogen attached to them. With full hydrogenation, any port on a carbon atom where hydrogen can attach is filled; under partial hydrogenation, some of those ports are left unfilled.

Stockton's method consisted of mixing 85 percent natural peanut oil with 15 percent fully hydrogenated oil, then blending 5 percent by weight of this mixture with 95 percent blanched (skins removed) and roasted peanuts, so that the finished peanut butter contained about three-quarters of 1 percent hydrogenated peanut oil with a melting point between 137 and 140 degrees Fahrenheit, much higher than partially hydrogenated oil.[17] Fully hydrogenated peanut oil, as Stockton acknowledged, is "a hard, brittle solid"—or, as former Skippy plant manager and informal Skippy historian Frank Delfino says, "concrete."[18] But you need less of it to stabilize peanut butter than when using partially hydrogenated oil, only about 1 to 1.5 percent by weight of the peanut butter.

Stockton licensed or assigned his patent to H. J. Heinz to stabilize the peanut butter it had been making since 1909. Tim Gaus of the Heinz Corporate Information Center says, "I have no information about any possible relationship between the Stockton patent and Heinz."[19] But there was one, beyond the fact that both Heinz and Stockton were based in Pittsburgh. Michael Mullen, director of global corporate affairs for H. J. Heinz, says Heinz developed a process that kept the salt evenly distributed throughout the peanut butter.[20] Most patents for hydrogenating peanut butter don't mention salt, but the Stockton patent has a long paragraph about it. Also, Stockton's patent was granted on November 1, 1921; from 1923 on, Heinz peanut butter labels noted that it was patented on November 1, 1921.[21] Finally, Lee Avera, who began working in the peanut butter industry in the 1920s,[22] noted in his testimony to 1966 hearings by the

U.S. Food and Drug Administration (FDA) on a standard of identity for peanut butter that Heinz purchased and used the Stockton patent.[23]

Frank Delfino says because of the standard of identity imposed on peanut butter in the early 1970s by the FDA, all stabilized peanut butters now essentially use a variation of the Stockton process.[24] With true partial hydrogenation, up to about 8.5 percent by volume of the peanut butter is hydrogenated oil. That doesn't leave enough room to add sugar, salt, and other ingredients and still have the 90 percent peanuts the standard of identity insists on. Nonetheless, the Skippy-proud Delfino is a bit touchy on this point. "I wouldn't use the term 'Stockton method' when you're talking about Skippy," the otherwise-kindly octogenarian says, "because if you do, I'll croak you."[25]

Peter Pan is ordinarily credited as the first hydrogenated peanut butter, but even if you lump it in with its now-forgotten hydrogenated forerunner Delicia or Dainty, that's not accurate. Peter Pan was first hydrogenated in 1928, and Delicia/Dainty was on the market in 1924. But the laurels go to Heinz, whose hydrogenation pedigree dates to 1923.

★★★

The hydrogenation process consists of bubbling hydrogen into the bottom of a tank of vegetable oil in the presence of a catalyst such as powdered nickel.[26] This isn't done at the peanut butter plant, but in a separate facility. When vegetable oil is hydrogenated, two things happen: hydrogen atoms attach themselves to carbon atoms and the double bonds of electrons between some carbon atoms are replaced by single bonds between the carbon and hydrogen atoms. Vegetable oil molecules with double bonds have a bent or kinked structure, so they don't stack together easily, causing them to remain fluid. Molecules with single bonds are straighter, stack together easily, and are solid.

By replacing double bonds with single bonds, hydrogenation creates a more tightly packed crystalline structure in the vegetable oil, raising its melting point, according to Chris Craney, a professor of chemistry at Occidental College.[27] He uses the analogy of water and ice: Ice, having a more crystalline form than water, is more densely packed and solid. Water is more diffuse. Hydrogenated oil is like ice; natural oil is like water.

Peanut Butter

George Washington Carver's legendary pamphlet *How to Grow the Peanut and 105 Ways of Preparing It for Human Consumption* was first published by the Tuskegee Agricultural Experiment Station in 1916, about the time Swift's Derby Foods division started to make peanut butter. These instructions for making peanut butter were the pamphlet's fifty-first recipe.

★★★

Shell the peanuts; roast just enough so that the hulls (skins) will slip off easily; remove all the hulls by gently rolling, fanning and screening; grind very fine in any sort of mill, passing through several times if necessary; pack in cans, bottles, or jars, and seal if not for immediate use. Some manufacturers add a little salt and a small amount of olive oil; others do not, according to taste. For small quantities of butter a good meat grinder will answer the purpose. If the nuts are ground fine enough, no additional oil will be necessary.

At a peanut butter factory, after peanuts are roasted, blanched (skins removed), and ground up, hydrogenated vegetable oil is mixed in with ground-up peanuts, sweetener (sugar or dextrose), and salt. The mixture is heated to about 170 degrees during processing, then rapidly cooled to 120 degrees or less.[28] This crystallizes the hydrogenated fatty acids in the stabilizer, trapping the peanut oil released by grinding.

★★★

Hydrogenation originated in Europe around the turn of the twentieth century with the work of chemists Paul Sabatier of France and Wilhelm Normann of Germany.[29] Normann's patents were acquired by the British firm of Joseph Crossfield and Sons, and in 1909 American rights to the Crossfield patents were obtained by Procter & Gamble,[30] which put its hydrogenated cottonseed oil shortening, Crisco, on the market in 1911. (The name Crisco is taken from the initial sounds of "crystallized cottonseed oil.") Frank Stockton and Joseph Rosefield were the first to apply that process to peanut butter.

Although public concerns about hydrogenation have grown in recent years, the peanut butter industry was eager to trumpet its new process in the 1920s and 1930s: early tins of Peter Pan and Skippy carried the slogan "improved by hydrogenation" (figure 4.1). Initially, consumer publications were overtly hostile to the process. In its March 1945 issue, *Consumers' Research Bulletin* gave peanut butter three letter grades: A, B, and C. Noting that "hydrogenation produces a modification of the fatty acid content of the oil which is nutritionally undesirable,"[31] it said perhaps even the best hydrogenated peanut butters should receive no higher than grade B. In 1962, *Consumer Bulletin* said, "Hydrogenated oil is undesirable, and of questionable wholesomeness."[32] But by 1987 *Consumer Reports* had made

FIGURE 4.1 EARLY PETER PAN TIN

Early Peter Pan tin, from the late 1920s or early 1930s. If Swift, which made Peter Pan, ever paid a royalty to playwright J. M. Barrie or even thanked him for the use of his character, there's no record of it. (Courtesy of Allan Dean Walker)

its peace with hydrogenation, saying, "While hydrogenated oil is a saturated fat, not enough is added to increase the saturated-fat level in a significant way."[33]

Originally, only hydrogenated peanut oil was used in peanut butter. Dan Gorbet, now retired from his position as a peanut breeder for the University of Florida, feels that's the only oil that should be allowed.[34] But given the corporate food lobby's clout and preference for cheaper soy, cottonseed, and canola oils, he acknowledges that won't happen anytime soon. A problem with the soy and cottonseed oils peanut butter consumers may be unaware of is that they're often genetically modified.

When I interviewed Gorbet, I told him about Wild Harvest, a then-new brand of peanut butter whose label touted the claim "no genetically engineered ingredients." He derided this as salesmanship targeted to environmentalists, noting that peanuts have not been genetically modified (yet). But later in our interview, he caught himself.

"I mis-spoke earlier," he said. "When you start mixing in other crops, other oils, you do introduce the possibility of transgenic material being involved, because there's definitely transgenic material. The dominant type of soybean grown in the United States is Roundup Ready. Well, that's trans-genic."[35] As of 2001, 80 percent of U.S. soybeans were genetically modified organisms,[36] as was 68 percent of cotton.[37]

Much of the concern over hydrogenation has to do with trans fats, which are unhealthy because they lower the level of HDL (high-density lipoprotein) cholesterol (good cholesterol) in your bloodstream and increase the amount of LDL (low-density lipoprotein) cholesterol, which is considered unhealthy. Consumed in sufficient quantity, trans fats contribute to coronary heart disease by clogging and stiffening your arteries. You can't burn them off by exercising because their melting point is so high.

In order to avoid trans fats, the magazine *New Times Naturally* says, "Avoid any foods that list partially hydrogenated oil(s) in the ingredients."[38] But does peanut butter get a bad rap over trans fats? The Peanut Institute, the research arm of peanut-industry trade groups such as the Georgia Peanut Commission and the American Peanut Shellers Association, says yes, noting that manufacturers add about 1 to 2 percent of hydrogenated oil to peanut butter and that trans fatty acids are only a small portion of that.[39] One would expect such an opinion from a peanut-industry trade organization, but they're in good company.

In a 2001 study, Tim Sanders, a plant physiologist and research leader with the Agricultural Research Service of the U.S. Department of Agriculture in Raleigh, North Carolina, examined eleven brands of stabilized peanut butter, including Jif, Skippy, Peter Pan, and Reese's. He found that the amount of trans-fatty acids contributed by the partially hydrogenated vegetable oil stabilizer in peanut butter was not detectable; because of improvements in current equipment, much smaller amounts can now be detected, but they're so small as to be inconsequential.

His calculations using the amount of trans fatty acid in the stabilizer and the amount of stabilizer added to peanut butter indicated that there were less than .0032 gram per two-tablespoon serving.[40] When significant amounts of trans fats have gotten into peanut butter, Skippy's Frank Delfino says, it's been because of improper catalysts,[41] while Gary List, a leading expert on fats and oils,[42] says it's because of excessively high temperatures used during the hydrogenation process.[43]

If the amount of trans fat in stabilized peanut butter were multiplied 156 times, only then would it reach 0.5 gram per two-tablespoon serving, the level at which FDA standards require its presence to be noted on the label. While people don't always restrict themselves to the standard serving size, that's still pretty low. (Half a gram per two-tablespoon serving means that a food can contain 1.6 percent trans fat and still legally say it has zero trans fat. This raises legitimate public policy questions about what the FDA lets the food industry get away with, but peanut butter is nowhere close to that.)

Michael Jacobson, executive director of the Center for Science in the Public Interest, says, "I suspect that one cookie made with partially hydrogenated oil contains ten times as much trans fat as a tablespoon of peanut butter. It would be nice to get rid of all of the trans fat, but I wouldn't focus on that as being a real problem in peanut butter." Asked if natural peanut butter without hydrogenated oils is healthier than stabilized peanut butter, he says, "It might be a teeny, teeny bit healthier, but if there really is .003 grams of trans fat per serving, it really is trivial."[44] Jacobson adds that sodium, or salt, in peanut butter is of more concern to him.

"Sodium is a very significant cause of high blood pressure. Peanut butter is a source of sodium." But even there, he adds, "there are much bigger sources. The bread in a peanut butter sandwich probably has more sodium than the peanut butter. And any meal at a restaurant easily has 10 times as much sodium as you'll find in peanut butter." But while hydrogenation produces only a low level of trans fats in peanut butter, it poses another problem, as *Consumers' Research Bulletin* noted in 1945: hydrogenating a vegetable oil eliminates its nutritionally valuable linoleic acid.[45]

Hydrogenation isn't used just to extend the shelf life of products such as peanut butter and Crisco; it has a wide variety of industrial applications, such as converting lignite and coal into liquid fuels, and it's also used in the synthesis of nylon. But as of the early 1980s, it hasn't been the only method of stabilizing peanut butter: now there's fractional crystallization, commonly known as fractionation.

With this method, palm oil is chilled, causing a part (or fraction) of the oil to form crystals. The crystals are melted and chilled again. The fraction that crystallizes first is cooled again, and the process is repeated several times. The residue is palm oil that is essentially crystalline or solid at room temperature. You mix it with ground-up peanuts, resulting in stabilized peanut butter. This method is used by Jif, Skippy, MaraNatha, and other brands.

The label may list palm oil, palm fruit oil, or even organic palm oil. MaraNatha describes its peanut butter with fractionated palm oil as "no-stir," while Jif and Skippy call it "natural." But is it legitimate to call peanut butter with fractionated palm oil natural? Although Frank Delfino is a Skippy die-hard, he's dubious. "Somebody says, 'We don't do anything. We take out this fraction, so it's natural,'" he says. "Well, it may be natural someplace, but it's not natural in nature."[46]

Fractionated palm oil has ecological drawbacks as well. The growing use of palm plantations to generate palm oil for products such as no-stir peanut butter is causing the destruction of tropical rain forests, grasslands, and peat swamps throughout South America, Southeast Asia, Oceania, and Africa. Also, palm oil is highly saturated, so it increases bad cholesterol more than unsaturated oils like peanut, canola, soybean, and cottonseed oils. Palm oil is even more saturated than lard, by a margin of 51 to 41 percent.[47]

In the marketplace, stabilized peanut butter (primarily hydrogenated) is the easy winner over what is variously called natural, old-fashioned, or unstabilized peanut butter: in 2005, it was outselling it at a ratio of 9 to 1.[48] As for myself, I eat unstabilized or natural peanut butter almost exclusively. While hydrogenated oils aren't as bad as their harsher critics maintain, they don't make peanut butter taste better (although they do make it smoother), nor do they make it more nutritious. I'd rather pay for peanuts than chemically altered oils whose purpose is to extend shelf life and prevent oil separation. And since the widespread advent of refrigeration several generations ago, oil separation in natural peanut butter isn't a problem—you just stick it in the fridge. While refrigerated peanut butter doesn't spread as easily, turning the jar upside down lets the oils blend back in with the solids, and removing the peanut butter from the fridge once it gets down to the bottom of the jar and most of the oil has been eaten decreases the possibility of rancidity.

★★★

The working relationship between Joseph Rosefield and Swift lasted until 1932 and appears to have included Rosefield Packing Company's distributing Peter Pan on the West Coast.[49] But in 1932 Rosefield withdrew his patent from Swift. There were big changes at Swift in the early 1930s: In 1931 Louis Swift, son of founder Gustavus Swift, stepped down after nearly thirty years as company president, and in 1932 he retired. That year, his brother, Edward Swift, chairman of Swift's board of directors, died.

More important for our story, George Cantine Case died in July 1931.[50] Case had been the head of E. K. Pond, the peanut-butter-producing subsidiary of Derby Foods, which was in turn a subsidiary of Swift. Case had a cordial working relationship with Joseph Rosefield,[51] but when Case's successor tried to slash Rosefield's patent licensing fee, Rosefield left and took his patent with him.[52]

As his son, Jerome, told the FDA's hearings on a standard of identity for peanut butter in 1966, Rosefield licensed his patent to Swift until December 31, 1932,[53] and canceled the contract as of January 31, 1933.[54] Rosefield Packing Company then remodeled its plant in Alameda, California, allowing it to produce partially hydrogenated peanut butter, which it started doing in May 1933.[55]

When Rosefield yanked his patent from Swift, it promptly switched to another patent developed by inventor Leo Brown. He applied for it in June 1932, and it was patented the next year.[56] His patent is notable for its focus on spit, mentioning no fewer than four times that one of its virtues is that it prevents peanut butter from sticking to the roof of the mouth by mixing more easily with saliva than unstabilized peanut butter.

Swift's Derby Division appears to have chosen the name Peter Pan because of the popularity of the character created by British playwright J. M. Barrie (figure 4.2). "Peter Pan, you may recall, would never grow old," the advertising trade publication *Printers Ink* noted. "That is why the name was chosen."[57] It made sense to choose it in 1928: in New York, Eva LeGalliene's Civic Repertory Theater on Fourteenth Street opened its

FIGURE 4.2 WORLD WAR II–ERA ADVERTISEMENT

Peter Pan ad from 1944. The E. K. Pond and Derby divisions of Swift made Peter Pan from its inception in the late 1920s until the early 1980s. (www.vintagepaperads.com)

production of *Peter Pan*, which would run until 1933. A London version of the show had been running continuously for more than twenty years, and, adding a touch of notoriety, anonymous pranksters tarred and feathered the Peter Pan statue in London's Hyde Park that August, making the front page of the *New York Times*.[58]

Although the name capitalized on Peter Pan's fame, there's no evidence that Swift reimbursed Barrie for its use. Christine De Poortere, who holds the title of Peter Pan Director at Great Ormond Street Hospital Children's Charity in London, says, "Peter Pan peanut butter was launched in 1928, a year before James Barrie gifted his Peter Pan copyright to Great Ormond Street Hospital. As far as I know, the hospital has never received any payment or royalties for the use of the character and I have not been able to ascertain whether permission was granted by James Barrie himself at the time, whether he ever received any payment for such use, or even if he knew about it."[59] If Barrie or his estate wanted royalties from Swift for the use of his character, they would have to look in Neverland.

HOW PETER PAN LOST ITS GROOVE

The history of Peter Pan is the most difficult to trace of the three major brands,[1] as Swift and subsequent owners have practiced the dark arts of secrecy in a way designed to confound all but the most adroit corporate Sovietologists. We know that Swift bought Derby Foods and E .K. Pond in 1904, that by 1914 it was making peanut butter, and that Peter Pan dates to 1928. But for many of the fifty-five years it made Peter Pan, Swift kept its name at arm's length from it.

News articles about and advertising for Peter Pan ordinarily refer to Derby Foods, rather than Swift. A perusal of Swift & Company annual reports reveals no mention of Peter Pan until 1969 (but another Swift brand of peanut butter, Oz, is mentioned as early as 1940, while Swift and Swift Premium brands are mentioned intermittently in the early 1930s and 1940s).[2] A 1950 *Chicago Tribune* article claims peanut butter is one of Swift's newer products, adding that its factory at 3327 West Forty-seventh Place on Chicago's South Side, had been in operation for only two years.[3] In fact, it had been built in 1924. (Different floors of that factory manufactured canned meats, creating possibilities for cross-contamination that make it unlikely it could be built today.) The *Tribune* article doesn't even mention Peter Pan. Why was Swift so bashful about its ties to Peter Pan? Some think it's because of a 1920 consent decree imposed on Swift and the major Chicago meatpackers by the U.S. Department of Justice.

In 1917, concerned that the big Chicago packers were acting in a monopolistic manner, President Woodrow Wilson ordered a Federal Trade Commission (FTC) investigation. The FTC found evidence of monopoly,[4] and in a consent decree drawn up by Wilson's attorney general, A. Mitchell Palmer, on February 27, 1920,[5] Swift and the other major packers agreed to permanently withdraw from making a long list of foods unrelated to wholesale meatpacking. Later that year, after Swift signed the consent decree promising to get out of non-meat-related food lines, its Derby Foods division introduced Peter Pan.[6]

However, as Janie Ingalls in the anti-trust division of the U.S. Department of Justice notes, peanuts and, by implication, peanut products were not included under the terms of the consent decree.[7] So Swift's discretion about Peter Pan probably wasn't a function of its not wanting to run afoul of the Department of Justice. Its mystifying reluctance to be associated with it, though, and the lack of solid information about Peter Pan's early days, constitutes the Bermuda Triangle of peanut butter.

Swift did want consumers to know about "Derby's Peter Pan," though. In the early 1940s, Peter Pan was supposedly the first nationally advertised peanut butter; however, given that major companies like Beech-Nut and Heinz were making peanut butter by 1910, this claim has to be treated skeptically. During World War II, young women dressed up as Peter Pan made presentations to business and consumer audiences.

A 1944 article in *Sales Management* magazine notes, "Men being as scarce as they are today, Peter Pan . . . has built up a crew of 20 girl 'salesmen.' Each girl works in a trim forest-green dress with a feathered woodsy green cap and green shoes."[8] They spoke to distributors, retailers, and schoolchildren. In the latter case, they never mentioned peanut butter, but simply told the story of Peter Pan. In the mid- to late 1940s, Peter Pan ran comic-strip-style ads in which Peter Pan saves kids from one disaster or another and sponsored the radio adventure series *Sky King*, about a heroic pilot.

Not all Peter Pan advertising went according to plan. In a famous 1961 incident, TV host Art James was doing a live Peter Pan commercial on the game show *Say When*. As he thrust a knife into the jar, the bottom of the jar fell off and he was splashed with peanut butter.[9] Because it was live, there was no chance for a second take and James, more amused than horrified by the incident, had to struggle to retain his composure while getting through the commercial.

And a late-1960s Peter Pan ad touting the introduction of whipped peanut butter was never even broadcast. The McCann-Erickson advertising agency came up with a TV commercial to show how light and airy the product was. Someone suggested an ad featuring a hot-air balloon. Noted balloonist Don Piccard agreed to let the agency use his balloon if he could appear in the commercial, and the agency chose Southern California's Conejo Valley for the filming.

Shortly after firing up the balloon, though, the cast and crew heard sirens. "What's that?" someone asked. "Trouble," the commercial's director said.[10] And it was: the fire department showed up to say it was illegal to have an open fire on the rangeland because of the danger to local crops, cattle, and homes. They were told to film their commercial someplace that couldn't catch fire.

The crew moved to a local schoolyard, with the fire department standing by. As soon as word got out about the hot-air balloon and film crew, several thousand locals descended on the site, creating a festive, carnival-like atmosphere, but making it difficult to keep the crowd out of camera range.

When the balloonist called "Ready," the balloon's ropes were cast off and it began to rise. The chase helicopter lifted off, carrying the camera crew. The cameraman warned the helicopter pilot not to get too close to the balloon for fear of creating excessive air turbulence. "I'll try not to," was the pilot's sanguine reply. "But this is only my second flight on a chopper. I usually fly crop dusters."

And the pilot did get too close to the balloon, causing it to veer sideways and allowing most of its hot air to escape. According to Terry Galanoy's book *Down the Tube*, this is how it played out:

> The spectators gasped. The camera crew forgot their cameras and looked on with horror.
>
> "Watch out!" somebody yelled at the balloonist. The balloon was falling.
>
> The balloonist looked frantically around for some protection. He usually had a helmet. There was none aboard. He reached for the nearest

helmet-looking object and jammed it on his head. It was a large bowl full of peanut butter.

Crash experts said later that the consistency of the goo protected his skull from the heavy shock when the balloon banged down hard on a supermarket parking lot.

Two ladies who had just left the supermarket were wheeling their groceries by as the balloon came crashing down.

"Don't even look at it," one said, staring straight ahead. "They're just trying to get your attention."[11]

Peanut Butter Garlic Bread

¼ cup smooth or crunchy peanut butter
¼ cup olive oil
1 clove garlic, crushed
⅛ teaspoon salt
1 loaf French bread

Mix peanut butter with olive oil, garlic, and salt.

Slice French bread in 1-inch slices not quite through bottom of loaf.

Spread peanut butter mixture between slices.

Wrap in aluminum foil and bake in hot oven (400 degrees) 10–15 minutes. Serve hot.

★★★

Yield: 6–8 servings.

FROM WILLIAM I. KAUFMAN, *THE "I LOVE PEANUT BUTTER" COOKBOOK* (GARDEN CITY, N.Y.: DOUBLEDAY, 1965). REPRINTED WITH PERMISSION OF JACQUELINE KAUFMAN AND IVA KAUFMAN.

Through the years, Peter Pan has gotten generally favorable reviews from consumer publications such as *Consumer Reports*; it's been lauded variously for its spreadability, sweetness, and having a lot of peanut chunks in its crunchy variety. But in 1972 both samples of Peter Pan crunchy tested by *Consumer Reports* contained insect fragments and rodent hairs. "We doubt that a health hazard is posed by the relatively small amounts of insect fragments and rodent hairs we found," the magazine noted. "But they are esthetically objectionable."[12]

Even more objectionable was the first *Salmonella* outbreak in peanut butter in U.S. history, which happened to Peter Pan in 1971 or 1972. Swift was able to keep a lid on the situation, and neither the public nor the government became aware of it, although some in the peanut butter industry did.[13] At the time, Sanford Bass was traffic manager for the Derby Foods division of Swift in Chicago. Now retired in Topeka, Kansas, he shared his recollections of the incident with the Web site consumeraffairs.com.

"The culprit in this situation was three strains of *Salmonella* resulting from poultry products produced at the same plant," he said. The possibility for cross-contamination that had always existed in the plant had finally been realized. "We were down for several months until we could effectively clean the piping system to prevent further contamination.

"We recalled [the peanut butter] to our broker warehouses, loaded it into thirteen box cars, and buried it in a phosphate mine owned by Swift in Agricola, Florida," Bass added.[14] Agricola, seventy miles east of the Tampa–St. Petersburg area, was at that time a ghost town, but it had been a thriving Swift company town during the first half of the century.

As the plant's traffic manager, Bass coordinated the shipping of the *Salmonella*-tainted peanut butter. He doesn't know if the government was notified of the recall. "I had no knowledge of reporting procedures of these problems to government agencies, nor was it my responsibility," he says. "This was the function of management." It appears that Swift management didn't perform that function: according to a report by the Centers for Disease Control and Prevention about the 2007 Peter Pan *Salmonella* outbreak, "This is the first reported outbreak of a food-borne illness caused by peanut butter consumption in the United States."[15] It isn't clear how much of the peanut butter got out to the public, nor how Swift retrieved the peanut butter and disposed of it while keeping the government and public in the dark.

The 1980s were, like the 1920s, a period of unabated business boosterism that Sinclair Lewis would no doubt have felt at home satirizing. During that Reaganesque decade, Peter Pan went through several ownership changes in rapid succession: in 1983, Swift sold it to Esmark, which merged it with its Hunt-Wesson Foods operation on the West Coast. The next year, Beatrice Foods bought Esmark and started to build a new Peter Pan plant in Sylvester, Georgia (figure 5.1).[16] The plant was completed in 1986,[17] the year Beatrice was acquired by Kohlberg, Kravis, and Roberts, the New York–based investment firm whose aggressive tactics in taking over companies and dismantling them in order to reap large, short-term profits were highlighted in *Barbarians at the Gate.*

In 1990 ConAgra bought Beatrice. ConAgra had started in 1919 as Nebraska Consolidated Mills. It expanded through the years and bought more than 100 processed-food brands in the 1980s and 1990s. Among its products are Butterball frozen turkeys, Chef Boyardee pasta, Slim Jim meat snacks, Banquet TV dinners, Gulden's mustard, and Eggbeaters.

Sylvester, Peter Pan's new home, was a small southern town rather than a big northern city. Signs at the edge of Sylvester proclaim it the peanut

FIGURE 5.1 PETER PAN SYLVESTER PLANT

The Peter Pan plant in Sylvester, Georgia, was built in 1986. Today owned by ConAgra Foods, it was extensively redesigned following a *Salmonella* contamination that began in 2006 and was discovered in 2007. (Photo by the author)

capital of the world, a designation claimed by several other communities in the peanut belt. But this town of 6,000 in southwestern Georgia is small by most standards: when I called its public library in 2008 and asked if I had reached the reference desk, an amused woman's voice answered in a soft southern accent, "This is the only desk."

The year before, Peter Pan had suffered its second *Salmonella* outbreak, and this time there was no concealing it from the public or the government.

In 2005, a new plant manager, twenty-five-year-old Tom Gentle, began work at the Peter Pan plant, telling the *Sylvester Local News*: "Anything that comes out of here could be on one of our children's sandwiches at lunch. It has to be perfect when it goes out the door."[18] Local residents described the plant as "scrupulously clean,"[19] but that's not how William Marler of Seattle, one of the lead attorneys in the eventual lawsuits against ConAgra, saw it. "We got a court order to go in there," he says. "They did some cleaning before we got there. But it was pretty Third World–like."[20]

Consuming *Salmonella* bacteria can cause diarrhea, cramps, vomiting, fever and chills, and even death. A distant early warning of the Peter Pan *Salmonella* outbreak came in 2005, when inspectors of the U.S. Food and Drug Administration, alerted to problems in the Sylvester plant by a former employee, went there and asked why a batch of Peter Pan had been destroyed. ConAgra acknowledged it had done so, but refused to say why unless the FDA filed a written request with corporate headquarters in Omaha.[21] It never did.[22]

In August 2006, *Salmonella* cases started to appear around the country;[23] the Centers for Disease Control noticed an increase that November, but the source of the outbreak wasn't clear. In early February 2007, the CDC noticed an alarming spike in cases[24] and notified the FDA, which, along with state and local health authorities, traced the outbreak to the Sylvester plant.

After the recall of Peter Pan was announced, attorney William Marler started getting phone calls from people asking him to sue Peter Pan. He soon learned Peter Pan was made by ConAgra, with which he had had a litigious relationship dating back to its 2002 ground beef recall. He e-mailed a ConAgra attorney he'd previously dealt with at corporate headquarters in Omaha, saying, "I'm going to sue you." The attorney e-mailed back, "I figured that."[25]

On February 14, 2007, a recall was announced for Peter Pan and Great Value, the Walmart house brand, which was also produced at ConAgra's Sylvester plant (figure 5.2).[26] To its credit, ConAgra kept all of the plant employees on salary during the six months the plant was down.

In the end, ConAgra was responsible for 714 reported cases of *Salmonella* poisoning in forty-seven states.[27] (The CDC estimates that for every person counted in an outbreak, about thirty-eight others remain uncounted, so the outbreak was probably much larger.) Allegedly among them: eleven-year-old Krystina Brugh of Indiana, who suffered kidney failure after eating Peter Pan. Her father donated one of his kidneys to her.

Residents of Sylvester stood behind one of its biggest local employers, sometimes recklessly so. Pearson Golden, owner of a seed and feed store

FIGURE 5.2 RECALLED JARS OF PETER PAN

The Peter Pan *Salmonella* contamination in 2006–2007 resulted in 714 reported cases of illness. The problem was traced to moisture (from the Sylvester plant's leaky roof and a faulty sprinkler system) polluted with bird droppings and bacteria from raw peanuts and peanut dust. (AP photo/John Bazemore)

in downtown Sylvester, refused to part with his jar of Peter Pan, even though it carried the "2111" product code indicating it was part of the recall. "I'm going to eat it," Golden told the Associated Press. "Put it back on the shelves again because my supply is running low."[28] (If his jar wasn't made in July, August, or September 2006, when most of the tainted peanut butter was produced,[29] he was probably safe, but it isn't clear if he actually chose to put himself in the running for a Darwin Award or not.)

ConAgra Foods said moisture from the plant's leaky roof and a faulty sprinkler contributed to the *Salmonella* outbreak.[30] The moisture had mixed with dormant bacteria that probably came from raw peanuts and peanut dust, and the *Salmonella* somehow came in contact with the peanut butter before packaging. To make matters worse, the plant's leaky roof contained not only water but bird droppings.[31]

Consumer advocates expressed outrage when it turned out the federal government had known for years about problems at the Sylvester plant (and in spinach fields in California that were the source of an *E. coli* outbreak), but done nothing about them. "The Bush administration did a lousy job in preventing food-borne illnesses," says Michael Jacobson, director of the Center for Science in the Public Interest. "[There was] no support for increasing the powers of the Food and Drug Administration. And there was continually reduced funding over [its] last five or six years."[32]

Paul Krugman of the *New York Times* noted that under George W. Bush, the FDA was dominated by what historian Rick Pearlstein called *E. coli* conservatives, more supportive of corporate autonomy than public health. "The Bush administration won't issue food safety regulations even when the private sector wants them," Krugman said. "They are influenced by an ideology that says business should never be regulated, no matter what," an ideology Krugman called literally sickening.[33]

The Peter Pan plant reopened for partial operations in August 2007; ConAgra invested $50 million in upgrades—among them, redesigning the plant to keep the raw peanuts farther away from the finished peanut butter. It also hired food safety expert Paul A. Hall as vice president of global food safety and established a food safety advisory committee chaired by Michael Doyle, director of the University of Georgia's Center for Food Safety. However, these steps did not keep Walmart and other private-label brands that had been made at the Sylvester plant from heading for the exit.[34]

In October 2007, the plant resumed full operations, marking the occasion with a celebration that included a ribbon cutting and barbecue dinner for employees. Among the speakers was Debbie Cannon, a staffer for Senator Saxby Chambliss (R-Ga.), who told those attending, "God bless Peter Pan peanut butter and God bless America."[35]

It wasn't just the extreme laissez-faire philosophy of the Bush administration that enabled the Peter Pan *Salmonella* outbreak. William Marler says there were factors unique to ConAgra. "My company [his law firm] is my company. It's personal to me," Marler says. "The quality of what we produce here is important. I think that one of the things ConAgra struggles with is that they don't have this culture of 'I am the one who created this.' Many of their companies, if not all, are brands they've purchased from someone else. So what they are is a brand company, an investment company in brands. Their interest is [in making] an investment, not necessarily in producing the highest-quality product."[36]

The Peter Pan case wasn't the first time ConAgra had sent contaminated food out to the public. In July 2002, ConAgra recalled 19 million pounds of ground beef from its Greeley, Colorado, plant, one of the largest meat recalls in U.S. history, because of contamination by the *E. coli* bacteria.[37] Later in 2007 ConAgra suffered its second *Salmonella* outbreak of the year, in its Banquet pot pies, produced at another plant.[38] Dean Hollis, the ConAgra executive in charge of the division that made peanut butter and pot pies, resigned in November 2007.[39] But that didn't stop ConAgra's problems: in June 2009, three workers died and forty-one were injured when an explosion caused part of the roof to collapse at ConAgra's Slim Jim meat snacks plant near Raleigh, North Carolina.[40]

Most large corporations are not eager to cooperate with outsiders: As Tina Neer, manager of corporate communications at Smuckers, told me when I called to ask some questions about Jif, "Brand management is one of our key daily things. So if we can't have control over what's being published, we just can't participate."[41] But ConAgra, press-shy at the best of times, would prove even more recalcitrant after its string of problems.

On the local level, Peter Pan workers are not from Sylvester, but nearby towns like Tifton and Albany. As a result, reporters from the *Sylvester Local News* don't even know who the Peter Pan workers are. "It's all very hush-hush," says Sherry Walls, who was working as a reporter for the *Local News* in 2007.[42] She got another example of ConAgra's code of *omertá* in her dealings with Tom Gentle. When the outbreak hit, he was sacked as plant manager. But Walls called him several times while working on articles after he was replaced, and he answered her questions as if he were still the plant manager.[43] She was in the dark for a week until it somehow came out.

After the outbreak, a ConAgra spokesman said reporters would never again be allowed into the Peter Pan plant,[44] supposedly for competitive reasons, although it seems it'd be eager to show off its $50 million renovation. Nonetheless, I e-mailed ConAgra on August 6, 2008, before heading to Georgia, saying I was hoping to meet the plant manager and get a tour of the plant. ConAgra's spokesman responded the next day to say neither would be possible and, as a sort of consolation prize, provided me with a brief excerpt from the Peter Pan Web site about how peanut butter is made.

Undaunted, I called the plant on August 20, spoke with the security guard who answered the phone, and asked to speak with a plant official whose name I'd been given. The guard connected me to the official's voice mail, but before I could leave a message, a robo-voice said my message had not been recorded and hung up. When I passed through Sylvester at the end of August, I drove up to the plant anyway and snapped a few pictures. Although the plant wall featured a typically benign corporate bromide ("Sylvester Team Vision: One Team, working together, becoming the #1 Peanut Butter brand . . . one spoon at a time" [figure 5.3]), it also felt a little creepy: signs warned "No trespassing" and "Parking facilities under surveillance and security patrols." Although it reveals a lack of valor on my part, I did not attempt to enter the plant.

Then there's the matter of the plant's peanut roaster, supposedly the largest in the world. I e-mailed ConAgra to ask how big it is, and how many pounds of peanuts it can roast in an hour. A spokeswoman told me the information was not available, again for competitive reasons. If I get notes from Jif and Skippy promising not to take advantage of Peter Pan, I asked, would she tell me then? I never heard back from her. (Incidentally, the answer, according to the History Channel's *Modern Marvels*, is "more than 150 feet long.")[45]

In early 2009 it looked like I had caught a break when I spoke with Susan Bond, the ConAgra official responsible for oversight of scientific and regulatory affairs. Our contact was unusual in that she sought me

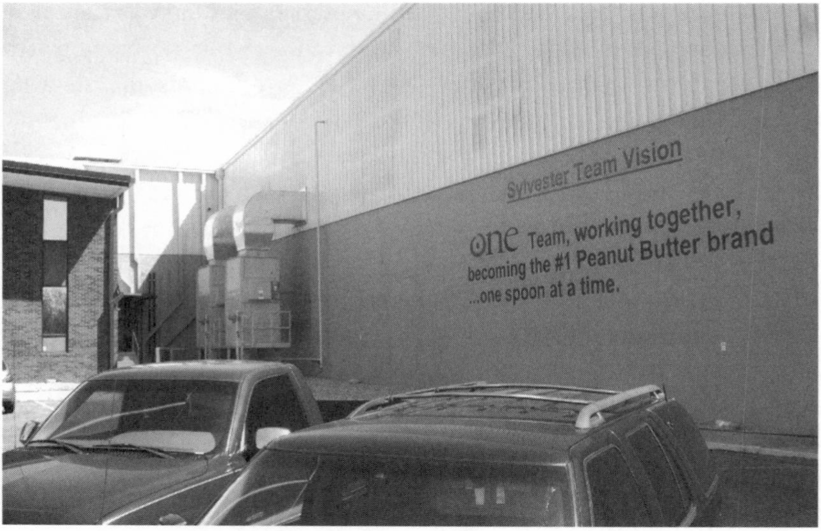

FIGURE 5.3 "ONE TEAM, WORKING TOGETHER" SIGN

Despite this motto on the wall of ConAgra's Peter Pan plant, Peter Pan is a distant third behind Jif and Skippy in the race for peanut butter market leadership. (Courtesy of Sherry Walls/worthit2u.net)

out, having seen a posting of mine on the Web site of the U.S. Food and Drug Administration, where she had previously worked. Pleasant and outgoing, she said ConAgra was the one food company they didn't see much when she was at the FDA. "They didn't come in—just kind of paranoid almost, you know?" she said. "Things have really changed, but there's still a lot of that 'I don't know if we can speak to people' mind-set."[46] She spoke well of current ConAgra Foods CEO Gary Rodkin as being very proactive and transparent. (If things are transparent now, I wondered, what must they have been like in the bad old days?) She also suggested I contact the Peter Pan brand manager and promised to look around on my behalf. But the brand manager never got back to me, nor did Susan.

Three years before the 2007 Peter Pan *Salmonella* outbreak, an article in its old hometown newspaper, the *Chicago Tribune*, called Peter Pan and other well-known brands such as Wonder Bread, Duncan Hines cake mixes, and Old Style beer "orphans" neglected as a result of massive consolidation in the food industry and pushed out of prime shelf space at grocery stores.

"Huge food companies like Kraft, Kellogg, and Procter & Gamble spread distribution and marketing costs across a number of $1 billion brands," it noted. "Such economies of scale free up hundreds of millions to improve everything from manufacturing and packaging to paying for the best shelf space to using their clout to get the best advertising rates.

"Have-nots," the article continued, "have been bought and sold many times by owners looking for short-term gains. That usually leaves them staggering under mounds of debt and without sufficient cash for competitive advertising or to innovate or improve product quality, manufacturing, or distribution."[47]

While the article's claim that Peter Pan had been the country's dominant brand for forty years after its introduction in 1928 is questionable, its assertion that it's fallen on hard times isn't. By 1975 it was in third place, with a 20 percent market share.[48] In 2006 it held only 11 percent of the crunchy market and 13 percent of the creamy,[49] and in the wake of the 2007 *Salmonella* outbreak, it's probably lower still.

The first brand to market usually becomes the market leader. But Peter Pan is now a distant third, despite having the crunchiest crunchy of the Big Three. Peter Pan was the boy who would never grow old, but the fortunes of his peanut butter have shown the ravages of time. Meanwhile, the peanut butter founded when Peter Pan tried to slash royalty fees to its owner for his patented hydrogenation process would leave Peter Pan in the dust.

SKIPPY

"HE MADE HIS FIRST JAR OF PEANUT BUTTER IN HIS GARAGE"

Although Skippy came on the market only five years after Peter Pan, it was a different business climate and a different world. After the stock market crash of October 1929, the Roaring Twenties gave way to the Great Depression, which hit bottom in 1933, the year Skippy was launched. Forty million Americans were plunged into poverty. Businessmen went from owning their own homes to renting rooms to becoming homeless. Okies like John Steinbeck's Tom Joad saw their farms fall victim to massive dust storms and migrated to California to live hard lives recorded in *The Grapes of Wrath*. Down-on-their-luck people selling apples on city sidewalks became a common sight, as did hobos riding the rails. Over cameo portraits of Andrew Carnegie and other industrialists, the headline of a 1932 full-page ad in the *National Nut News* proclaimed, "Their Confidence Was Justified . . . America Came Through . . . America Has Beaten 19 Major Depressions—She Will Beat This One."[1]

As an inexpensive source of protein, peanut butter was a good food for hard times. But it wasn't hard times for everyone. In 1938, at age twelve, William F. Buckley Jr. was packed off to boarding school in England, taking with him a fondness for peanut butter. Every two weeks, his father sent him a case of grapefruit and a large jar of peanut butter. Buckley offered to share his good fortune with his British schoolmates. "They grabbed instinctively for the grapefruit—but one after another actually spit out the peanut butter, which they had never seen before and which only that very year had become available for sale in London," Buckley later wrote, adding, "No wonder they needed American help to win the war."[2]

Of the major brands, Buckley liked Skippy best, although his favorite was Red Wing peanut butter of Fredonia, New York,[3] which made house brands for various supermarket chains. Skippy, though, inspired him to wax poetic:

I know that I shall never see
A poem lovely as Skippy's peanut butter.[4]

While Buckley's peanut butter scholarship was questionable (he attributed its discovery to George Washington Carver), his lifelong enthusiasm was indisputable. When he died in 2008, his son, writer Christopher Buckley, told a crowded memorial service at St. Patrick's Cathedral in New York that in his coffin were his favorite rosary, his television remote control, and a jar of peanut butter. "No pharaoh off to the afterlife goes better equipped than he does," Buckley quipped.[5]

Although Skippy would eventually become the nation's best-selling peanut butter for more than thirty years, it was originally envisioned as a high-end product, targeted more to the Buckleys than the Joads. "Distribution was aimed at the quality market [when it was introduced in 1933]," according to a 1945 article in the trade magazine *Sales Management*. "The product cost nearly twice as much as most of its competitors . . . [then] they discovered that their customers were not in the quality group they had aimed at, but in the middle-income group."[6]

Skippy peanut butter was the brainchild of Joseph Louis Rosefield (birth name Rosenfield), a native of Louisville, Kentucky, and one of three children of Manuel and Carrie Rosenfield. Joseph was the grandson of immigrants from Wurtemberg,[7] the southern province of Germany that includes Stuttgart. Wurtemberg's entrepreneur-inventors included Gottleib Daimler, founder of Mercedes-Benz, and Count Ferdinand von Zeppelin, creator of the turn-of-the-twentieth-century airships. Among the province's principal exports were beer, wine, and spirits. The Rosenfields themselves turned out to be an export as well—by 1880, Manuel was running a men's clothing store in Louisville. Business must have been good, as they not only had two infant children, Sarah and John, but two servants. Their third child, Joseph, was born on December 18, 1882.

In the late 1890s, the Rosenfields heeded Horace Greeley's admonition to go west and by 1898 were living in Cripple Creek, Colorado.[8] Some 9,500 feet above sea level and just below the timberline in the front range of the Rocky Mountains, the town was the site of the last great Colorado gold rush. The miners lived hard and drank hard; true to his Wurtemberg roots, Manuel was proprietor of the Old Kentucky Liquor Company, where both his sons worked. Cripple Creek was a violent place, with a Wild West mentality and bloody battles between mine owners and labor unions. At one point, there was a killing a day, and, on November 11, 1898, when Joseph Rosenfield was fifteen, his nineteen-year-old brother, John, shot a man dead: as a deputy constable, he killed a drunken blacksmith who attacked him. The case was found to be justifiable homicide.[9]

By 1904 the Rosenfields had moved to Pueblo, on the high plains of Colorado. That May, Joseph was married in Boulder. According to the *Boulder Daily Camera,* he married Mary Call of Cheyenne, Wyoming, on May 13.[10] But Census records indicate his bride was Mae Sutherland of Paterson, New Jersey (figure 6.1).[11]

FIGURE 6.1 JOSEPH AND MAE ROSEFIELD

Skippy founder Joseph Rosefield and his wife, Mae, probably onboard the cruise ship *Lurleen* as it arrived in Honolulu in the 1940s or early 1950s. A hard-driving businessman, Rosefield started Skippy in 1933, during the depths of the Great Depression, and made it the number-one brand of peanut butter in the United States from about 1945 through 1980. (Courtesy of Frank Delfino)

By 1910 the Rosenfields had moved again, to Denver. Joseph's father, Manuel, now a widower, was living with him and his wife, Mae, but twenty-seven-year-old Joseph was now head of the household and the proprietor of the Old Kentucky Liquor Company. He and Mae had two sons, Jerome (figure 6.2) and Marvin (figure 6.3) and a daughter, Virginia. Three years later, they moved again, to Alameda,[12] on an island on the east side of San Francisco Bay next to Oakland.

FIGURE 6.2 JEROME ROSEFIELD

Joseph Rosefield's son, Jerome, handled marketing for Skippy. Preoccupied with quality control, he would go into out-of-town grocery stores on vacations and remove Skippy jars past their sell-by dates from the shelves. (Courtesy of Frank Delfino)

FIGURE 6.3 MARVIN ROSEFIELD

Joseph Rosefield's son, Marvin (seen here with his secretary), served as plant manager and enforced the ban on adult male visitors to the Alameda, California, plant because of concerns that they might pirate its unpatented production equipment. (Courtesy of Frank Delfino)

As Joseph Rosefield's grandson Rick Rosefield tells it, the move was happenstance. "He stopped to visit friends on his way to Los Angeles," he laughs. "He wasn't coming to Alameda."[13] But that—and later, when he was successful, nearby Piedmont—was where he stayed: he apparently knew some people there and took a liking to the town. It isn't clear whether he changed his name because it sounded too Jewish (there's no evidence of Jewish ancestry in his family, although son Marvin was denied a country-club membership in the 1950s on the suspicion he had Jewish roots),[14] because it sounded too German (this was about the time of World War I), or because it represented a new start in California. But whatever the reason, it appears he left Colorado a Rosenfield and arrived in California a Rosefield.

Instead of continuing in the liquor business, he first worked as an icebox salesman, then a food salesman, traveling up and down Alameda Island on the community's trolley system, known as the Interurban Electric Railroad.[15] About 1915, he founded the Rosefield Packing Company,[16] working out of the 150-square-foot garage of his house at 1339 Burbank Street in the Burbank-Portola neighborhood of Alameda, an area of comfortable bungalows and palm trees on San Francisco Bay. Although he packaged and sold different food products, there were only two he made himself: pickles and peanut butter. "He built the machinery himself and made his first jar of peanut butter in his garage," says George Mackin, a longtime Rosefield employee.[17] At the time, there were about a dozen manufacturers of peanut butter in the San Francisco Bay area.[18]

Joseph Rosefield's family and friends recall him with admiration. Rick Rosefield says he was of medium height, athletic, with red hair before he went bald, confident and self-assured, with a strong character and convictions. Although somewhat reserved, he was a superb salesman and liked his coffee boiling hot.[19] Thomas Fuller, who started working for Rosefield in 1951, says, "He was a fantastic, brilliant man. He made a presentation to Congress once that they said was one of the finest that had ever been made. It was about the railroad [shipping] rates."[20] (Because the San Francisco Bay area is so far from the peanut fields of the South, railroad shipping fees would always be a source of concern for Rosefield.) He could laugh a little, says George Mackin, and Lee Avera, another employee, later recalled his participating in chocolate-éclair-eating contests with

Peanut Butter and Pickle Sandwich

Before the Rosefield Packing Company turned its attention exclusively to the manufacture of peanut butter, it was one of the largest pickle makers in the state of California. So it's only appropriate to include this quick-and-easy recipe.

Spread peanut butter on two slices of bread.
Cover one of them with pickles.
Put them together and eat.

employees when business was slow.[21] Ultimately, though, Rosefield was all business. Mackin stated, "He was one of the fairest, squarest businessmen I have ever been privileged to work for." He was also demanding, Mackin adds, but properly compensated you for your efforts. "Everyone was well paid," he says. "People used to be amazed at the money I was making for the job I had."[22]

The Rosefield Packing Company would be the most successful business to come out of Alameda, but its beginnings were modest. In his garage on Burbank Street, Joseph Rosefield handled coffee, tea, pickles, mayonnaise, mustard, jam and jelly, and dried fruits. His sales trips along the Interurban Electric Railroad, stopping off at different markets to sell them, were what got him interested in peanut butter.

"In those days, they sold peanut butter in bulk, in barrels. And they put it into something like takeout containers from Chinese restaurants. They had a lot of trouble with rancidity and used to have to throw it away pretty frequently," says Rick Rosefield. "And with the oil separation, it was bothersome having to mix it all up each time somebody would want some. The merchants used to complain to my grandfather about that, which is what got him interested in doing something about it."[23]

FIGURE 6.4 ROSEFIELD PACKING COMPANY PLANT (LATE 1920S/EARLY 1930S)

This photo of the original Rosefield Packing Company plant in Alameda, California, dates to the late 1920s or early 1930s, before it made Skippy. The billboard features Luncheon, the natural or unstabilized brand of peanut butter the plant then produced. Vats that stored pickles, which the company stopped making around World War II, are visible on the left. (Courtesy of Frank Delfino)

By the 1920s the Rosefield Packing Company was making its first brand of peanut butter, Luncheon (figure 6.4). Like all peanut butters of its day, it was old-fashioned or unstabilized. As early as 1918 Rosefield Packing also made Choc-Nut Butter, a mixture of chocolate and peanut butter[24] that wasn't successful. It isn't clear if there were problems with the design or marketing or if it was just ahead of its time, but five years later Reese's came out with its still-successful peanut butter cups.

Rosefield then developed a more successful concept and patented it: stabilizing peanut butter by hydrogenating peanut oil. He may have worked with a chemist on this, but the chemist's name has long since been lost. Rosefield's patent, applied for in 1921 and granted in 1923, wasn't the first time hydrogenation had been applied to peanut butter: that was Frank Stockton's patent, which Stockton applied for weeks earlier and which was also patented in 1921. Stockton's patent used full hydrogenation, while Rosefield's used partial hydrogenation. Full hydrogenation, Stockton acknowledged, produced a "hard, brittle solid"[25]—or, as longtime Skippy engineer and executive Frank Delfino derisively calls it, "concrete,"[26] which didn't allow the peanut flavor to release upon the tongue as fully as partial hydrogenation did.

Rather than develop hydrogenated peanut butter himself, Rosefield licensed his patent to the Derby Foods division of Swift & Company in 1923 or 1924. In the mid-1920s, Derby first made a product in stick form, like butter, named Delicia[27] or Dainty.[28] When that wasn't successful, Derby packaged peanut butter in a tin under the name Peter Pan. Apparently, Rosefield went with Swift because he didn't have the money to build a plant to utilize the process himself. But in July 1931, George Case, the head of Derby Foods, died. Rosefield had had good relations with him, but Case's replacement tried to cut Rosefield's royalty from one cent a pound of stabilized peanut butter to half a cent.[29] Rosefield balked and in December 1932 ended their business relationship. In the depths of the Depression, he prepared to start making stabilized peanut butter himself.

The patent used for Peter Pan was only one of ten peanut butter patents Rosefield either developed or had assigned to him.[30] In addition to being a businessman, Rosefield was something of a visionary. During the 1920s, his son, Jerome, later recalled, his father formed the Rosefield Development Corporation: "[It] became kind of a gleam in his eye," Jerome said. "We would continue to manufacture, but he started to look in other directions, getting patents in the development of other food products . . . and in my opinion developed some and was granted patents 10 or 50 or 100 times as valuable as Skippy. He decided to get out of the manufacturing business and strictly into the development field. [But] the Crash came along and took care of that idea, and we were lucky to remain alive."[31]

In 1935 the L. O. Taft Company, a food wholesaler in Salt Lake City, was distributing Skippy.[32] That year, it may have helped test-market a new product for the Rosefield Packing Company: chunk-style peanut butter.[33] Jerome Rosefield later explained the origins of "a crunchy product which can be spread, but preserves the illusion of whole peanuts."[34]

As Rosefield's head of marketing, Jerome spent a lot of time talking to consumers. When he met people who had tried Skippy but didn't like it, he asked why and was surprised by one frequent answer: it was too smooth, which he considered one of its greatest selling points. "We decided that if that's the way some of them wanted it, we would produce a product for what we considered a very small segment of the public. We chopped peanuts and mixed them in the finished product and produced a product called 'chunk,' which we took to Salt Lake City and put on the shelf," Jerome later said. "Quite a few people liked it, and it became part of our line."[35] For Jerome, the whole idea of peanut butter was to make it as smooth as possible, so the idea of crunchy struck him as somewhat perverse.[36] But as a businessman, he believed the customer was always right, so chunk it was.

Accounts differ as to when Skippy introduced chunk style. *The Magic of Peanut Butter*, a book published by Sterling, says it was first introduced shortly after Skippy came on the market in 1933.[37] Jerome Rosefield put the date at 1936 or 1937,[38] but this was at his testimony before the FDA's standard-of-identity hearings for peanut butter in 1966, and he would be the first to say he didn't have a good memory for dates.

Crunchy peanut butter was only one of several innovations from the Rosefield Packing Company during this period: the company pioneered hydrogenation, and 1935 was also the year Skippy introduced wide-mouthed jars,[39] now standard in the peanut butter industry (figure 6.5).

World War II brought heightened interest in peanut butter, as the government realized it was a cheap, nutritious, and easy-to-supply food for American soldiers fighting overseas. "C-rations and K-rations had peanut butter in them, in a tin can with a key to open it," recalls Wisconsin veteran Fred Keller. "I took it across France. You could also take the can opener from your dog tags, open the can, and spoon the peanut butter onto your hardtack [a durable biscuit]. The can opener came in handy, as if you're out in the countryside and your tin-can key didn't work, you couldn't use your bayonet to open the peanut butter tin."[40] In 1942, stabilized peanut butter outsold natural for the first time, possibly because of all the stabilized peanut butter the government shipped to American troops in Europe and the Pacific.

With meat rationing, peanut butter was a good way for people on the home front to get protein, although in *Breakfast at Tiffany's*, Holly Golightly has a hard time finding it in wartime midtown Manhattan. (After going to Central Park, author Truman Capote's narrator says, "The rest of the afternoon we were east and west worming out of reluctant grocers

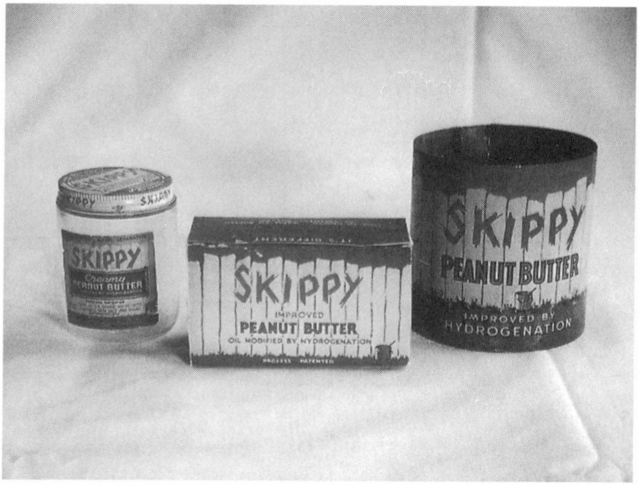

FIGURE 6.5 EARLY SKIPPY JARS AND BOXES

Early Skippy containers: a jar, a box, and a tin. A brick-like form of peanut butter was sold in boxes for a while, but it proved unpopular and was discontinued. (Courtesy of Frank Delfino)

cans of peanut butter, a wartime scarcity; dark came before we'd rounded up a half-dozen jars, the last at a delicatessen on Third Avenue.")[41]

Although World War II proved a bonanza for the peanut butter industry, it almost spelled the death knell for the Rosefield Packing Company: the Navy wanted the land its factory was on for military housing. At the time, it was still in the pickle-manufacturing business, and Rosefield Packing did lose the land out back where it had its pickle vats. But Joseph Rosefield saved his peanut butter factory. "Rosefield happened to be in Washington, D.C.," says longtime Skippy employee and historian Frank Delfino. "He pounded on the desk and said, 'You're putting us out of business. And right now, you need this kind of food for people. You can't find meat, but you can buy peanut butter.' So they came to a compromise: government housing was built where the pickle vats had been, but the plant was saved."[42] World War II had another consequence for Skippy and the peanut butter industry: before the war, peanut butter had been sold primarily in tins, but now tin plate was needed for the war effort, so glass jars became the new industry standard.

Skippy peanut butter expanded rapidly. In 1980 Jerome Rosefield said it had been sold in six western states in 1937; by 1940 (the first year it turned a profit) it was in fifteen to twenty states, still mainly out west. It came to New York in 1944, Philadelphia in 1945, and New England in 1946.[43] A 1945 article in *Sales Management* magazine sees it differently, saying the New York market was the last one opened.[44] By 1946 or 1947, Skippy was the best-selling peanut butter in the United States,[45] a title it would not relinquish until 1980 (figure 6.6).

The success of Skippy peanut butter transformed the Rosefield Packing Company.

In 1937 the company sold mustard, peanut butter, relishes, pickles, and tapioca under the brands Skippy, Luncheon, Butternut, Rosefield (the label featured a rose), and Del Rio.[46] But by 1942 the company was making only one product, peanut butter, and the Rosefield and Del Rio labels had disappeared.[47] Bert Gannon, who started working for Rosefield in 1942, recalls that one of his first jobs was to break up the old pickle barrels that Rosefield Packing no longer used.[48] Skippy's success also transformed the Rosefields into community leaders. Joseph Rosefield; his wife, Mae; his children; and their wives would become active in a long list of civic organizations.

FIGURE 6.6 ROSEFIELD PACKING COMPANY PLANT (1940S)

Skippy's Alameda plant sometime during the 1940s, when Skippy surpassed Peter Pan to become the nation's leading brand of peanut butter. (Courtesy of Frank Delfino)

When Skippy turned profitable in 1940, it began to advertise. As the distribution of Skippy expanded, Rosefield Packing sponsored *Skippy Hollywood Theater,* a radio show broadcast nationally throughout the 1940s. The Rosefields would move to increasingly nicer houses in Alameda, then abandon Alameda for tonier nearby Piedmont. For Joseph Rosefield, it was a long way up from the house with the 150-square-foot garage on Burbank Street in Alameda.

SKIPPY ON TOP

After World War II, Skippy cemented its leadership status in the peanut butter industry, chalking up $6 to $7.5 million in sales a year between 1947 and 1949.[1] Its sales reputedly exceeded the total of the next three nationally advertised brands combined,[2] which may have been Peter Pan, Heinz, and Beech-Nut. In the 1950s, Skippy advertised on the TV show *You Asked for It* and in the 1960s on *Dennis the Menace* and *The Flintstones*. Annette Funicello, famed as a Mouseketeer and the costar of agreeably frivolous beach movies with Frankie Avalon, served as a commercial spokesperson. But nothing says "iconic American brand" quite like having Norman Rockwell do your magazine ads.

In the spring of 1963 Rockwell, the most iconic of American artists, did four drawings for the Whispering Sweepstakes, a full-color Skippy ad campaign that ran in the *Saturday Evening Post*, *Ladies' Home Journal*, and *American Home*.[3] The first drawing shows a husband whispering to his wife about the virtues of Skippy; in the second, the wife whispers to her daughter; in the third, the daughter to her brother; and in the fourth, the smiling boy, who bears a faint resemblance to *Mad* magazine's Alfred E. Neuman, turns to the reader, jar of Skippy in his hand, to extol its virtues. Contest entrants competed for a round-the-world trip on a new Pan Am Boeing 727, which Eastern Airlines called the "Whisperjet." Guild, Bascom & Bonfigli, the ad agency that devised the slogan "If you like peanuts, you'll like Skippy," ran one more Rockwell sweepstakes ad for Skippy, in which Rockwell painted a family portrait of the winner's family.

Behind the image was a genuine devotion to quality. "Skippy wanted peanuts that were freshly shelled," says Frank Delfino. "Of course, the shelling plants didn't like that, because they'd go through and shell everything, stick it in the warehouse and then shut the plant down. With Skippy, they had to keep the plant operating year-round."[4]

That's how Joseph Rosefield's grandson Rick recalls it. "The standard of manufacturing was a point of pride for everybody, whether you were a shipping clerk, a warehouseman, or the guy mixing it," he says. "It was just that kind of a company."[5] On family vacations, his father Jerome would go into out-of-town grocery stores to make sure Skippy jars hadn't passed their expiration date.[6] After World War II, the Rosefield Packing Company set up its own research lab, run by Lee Avera, and an engineering division, headed by R. J. Siefert.[7]

There appears to have been a good esprit de corps at Rosefield Packing. In 1948 a dockworkers' strike on the West Coast, led by firebrand union activist Harry Bridges, shut down Skippy's Alameda plant for three or four months; workers there were members of Local 6 of the International Longshoremen and Warehouse Workers' Union (ILWU).[8] As the story came down to Rick Rosefield, though, "A couple of people were walking up and down in front of the plant and the rest of them were inside working. They came in the back door. When the union found out what was happening, they pulled all the Skippy people and had them go picket somebody else and had non-Skippy employees picketing Skippy."[9]

Longtime Skippy employee Thomas Fuller told me he didn't even like to hear the names of Skippy's competitors.

"You're very loyal to Skippy," I said, "if the very mention of Jif or Peter Pan—"

"Shut up," he interrupted.[10]

(Jif employees, it turns out, are equally patriotic: Paul Kiely, who managed Jif's Lexington plant in the late 1980s, grew up in a Skippy family. But every year when he goes home to visit his sister, he removes the jar of Skippy from her pantry and replaces it with Jif.)[11]

Postwar Skippy employees fondly recall one of the quirks of the Rosefield Packing Company: its ban on male visitors, although the precise nature of this ban varies with the telling. "When the family owned [Skippy], there was a strict ruling that no males be brought into the factory, because they were concerned that they might copy the equipment," says Rick Rosefield. "It wasn't patented. Until near the end of family control, Girl Scouts could tour the plant, but Cub Scouts couldn't."[12]

Frank Delfino says children of either gender were allowed—it was adult males who couldn't come in. Around 1950, he was told, a peanut equipment salesman got into the plant. "Within a few months, that company had a complete schematic drawing of the plant," he says. "From that point on, no men were allowed in the factory. Only women and children."[13]

But the era of family control of Skippy was coming to an end. In 1955 Rosefield Packing was purchased by Best Foods, makers of Hellman's and Best Foods mayonnaise, for $6 million, ending forty years of Rosefield ownership. Best Foods offered $24 a share for 250,380 shares of stock, 52 percent of which was owned by the Rosefield family, the remainder by 700 other stockholders.[14] "My grandfather wanted to sell the business considerably earlier, but his two sons outvoted him," Rick Rosefield says. "When my aunt passed away [Marvin's first wife, Marjorie], my uncle decided there was no reason to work any longer, so he voted with my grandfather and they decided to sell the business."[15]

Years earlier, Jerome confirmed this analysis: "January 1, 1955, we sold our company to Best Foods. I did not want to sell, but my father and brother did, and I went along with it." Asked if he went to work for Best Foods as part of the sale, he said, "Yes, I was sold down the river."[16] Jerome was well known as a shrewd marketer, and Best Foods wanted him on board as it took the reins. Marvin may have stayed on briefly as well. During the three years it owned Skippy, Best Foods added a plant in Dallas to go along with the original Alameda plant and factories the Rosefields had added near Minneapolis and in Portsmouth, Virginia.

Frank Delfino started working for Skippy in the spring of 1955 as a twenty-five-year-old. Although he came in at the end of the Rosefield era, he was more impressed with the Rosefields than the new management from Best Foods. Around the time of the sale, there was a crop failure and a nationwide peanut shortage. A peanut broker tried to interest Marvin Rosefield in a shipment of peanuts from Brazil, but they didn't meet his quality standards. The broker then contacted Best Food headquarters in Englewood Cliffs, New Jersey, and convinced the company to buy the peanuts.

"When the peanuts arrived in Portsmouth, they unloaded themselves," Delfino says. "They were so infested with beetles that it became a major

Peanut Coffee

According to his grandson Rick, Skippy founder Joseph Rosefield liked his coffee boiling hot. He probably didn't make it from peanuts, but he could have done so with this recipe.

★★★

Here again the Peanut fills a useful end, especially in times of scarcity, or high prices for coffee. Taken alone, and without any addition whatever of the pure berry, the Peanut makes a quite good and palatable beverage. It closely resembles chocolate in flavor, is milder and less stimulating than pure coffee, and considerably cheaper than Rio or Java. If mixed, half and half, with pure coffee before parching, and roasted and ground together, the same quantity will go as far and make about as good a beverage as the pure article, and a better one than much of the ground and adulterated coffee offered in the market. Indeed, if people will adulterate their coffee, it were much to be wished that they would use nothing more harmful than the Peanut for this purpose.

For making the beverage, the Peanut is parched and ground the same as coffee, the mode of decoction the same, and it is taken with cream and sugar, like the pure article.

FROM BRIAN W. JONES, *THE PEANUT PLANT: ITS CULTIVATION AND USES* (NEW YORK: ORANGE JUDD, 1885), 58. COURTESY OF ANDREW F. SMITH.

program to handle them. They had to put them in a separate warehouse and fumigate the nuts to kill off the beetles. All the skins had to be destroyed. Portsmouth [where Skippy had opened a plant in 1945] had just built a new garbage incinerator, and it took about two weeks to burn up all the skins."[17] A major difference between the philosophy of Best Foods and Rosefield Packing, Delfino adds, was that Rosefield Packing would not manufacture a product until it was sold. So it always had back orders. "They were assured that whatever they made would go out fresh. That's what really built the business," he says. "Well, to Best Foods, that was crazy. You should run the plant wide open, and if you're not selling it, just stack it in the warehouse. So you sell stale product."[18]

In 1958 Best Foods was acquired by Chicago-based Corn Products Company.[19] One of the world's largest corn refining and ingredient companies, it changed its name to CPC International in 1969 and owned Skippy until 1995.[20] The year 1958 was also a watershed for the Rosefield family's involvement with Skippy. On November 8, patriarch Joseph Rosefield died at age seventy-five in an Oakland hospital.[21] And Jerome retired before the sale of Best Foods to CPC, ending the Rosefields' twenty-five-year involvement with Skippy.

Frank Delfino represented the third generation of leadership at the company. A chemical engineering graduate from the University of California at Berkeley, he would become chief engineer at the Alameda plant and then serve as the first plant manager of the flagship Skippy plant built in Little Rock, Arkansas, in 1977. An elfin sprite with a sharp wit, idiosyncratic nature, and willingness to challenge authority, he and his wife, Janice, later lived in a comfortable Castro Valley house with a half-acre fruit and vegetable garden behind it. I was served a delicious spinach soup from that garden when I visited them in the winter of 2008.

"Frank is a unique, genius-level type of person who knows more about peanut butter than I ever will," says Carl Bleier, who served as administrative manager at the Little Rock plant. "He loved what he did, and he loved Skippy." But, he adds, "Frank will stop a parade in its tracks. You could be president of the company—I don't care who you were, if it was not right, Frank was going to let you know."[22]

Around 1963 Delfino helped Skippy add to its impressive streak of peanut butter industry innovations, coming up with the first electronic color-sorting system to help detect peanuts infected with aflatoxin, a naturally occurring toxin produced by a mold in nuts and grains. Before then, much of the work of detecting aflatoxin-contaminated peanuts had been done by hand, a slow and laborious process. "Aflatoxin changes the starches in peanuts into sugars," Delfino explains. "And when you roasted them, they got darker. So you picked out the dark peanuts, and that reduced the aflatoxin content."[23]

Delfino was too modest to tell me this innovation was his; this was something I learned about only later. But his modesty got me in trouble when I told him I'd read somewhere that careful hand-picking was more selective and accurate than photoelectric color sorting. "Where did you get that bullshit?" he demanded. "If you're going to make one pound of peanut butter that's absolutely pristine, you can hand-sort the peanuts. But if you're going at the rate of 200 jars a minute, you're not going to hand-sort a damned thing."[24] He had stopped my parade in its tracks.

★★★

Accounts differ as to when Joseph Rosefield moved his business from his garage into the back of a furniture plant at 1916 Webster Street in Alameda, converting part and then all of it into a peanut butter factory. Some accounts say 1915,[25] others 1918,[26] and one 1930,[27] although that seems improbably late. But CPC International increasingly regarded that facility as a white elephant. It was the oldest and least efficient of a network of plants that now included Minneapolis; Portsmouth, Virginia; Dallas; Santa Fe Springs in Southern California; and Baie-d'Urfé, near Montreal. In the fall of 1974, CPC decided to close the birthplace of Skippy peanut butter.

The Best Foods division of CPC was only one of the conglomerate's many divisions, and Skippy peanut butter represented only a minor portion of the parent company's sales. Plant management said it would try to find work elsewhere for the sixty plant workers, many still members of ILWU Local 6, but made no promises.[28]

On October 18, 1974, people worked until they ran out of peanuts, and employees on the final shift signed the last case of peanut butter.[29] Frank Delfino was the last person in the plant. One day, he went into the vault and found the blueprint for the meat-processing plant in Chicago where the Derby Foods division of Swift started making stabilized Peter Pan with the Rosefield patent in the 1920s. Delfino still has the last jar of peanut butter made at Alameda, a twenty-eight-ounce jar of Skippy creamy with a use-by date of October 18, 1975. The building that housed the Skippy plant was taken over by the Alameda Housing Department and remained in place until 1998, when it was torn down to make way for a shopping center.

On a cold, rainy, and windy January day ten years after the plant was demolished, Frank Delfino and I pulled up to the site, now a Walgreen's pharmacy. There was a small, dark-blue marble historical monument to Skippy out front (figure 7.1). It looks like a grave marker, I told Delfino. "It

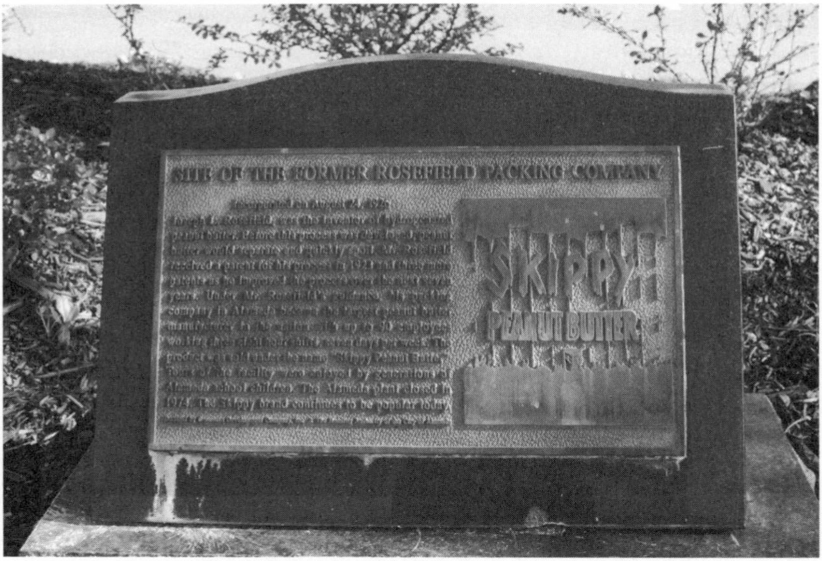

FIGURE 7.1 SKIPPY MONUMENT

Today a chain drugstore stands on the site of the original Skippy peanut butter plant at the corner of Webster Street and Atlantic Avenue in Alameda, California. This historical monument is all that remains to mark the site. (Courtesy of Dennis Evanosky)

is," he replied sadly. But the shuttered Alameda plant also served as the birthplace for Skippy's new flagship plant in Little Rock, Arkansas.

In a small office on the second floor of the now-closed plant, Delfino worked with a designer to come up with a blueprint for Little Rock. Larry Shearon, who worked for Delfino in Little Rock after the plant opened in 1977 and later became plant manager, recalls how informal the arrangement was. "Because the doors were locked, I used to have to stand outside and throw stones at the second-floor window," Shearon says. "Frank would look and wave, then come down and let me in."[30]

The site in Little Rock, at 8201 Frazier Pike along the Arkansas River in the Riverport Industrial Park, was chosen because Little Rock is a national transportation hub; studies showed Skippy could deliver peanut butter to Alameda more cheaply than it could be made there.[31] And although Arkansas is one of the few southern states that doesn't grow many peanuts, it's closer to those old peanut fields back home than Joseph Rosefield was in Alameda, which was why he had spent a lot of time in Washington lobbying for better rail-freight rates.

In addition to its prime location, Arkansas had another virtue for the owners of Skippy: It was a right-to-work state without a strong union presence. "There were a lot of issues back then with unions," Carl Bleier says. "We were going to have a team concept, or social system [in the plant], and its climate as a nonunion facility . . . was really why it was selected."[32]

Larry Shearon adds that there had been past labor troubles for CPC with Skippy. "So there would be no problems with their other plants, they told the, I guess, Oil, Chemical and Atomic Workers Union that they'd look the other way if they came in and organized the Santa Fe Springs plant," he says. "I think they felt that was a mistake, because it led to labor problems, and they had no flexibility to manage a modern plant in a modern way."[33] There were several attempts to organize the Little Rock plant, but Shearon says none were successful because working conditions were so congenial there was nothing unions could offer workers that they didn't already have. CPC executives met with the state's governor, Bill Clinton, who expressed a keen interest in attracting more industry to the state, and the deal was sealed (figure 7.2).

Carl Bleier, a New Jersey native and the plant's first administrative manager, had been working at Best Foods headquarters in Englewood Cliffs, New Jersey, and did not want to go to Little Rock, regarding it as a one-horse southern town. "We used to take a flight out of Newark Airport on Braniff," he says. "I remember landing in Little Rock on a Sunday, leaving the airport, and the town was basically closed. The plant was in the middle of nowhere. I could look out my office window and see them putting fertilizer on cotton fields."[34] (Larry Shearon says it was soybeans.) But Bleier and his wife adapted. "The quality of life was very good," he says. "We made a lot of friends and wound up enjoying it very much."

One of the things he enjoyed was the plant's unique design and social system. When CPC built the Little Rock plant, it reengineered not only the physical design of the plant, but the social relations and interactions of those working there as well. To do that, CPC worked with two psychologists during the planning process: Carl Bramlett, a psychologist from Georgia State University, and Lou Davis, head of the Center of Quality of Working Life at UCLA's Institute of Industrial Relations, which did

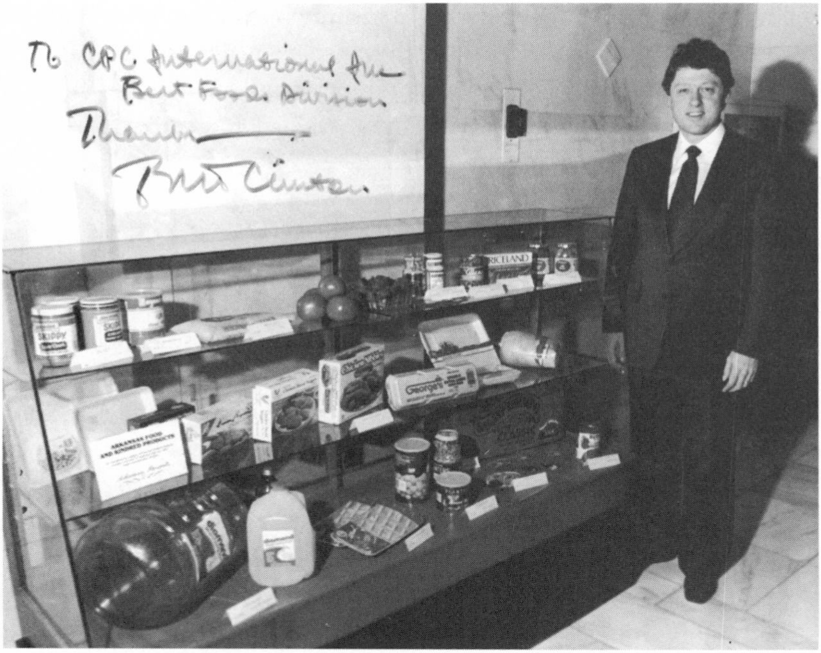

FIGURE 7.2 GOVERNOR BILL CLINTON

Governor Bill Clinton stands in front of a display case of products made in Arkansas, including, at top left, Skippy peanut butter. Skippy moved its plant to Little Rock in 1977, a process Clinton helped facilitate. (Courtesy of Larry Shearon. Photo: Arkansas Industrial Development Commission)

pioneering work in creating more effective and less hierarchical organizations based on active worker participation.

The plant's physical innovations included reconfiguring the production equipment so people in the production area could see and communicate with people in the packaging area.[35] In terms of social design, everyone was on salary; no one received hourly wages (they still got time-and-a-half for overtime, though), and everyone had the same benefits plan. There were no supervisors; everyone worked for one of six teams: roasting and sorting, processing and packaging, preparation and repair, shipping and receiving, administration, and management. "There were no 'jobs,'" says Larry Shearon, "just a lot of tasks to be done, and anyone with the skill set and certification could do them. If you looked at a traditional Skippy plant, there would be someone whose job was 'fork lift driver' or 'quality-control technician.' None of that existed in Little Rock, and, as far as I know, still doesn't."[36]

The original Skippy plant in Alameda had one assembly line, as did the second plant, near Minneapolis. All subsequent plants had two lines, including Little Rock, but Little Rock's assembly lines were more high-speed. "The plant had a unique design," says James Hirchak, the plant's original personnel manager. "It was the first fully automated plant to make Skippy. From both a technology and organizational perspective, it was advanced. It was an experiment for the Best Foods Division of CPC."[37] As Little Rock moved into production, Skippy's other plants closed: one by one, Minneapolis, Dallas, Portsmouth, then Santa Fe Springs shut down. As of 2008, the only plant besides Little Rock still making Skippy was Baie-d'Urfé, near Montreal.[38]

The pressure for resisting the rise of Jif, which was taking an increasing amount of market share and threatening the dominance of Skippy, fell on Little Rock. "The whole time I was there, we were under a lot of pressure from Procter & Gamble, from Jif," says Larry Shearon. "There was the whole 'Choosy mothers choose Jif' thing. There was a concerted effort on their part to convince people that a sweeter peanut butter was the [real] product, which Skippy tried to resist."[39] But that resistance went only so far, especially when Jif passed Skippy around 1980 to become number one. "[During the 1980s,] ads stressed that Skippy contained less sugar than other brands," the *Encyclopedia of Brands* notes. "One of these sweeter competitors, Procter & Gamble's Jif, had been slowly increasing its market share since the early 1970s. In early 1988, a reformulated, sweeter Skippy was launched in an attempt to hang onto customers with sweeter tastes."[40]

James Hirchak says there were two main problems. "Jif passed Skippy because of spreadability and sweetness," he says. "Jif was easier to spread, and it was a sweeter peanut butter. Sweetness was the foremost issue."[41]

Frank Delfino says Procter & Gamble's marketing muscle also played a role. "I would say that Jif got to be number one by advertising," he says. "The product really isn't any better. They just flooded the market with advertising. Typical Procter & Gamble stuff."[42]

In 1995 CPC spun off Best Foods.[43] It was again an independent company until 2000, when it was acquired by Unilever,[44] a huge (2005 sales:

$50 billion) Anglo-Dutch conglomerate founded in 1930 by the merger of British soap maker Lever Brothers and Dutch company Margarine Unie. It was a marriage made by palm oil, an important ingredient in both soap and margarine. Unilever's product line now includes Lipton tea, Hellman's mayonnaise, Dove soap, Bertoli olive oil, Ragu spaghetti sauce, Birds Eye frozen foods, Breyers ice cream, Lux soap, and Calvin Klein fragrances. It even makes another peanut butter, the tasty Dutch brand Calve Pindakaas.

Like any company in the peanut butter business, Unilever would have to deal with the real dangers of plant operation, such as roaster fires. "Peanut skins are spontaneous combustion waiting to happen," says Frank Delfino,[45] and as if to prove him right, the day before Halloween in 2008, a roaster in the Little Rock plant caught fire, and the blaze spread through the plant's ventilation system, causing $300,000 in damage.[46] Then there were the unreal dangers, hobgoblins of post–September 11 hysteria. In a 2002 article, the *Arkansas Democrat-Gazette* noted the plant is "announced by a single Skippy sign on a parking lot restricted to authorized personnel only," adding "that seems reasonable in these parlous times when even peanut butter factories are in danger of being terrorized."[47] Protect your peanut butter plants, patriotic Americans: the evil ones walk among us.

Perhaps the company regarded me as a threat to peanut butter security, but I didn't learn much about Skippy from Unilever. When I called the 800 number given on Skippy's Web site, the operator told me a Skippy brand specialist would get back to me. None did. A few days later, I went to Unilever's British Web site and asked for contact information for a Skippy official in the United States. An official with Unilever U.S. Media Relations got back to me the next day. She said she'd pass my request along to an appropriate person.

Later that day, I received an e-mail from Unilever U.S. Media Relations telling me my inquiry was important and would receive a response in a timely manner. That response turned out to be a letter saying the information I had requested was unavailable, although all I'd asked for was someone who would talk to me about Skippy. Included was a booklet of discount coupons for Unilever products. A week later, on December 21, 2006, I heard from Unilever U.S. Media Relations. I was informed that

I would be put in touch with someone at the Little Rock plant (this never happened) and that we could talk during the new year.

On January 10, 2007, I e-mailed Unilever U.S. Media Relations a list of questions. I received a response on February 2, telling me the Skippy brand manager was unavailable to answer any further questions. I was referred to Unilever's book about Skippy, *The Magic of Peanut Butter,* which consists of recipes using Skippy and a not-always-accurate Skippy time line. I wrote back asking for the brand manager's name and asking when he or she would be available. Unilever couldn't reveal the name, but if I still needed assistance, I should check back in a month. I did, but no one ever got back to me.[48] It was as if the giant Anglo-Dutch conglomerate Unilever was continuing Joseph Rosefield's tradition of keeping men not employed by Skippy out of the plant.

JIF

"BUT IS IT STILL PEANUT BUTTER?"

In World War II, William T. Young served stateside as an officer in the ordnance branch of the U.S. Army, procuring and maintaining military supplies. After demobilization, Young, the son of a Lexington, Kentucky, dry-cleaning shop owner, wanted to start his own business but couldn't get a bank loan. His father-in-law, a peanut sheller in Blakely, Georgia, offered to lend him $25,000 if he'd do something involving peanuts.[1] Young had studied mechanical engineering at the University of Kentucky and knew what equipment would be needed, so in 1946 he started his own peanut butter company, calling it Big Top.[2] Twelve years later, it would give birth to Jif.

During the postwar period, the peanut industry was revolutionized by new equipment. In 1950, J. L. Shepherd and W. D. Kenney, agricultural engineers at the University of Georgia's Coastal Plain Experiment Station, developed a new peanut harvester.[3] Until then, peanut harvesting had been labor-intensive, with many field hands needed to dig up peanut plants, shake the dirt off them, lean them against a stackpole, and dry them. The plants remained in the fields for weeks, where they were exposed to the elements before being hauled to old-style stationary pickers for separation from the peanut plant. The new harvester made it possible for a farmer to simply ride through his fields, harvesting several rows of peanut plants at a time, and depositing them back on the ground, where they needed to sit for only several days. By the mid-1950s, stackpoles were no longer in use.[4]

But the peanuts still needed to be separated from the plant. In November 1950, the Lilliston Company of Albany, Georgia, successfully demonstrated a fully mechanized peanut combine. It picked peanut plants off the ground as they sat in windrows, separated the nuts from the plants, cleaned and bagged them, then threw the vines back onto the ground, where they could either fertilize the ground for the next year's crop or be rolled into bales of peanut hay. The combine cut field work from thirty man-hours per acre to four and the number of field hands needed from twelve to three, and saved the peanut farmer $40 per ton of peanuts harvested (in 1950 dollars).[5]

Peanut farmers' ability to harvest their crops more efficiently contributed to the postwar boom in peanut butter sales, according to John Johnson, curator of the National Peanut Museum in Tifton, Georgia. "If you have anything that improves the volume of production of any crop, now you can mass-produce it," he says. "Entrepreneurs are going to take advantage of that. That kind of production increase will definitely cause an increase in consumption."[6]

For small peanut farmers of the South as well as their corn-growing brethren in the Midwest, though, the new machines were a mixed blessing. Reflecting on the decline of the town of Moneta in Iowa's corn belt, author Vicki Myron notes, "Some farmers bought new machines, then bought out their neighbors and doubled their production, then used that money to buy out more neighbors. Farm families began to disappear."[7] It wasn't just stronger farmers buying out their less prosperous neighbors. It was also boom times for agribusiness, as large agricultural corporations such as Archer Daniels Midland, Monsanto, and Cargill expanded at the expense of family farmers.

During the 1950s and beyond, one prominent southerner's fondness for peanut butter would become part of his legend. The book *Are You Hungry Tonight?* notes that while Elvis Presley probably did not invent the fried peanut butter and banana sandwich, it became his signature dish.[8] "The peanut butter and banana sandwich is part of the whole Elvis mystique," says Robert Thompson, professor of media and culture at Syracuse University, adding that the lowbrow sandwich was evidence of Elvis's common touch. "He wasn't only the King, he was one of us."[9]

Presley would eat as many as twelve to fifteen at one sitting,[10] according to the NPR show *Splendid Table*, which encourages those who take their devotion to the King seriously to fry their Elvis sandwiches in bacon fat rather than butter. Ellie Volk of Buffalo, New York, might be such a person: In Memphis in 2002 to commemorate the twenty-fifth anniversary of the singer's death, she admitted, "I don't even like peanut butter. But if Elvis wanted me to eat a peanut butter and banana sandwich, if it meant that I could sit next to him, I'd do it."[11]

Production of peanut butter rose in the postwar period. In 1936, some 200 million pounds of peanuts were used to make peanut butter in the United States.[12] By 1947, that figure had risen to 325 million pounds,[13] and by 1958 to 400 million pounds,[14] double the amount of twenty years earlier. Large peanut crops at the end of the 1950s also contributed to the growing availability and popularity of peanut butter,[15] as did the fondness of World War II GIs, who had it in their rations overseas and came back and fed it to their baby-boom children.

Which made it a good business for William T. Young. Located in the bluegrass region of north-central Kentucky, eighty miles south of Cincinnati, Lexington was known as the Thoroughbred City for its horse farms and auctions and Keeneland race track. With the founding of Young's Big Top, Lexington was one of a shrinking number of cities to still have its own peanut butter company (figure 8.1).

From the start, Young showed an adroit sense of marketing. In addition to selling peanut butter in standard jars, he sought to distinguish Big Top from other brands by putting it in goblets and tumblers with collectible designs (figure 8.2). In 1956 and 1957, Big Top jars featured song titles such as "The Mulberry Bush," "America," "The Eyes of Texas," and "On the Banks of the Wabash."[16]

"There really is not much to differentiate peanut butter," says William T. Young Jr. "One of the things my father did was to come up with inexpensive glassware made by Hazel-Atlas Glass. People got in the habit of collecting it. If they wanted twelve glasses of the same type, they had to go out and buy twelve jars of peanut butter."[17] In the late 1940s and early 1950s, Big Top grew steadily from a small local operation to a leading brand in the Upper Midwest.[18] Its success attracted the attention of Procter & Gamble, eighty miles up the road in Cincinnati.

"My father was sitting in his office one day, and a fellow walked in off the street and wanted to talk to him," Young says. "He would talk to any-

FIGURE 8.1 BIG TOP FACTORY

The Big Top peanut butter plant in Lexington, Kentucky, in a photo taken in 1946, shortly after it opened and almost ten years before it was acquired by Procter & Gamble to make Jif. (Courtesy of Ron Garrison. Photo: *Lexington Herald-Leader*)

body. The guy asked if he had any interest in selling the company. My father had never been approached before and didn't know what to say. He said, 'Possibly,' depending on what the offer was. This guy said, 'I represent a client interested in purchasing your company.' The guy was John Weinberg, son of Sidney Weinberg, a founding partner of Goldman Sachs. This was the first job John had had in the field, representing Procter. John later ran Goldman Sachs for a number of years. But in the mid-fifties, he was just a boy. He and my father hit it off real well, and that's how it came together."[19]

On August 22, 1955, Procter & Gamble bought W. T. Young Foods. P&G acquired all shares of stock in Young Foods in exchange for an undisclosed number of shares of P&G stock.[20] The Cincinnati-based company, best known for soap and household cleaners, had decided to expand its small line of food products. "Procter & Gamble had limited experience in food—they're a soap company," says Ted Woehrle, who served as assistant brand manager and then brand manager for Jif in the late 1980s and early 1990s. "But they did make Crisco shortening going back to the early 1900s. Crisco had emulsification technology—emulsifiers help water and oil mix together. Someone connected with that emulsifier technology said,

FIGURE 8.2 BIG TOP PEANUT BUTTER AD

As a sales gimmick, Big Top peanut butter was sometimes sold in goblets made by the Hazel-Atlas Glass Company, such as the one pictured in this 1957 ad. Clever promotions by William T. Young, Big Top's founder, made Big Top a strong regional brand in the Upper Midwest and drew the attention of Procter & Gamble, which used Big Top to get into the peanut butter business. (www.adsbydee.com)

'This emulsifier can help to develop a smoother, creamy, tasty peanut butter.' So they bought Big Top."[21]

Young remained at what was now the W. T. Young Foods division of Procter & Gamble for two years, to assist the new owners. The P&G stock he was paid in would serve as the basis for his extraordinary business career. On the day Procter & Gamble bought W. T. Young Foods, it was selling for $100 a share. In 1956 it split two for one. By 1961 it had climbed to $152 and split two for one again. By 1992 there had been four more such splits.[22] Young still held P&G stock more than forty years after he sold Big Top, and according to John Gretz, who worked as an engineer at the Jif plant in Lexington, "He was glad he did. He had done real well with it."[23]

After selling Big Top peanut butter, William T. Young founded a storage and transfer business in the Lexington area and joined the board of directors of Royal Crown Cola, which he chaired for nearly twenty years. His razor-sharp business acumen impressed Procter & Gamble, which used the services of the W. T. Young Storage Company. But in the late 1980s, Jif plant manager Paul Kiely felt their business relationship needed to be pared back. "I went in to tell Mr. Young we had too much stock in his warehouse and didn't want all of it there; we could be more efficient on-site," Kiely says. "He just sat there and looked at me and said, 'I wondered when you guys were going to figure that out.' I was in my early thirties and he was about seventy, but he was sharp as a tack."[24]

In later years, the snowy-haired business magnate became a leading citizen of Lexington, admired for his public service and philanthropy. Usually dressed in a dapper tweed coat, he was known as a true gentleman who wrote carefully crafted and timely thank-you notes. The only blot on his escutcheon was the Humana Hospital affair.

In the early 1980s, while serving as chief of staff to Kentucky governor John Brown, Young lobbied Kentucky's Hospital Licensure Board to approve an application from Louisville-based hospital chain Humana for a new hospital in Lexington. A month after the board approved the hospital, Governor Brown announced a freeze on hospital construction in Louisville and Lexington. Young was at one time the single largest stockholder in Humana, so the increase in his stock portfolio from his lobbying efforts must have more than made up for his nominal $1 a year salary as chief of staff to the governor. In the wake of this episode, he resigned from Governor Brown's staff, the University of Kentucky Board of Trustees, and the state's Council on Higher Education, but the incident failed to do lasting damage to his public image.[25]

Young also turned to the hobby one might expect of an affluent Lexington gentleman: horses. In 1972 he bought the first 110-acre parcel of what would grow into Overbrook Farms, one of Kentucky's finest horse farms. His original intent was simply to restore a small historic cottage on the property. "Like its owner, [it was] elegant and understated," said the *Lexington Herald-Leader*, "a place of manicured pastures, winding roads and barns that Mr. Young designed to resemble traditional Kentucky tobacco barns."[26]

Like most everything else he touched, it turned to gold. His horse Tabasco Cat won the Preakness and the Belmont Stakes; Timber Country won the Preakness; Editor's Note won the Belmont Stakes; and in 1996, his colt Grindstone won the Kentucky Derby (figure 8.3). "I'm not a wizard and I'm certainly not a horseman," Young said with aw-shucks modesty. "I just try to bring a little common sense to what we do."[27] He displayed a

FIGURE 8.3 WILLIAM. T. YOUNG

William T. Young, founder of Big Top peanut butter, the precursor of Jif, was the son of a Lexington dry cleaner. He created a business empire that made him wealthy enough to have his own horse farm. He is seen here at Churchill Downs in 1996 after his colt Grindstone won the Kentucky Derby. On the left is winning jockey Jerry Bailey; on the right is his daughter, Lucy. (Courtesy of Ron Garrison. Photo: *Lexington Herald-Leader*)

similar modesty toward his philanthropy, which included giving so much toward construction of the library at the University of Kentucky that it bears his name, as does the student center at Transylvania University, a private liberal arts college in Lexington. Asked in 1999 how much he and his family had given away, he said $60 million, off-handedly adding "more or less."[28] And he owed it all to peanut butter.

Procter & Gamble now found itself in the peanut butter business. Unlike W. T. Young Foods, it was a venerable American institution, started by William Procter and James Gamble in Cincinnati in 1836, the year the Battle of the Alamo was fought, Charles Darwin sailed on *The Beagle*, and Arkansas joined the Union. P&G made soaps and candles and by 1890 was selling more than thirty different kinds of soap, including Ivory.

The company has a legacy of innovative and successful advertising, including full-color ads in national magazines, and of sponsoring and producing domestic serial dramas, first on radio, then, in the 1950s, on television, helping to coin the term "soap opera" in the process. Its roster of well-known products includes not only Ivory, but Tide detergent, Luvs diapers, Downy fabric softener, Duncan Hines cake mixes, Pantene shampoo, Bounty paper towels, Olay face cream, and Charmin toilet paper. It has prospered by all of them: in 1988–1989, P&G had sales of $21.4 billion.

One of Procter & Gamble's first decisions was to change the name and formulation of Big Top peanut butter, calling it Jif, probably to convey a sense of convenience to harried post–World War II housewives. (In electronics, a "jiffy" is a unit of time, one-fiftieth of a second, making it similar to a New York minute.) According to Jif's Web site, the name was chosen because it's easy to say, spell, and remember. It made its first big splash on America's grocery shelves in 1958.[29]

In addition to taking over William Young's peanut butter plant in Lexington, Procter & Gamble converted a factory it owned in Portsmouth, Virginia, to the production of Jif. Previously the plant had been used to make Crisco. In its early stages, Jif didn't have as much of a key peanut butter ingredient as its competitors: peanut oil, which was removed for use in other products.[30] Customarily, peanut oil is not removed during peanut butter production, but Procter & Gamble had other ingredients it wanted to put in its peanut butter, and it would attract the attention of the U.S. Food and Drug Administration for doing so.

Jif appears to have found another way to pare back the presence of peanut oil in peanut butter: Since the 1920s, the hydrogenated oil put into peanut butter to stabilize it had been peanut oil. But starting around 1958, when Jif first came on the market, the peanut butter industry switched to other vegetable oils, such as soy, cottonseed, and canola or rapeseed.[31] While hydrogenated oils have more in common physically with each other than they do with their source oils, peanut butter purists do not regard this as a happy milestone in the history of the product.

By putting a peanut butter plant in Portsmouth, Jif joined market leader Skippy, which had had one there since 1945. The Jif plant was on Elm Avenue near the Naval Shipyard. The Skippy plant was at the intersection of High and Confederate Streets, where it spread the aroma of roasting nuts across the Mount Hermon neighborhood. Because each plant eventually made 30 percent of its respective brand, Portsmouth called itself the Peanut Butter Capital of the World.

Jif had a more complex formula and sweeter taste than Big Top; one Lexington plant worker, William Covington, says it was also darker.[32] David Guin, who managed the Lexington plant from 1967 through 1987, says Jif had more of a molasses taste[33] (molasses was added in 1969),[34] while Don Taylor, who worked in quality control at Lexington, says honey was added to Jif but not Big Top.[35] People who worked for Skippy are convinced that this sweetness, along with Procter & Gamble's marketing muscle, is why Jif eventually passed Skippy to become the market leader.

Throughout its corporate history, Procter & Gamble has been responsible for numerous innovations, but it chalked up a baleful one when Jif first hit the market: no one had ever tried to market as peanut butter something that had so few peanuts in it. According to Jerome Rosefield, the son of Skippy's founder, the Best Foods lab analyzed Jif at its inception and found it contained 25 percent hydrogenated oil. "As big a company as they are, and as great as they are in their field, they don't know anything about peanut butter, and in my opinion, this is a very poor product," Rosefield said.[36] According to Don Taylor, early Jif contained emulsifiers, notably lecithin,[37] which comes from egg yolks; *Consumer Reports* said it was cooking fat.[38]

Even before Jif could be found in grocery stores, an insight into Procter & Gamble's attitude toward it could be found in the public musings of its top public relations executive. In March 1957, S. A. Shaddix told the *Norfolk Ledger-Dispatch*, "Peanut butter production is a logical extension of

Peanut Butter Cheesecake

Given Jif's well-deserved reputation for sweetness, a dessert recipe is in order here.

2 pounds softened cream cheese
1 cup sour cream
1 cup granulated sugar
2 teaspoons vanilla
¼ teaspoon ground allspice
¼ teaspoon ground cinnamon
¼ teaspoon grated lemon peel
3 eggs
2 tablespoons cornstarch
½ cup milk
1 cup creamy peanut butter
Cake crust (recipe follows)

Preheat oven to 350 degrees F.

Mix together cream cheese, sour cream, sugar, vanilla, allspice, cinnamon, lemon peel, and eggs. Set aside.

Dissolve cornstarch in milk and add to cream cheese mixture. Blend in peanut butter.

Pour filling into crust. Bake for 60 to 65 minutes.

Let cool completely.

★★★

CAKE CRUST

3 cups all-purpose flour
1 cup softened butter or margarine
⅔ cup granulated sugar
2 eggs

Combine flour, butter, sugar, and eggs, beating until smooth.

Press mixture onto bottom and sides of a 9-inch springform pan.

FROM LARRY ZISMAN AND HONEY ZISMAN, *THE GREAT AMERICAN PEANUT BUTTER BOOK* (NEW YORK: ST. MARTIN'S PRESS, 1985). REPRINTED WITH PERMISSION OF LARRY AND HONEY ZISMAN.

FIGURE 8.4 EARLY JIF JAR

The Jiferoo, a peanut-butter-loving kangaroo, was Jif's early icon. Its slogan was "You gotta jump for Jif . . . because Jif is creamy smooth." But consumer advocates pointed out that the creaminess came from having about half a cup of hydrogenated vegetable oil mixed in with every pound of peanuts. This sparked a decade-long fight between the U.S. Food and Drug Administration and the peanut butter industry over a standard of identity for peanut butter. (Courtesy of Dan Goodsell)

our interest in the fat and oil business." Noting that the Portsmouth plant had been used to make hydrogenated vegetable shortenings, he added, "Our experience with other products has, in effect, opened a new field and it all grew normally from our soap business."[39] Yum.

As word got out about the composition of Jif, consumer magazines leapt to the barricades. In October 1959, *Consumer Reports* noted Jif's slogan was, "You gotta jump for Jif . . . because Jif is creamy smooth." But this slogan, which appears tied to P&G's use of the Jiferoo (figure 8.4), a peanut-butter-loving kangaroo on Jif's label, did not amuse *Consumer Reports*. "Smooth it is," *Consumer Reports* said. "But it is not the 'touch of honey' which, as the TV commercial claimed, accounts for that creaminess. According to the Food and Drug Administration, there is about half a cup of cooking fat mixed into a pound of Jif's peanuts."[40]

Consumer Reports noted that the FDA had proposed a standard calling for peanut butter to contain 95 percent peanuts. "The Peanut Butter Manufacturers Association [which later merged with the Peanut and Nut Salters Association to form the Peanut and Tree Nut Processors Association], whose members do not want to miss any cost-cutting opportunities, is opposing the standard."[41] Taking a similarly dubious view of Jif, *Consumer Bulletin* said in September 1959, "Recently a product appeared on the market called Jif, 'the New Peanut Butter.' . . . This was indeed something new in edible products, but hardly peanut butter."[42]

Speaking before the Peanut Butter Manufacturers Association, FDA commissioner George Larrick said, "If manufacturers are to be permitted to substitute 20 or 25 percent cheaper vegetable oils for more expensive peanuts and call the product peanut butter, then the housewife needs the safeguards provided by the food standards section of the Food, Drug, and Cosmetics Act."[43] The comment apparently had some effect, *Consumer Bulletin* noted, "for an obscure little item in a food trade journal reported that Procter & Gamble was changing the designation of Jif from 'just peanut butter' to 'peanut . . . spread' on the ground that this item had always been a distinctive product."[44] (According to the *Encyclopedia of Consumer Brands*, it was not until 1960, when P&G increased the peanut level in Jif to 90 percent, that it could be marketed as peanut butter.)[45]

On July 2, 1959, the FDA proposed the standard of identity for peanut butter under which it had to contain at least 95 percent peanuts.[46] It invited written comments and got plenty from the peanut butter industry, none of them friendly. In 1959 the Peanut Butter Case (both the FDA and peanut butter industry lawyers would later speak of it in capital letters) began. It would spool out over twelve years of the Eisenhower, Kennedy, Johnson, and Nixon presidencies, lurching to its conclusion only in the spring of 1971. FDA historian Suzanne Junod notes, "A prominent attorney on the case later observed that the peanut butter standard put many lawyers' children through college."[47]

On November 28, 1961, after two years of talks with the peanut butter industry, the FDA decided to roll back the proposed standard of identity for peanuts from 95 to 90 percent and published that new standard in the *Federal Register*.[48] But if it thought that compromise would bring the process to a swift conclusion, it was wrong. On February 1, 1962, in response to objections by the peanut butter industry, the FDA decided not to publish a final order setting the standard of identity at 90 percent, saying the issue warranted further study.[49] The industry then proposed the peanut level be set at 87 percent.[50]

In the *Federal Register*, the FDA noted a litany of objections from peanut industry trade associations, manufacturers of peanut butter, and suppliers of ingredients. "Their objections were directed at one or more of the following," it noted. "The order in its entirety [and] the maximum limitation of ten per cent for optional [i.e., non-peanut] ingredients. . . . Some wanted additional optional ingredients to be specified and [there were objections to] the labeling requirements for optional ingredients." In a barely concealed tone of bureaucratic exasperation, FDA commissioner George Larrick added, "There were objections to substantially all provisions of the order."[51]

That year, Procter & Gamble, both a manufacturer of peanut butter and a supplier of ingredients, complained that the new standard would injure its business in stabilizers sold to the peanut butter industry and discourage research and restrict improvements to peanut butter. *Consumer Bulletin* wryly responded, "In the food trade, improvement all too often means making something complicated which started out by being made of simple, readily recognized ingredients."[52]

On November 10, 1964, the FDA revised other aspects of the peanut butter standard of identity but left the peanut level at 90 percent.[53] It again invited comments, and the peanut butter industry was again happy to oblige. By the following July, after studying extensive comments from the industry (which wanted the standard watered down) and consumers (who wanted the standard maintained or strengthened), the FDA decided to stick with 90 percent.[54] The stage was set for the peanut butter hearings.

The peanut butter industry formally asked the FDA to hold public hearings on the standard of identity, and the FDA agreed, setting October 18, 1965, as the date for the hearings to begin.[55] Implementation of the standard was delayed pending outcome of the hearings. On November 1, 1965, after two postponements, the hearings began.

The hearings were a David-and-Goliath confrontation. On one side was a battery of high-priced, high-powered, well-connected Washington lawyers representing Skippy, Peter Pan, Jif, and the Peanut Butter Manufacturers' Association, which wanted the level of peanuts in peanut butter reduced to 87 percent. On the other side was consumer activist Ruth Desmond, known as the Peanut Butter Lady, and her group, the Federation of Homemakers (which *Newsweek* described as "a clutch of gay-hatted housewives"),[56] which wanted it restored to 95 percent.

Desmond had started the Federation of Housewives in 1959 in response to P&G's adulteration of Jif. She was a well-mannered firebrand: once, sitting next to a senior vice president of General Foods at a conference on international food law, she politely but pointedly observed, "It amazes me how you gentlemen in the food industry are always so concerned about having quality food yourself. But you want the rest of us to eat sawdust."[57]

The hearings were held in Room 5131 of the Health, Education, and Welfare Building in Washington, D.C., a room, the *Washington Post* noted, that had peanut-colored paneling on its walls. The first witness was FDA chemist Prince Harrill, who talked about the history of peanut butter. Soft-spoken FDA attorney Michael Foley questioned him in less than an hour, but, typical of the peanut butter industry's penchant for prolonging the process, H. Thomas Austern, whom the *Post* described as "the persistent counsel for Procter & Gamble," "spent the rest of the day trying to roast Dr. Harrill." *Post* reporter Ernest Lotito praised hearing examiner William E. Brennan as "a man of infinite composure," but reserved his highest compliments for stenographer Claire Ring, calling her the hero of the day for having to wrestle with phrases like "palmitoleic hydrogenated glyceryl."[58]

A sample of pro-industry testimony at the hearings came from James Mack, the managing director of the Peanut Butter Manufacturers' Association, who said that without stabilizers, peanut butter would turn rancid quickly. Furthermore, he fear-mongered, "it would stick to the roof of your mouth, it would tear holes in your bread when you tried to spread it."[59] But Ruth Desmond wasn't buying. "The manufacturers want to be able to make it more and more like peanut-flavored [cold] cream," she said. "We want to keep this product traditionally simple. It's time to reverse this trend and take the chemicals out of food."[60]

Neither was Desmond impressed by the peanut butter industry's argument that imposing a minimum of 90 percent in peanuts in peanut butter would stifle innovation. Questioning Skippy official Lee Avera during the hearings, she bridled when he said, "I feel we must not and cannot freeze America or industry at its present levels of expertise in food manufacture, because we have too much to gain on the plus side."[61]

Desmond's retort: "May we not also gain very bad health, which would be on the minus side, from too much experimentation with improperly tested additives with respect to the lifetime effects?"[62]

Desmond attended the hearings day after day, preparing a simple dinner for her husband, Gordon, before she left the house, telling him, "I cannot leave them alone, those lawyers."[63] Her work in this and other cases earned the approval of consumer-rights icon Ralph Nader. "She was really the first person to go after these namby-pamby regulatory agencies," he said years later, calling her the only remaining heiress to a tradition of home-economics activism that started at the turn of the twentieth century with women like Carrie Nation.[64]

The hearings took twenty weeks and ran until March 15, 1966, producing a transcript of nearly 8,000 pages. But they did not settle the standard-of-identity conflict between the FDA and the industry, which would continue for another five years. On July 24, 1968, the FDA published its final order, setting the standard at 90 percent.[65] The industry appealed to the courts, and on May 14, 1970, the U.S. Court of Appeals for the Third Circuit affirmed the FDA's order.[66] The industry then appealed to the U.S. Supreme Court, which on December 14, 1970, declined to hear the industry's objection.[67] On March 3, 1971, the FDA order for the peanut butter standard of identity finally went into effect, twelve years after it was first published and ten years after it had been set at 90 percent.

Ben Gutterman, the official in charge of arguing the FDA's case in courts and hearings, later reflected on the Peanut Butter Case. "We were using the ninety percent figure; the industry was arguing for eighty-seven percent. If we had said eighty-three, they'd have gone to eighty. They were saying, 'Nutritionally, it's the same; price-wise, it's the same.' We were asking, 'But when does it stop being peanut butter?' That's what it was all about. We weren't saying that it was a bad product, only that it wasn't what the consumer expected to find under that name. Does she expect to buy peanut butter, or a mixture of lard and peanuts, with maybe some turnip greens ground up in there besides? If that's what the manufacturer wants, let him produce it, but under that name."[68]

His final thought on the matter: "It did drag on for a little while."

Another footnote to the hearings came from Skippy's Jerome Rosefield, who was supremely confident of Skippy's ability to fend off the challenge from Jif. "Mr. Blumenschine, chairman of the board and president of Best Foods, used to call me regularly [when Jif came on the market] and say, 'What are you going to do to meet Jif head-on in the marketplace?'" Rosefield testified at the hearings. "I said, 'We are not going to do anything.' He said, 'You don't realize—you have never been up against something like Procter & Gamble, a big company recognized as the greatest marketing force available. They will snow us under.' I said, 'I don't think their product is any good, and as long as I don't think so, I don't think the consumer will think it is any good, and if the consumer doesn't think it is good, it is not going to succeed.' "[69] Less than fifteen years later, Jif passed Skippy to become number one.

"CHOOSY MOTHERS CHOOSE . . ."

During and after the Peanut Butter Case, Procter & Gamble continued to grind out Jif in its Lexington plant at 767 East Third Street (renamed Winchester Road in the 1980s) and a satellite plant in Portsmouth, Virginia. After Jimmy Carter was elected president in 1976, Billie Jean Gibbons, then executive secretary to the Lexington plant manager, says there was a fuss when peanuts from his family farm came to the plant. "We would get peanuts in burlap bags," she says. "There were tags on them that said 'Carter's'—everyone wanted one, just because he was, or had been, president."[1]

While the bags from Carter's farm brought out the souvenir hunter in Jif employees, processing those bags was not fun and games. Rita Keys, who worked as plant safety officer, recalls the difficult working conditions for those who opened them. "These guys would stand up in the penthouse [the plant workers' nickname for the mezzanine], slit the bags open, and dump the peanuts down a grate. Gravity would bring peanuts down into the roasters and color sorters and into the processing area.

"It was a brutal job," she says. "All day they stood up there with knives, cut the bags open, and dumped these hundred-pound bags of peanuts. It was very, very hot up there, especially in the summertime. I would always make sure they were getting plenty of water, taking breaks, getting cool . . . we had bandannas with cooling stuff in them—no one ever fainted. That's amazing, I guess, in retrospect."[2]

In the late 1970s, Jif employees pioneered the delivery of peanuts to the plant by railcar rather than 100-pound burlap bags. John Gretz, who worked in engineering at Jif's Lexington plant, says "In about 1978 or 1979, we were sitting around in the break area with the plant manager and the director of the lab. The plant manager said, 'You know, they move soybeans in rail cars—why can't we move peanuts that way?' So we made arrangements to get a carload brought in at the Portsmouth plant, just to prove it could be done. And eventually it was adopted."[3]

By the late 1980s, as many as four railroad cars a day pulled into the Lexington plant, each loaded with 200,000 pounds, or 100 tons, of peanuts. Large hoses sucked them from the railcars into the plant's receiving bins. This method is now standard at large peanut butter plants. Between April 1987 and August 1989, Jif came up with another innovation: with plastics impermeable to oxygen now available, Jif became the first peanut butter to use plastic rather than glass jars.[4]

In addition to the 90 percent of nuts it's required to have, Jif consists of sugar, molasses, hydrogenated vegetable oil, mono- and diglycerides, and salt. The two sweetening agents make it one of the sweetest peanut butters on the market, something noted through the years by *Consumer Reports,* which routinely refers to Jif's "candy-like flavor" and "sweet, molasses-candy aroma" (1982),[5] "sweet nuttiness" (1987),[6] "sweet, nutty flavor" (1990),[7] "moderate sweetness" (1995),[8] and "molasses-like note" (2002).[9] Anyone who has eaten Jif will be hard-pressed to disagree: it's light, smooth, fluffy, and sweet. It tastes good, but it's like the peanut butter equivalent of cotton candy.

Since its construction in 1946, the Lexington plant, now the world's largest in terms of productivity, has undergone five major expansions. The volume of peanut butter running through its three production lines is phenomenal. Even in 1993, it could produce up to 750 jars a minute, enough peanut butter to make 2 billion sandwiches a year.[10] This would supply an average family's needs for 28,000 years.[11] Equally remarkable is that from the time peanuts arrive in railcars at the Jif plant until they leave in the form of peanut butter, they are not touched by human hands. I told Paul Kiely, who managed Jif's Lexington plant in the late 1980s,

Maple-Nut Sundae Sauce

Another Jif chapter, another dessert recipe to acknowledge its sweetness.

⅓ cup crunchy peanut butter
⅔ cup maple blended syrup

Mix peanut butter with syrup until mixture is smooth.

Serve over orange milk sherbet or vanilla ice cream.

★★★

Yield: 5–6 servings.

FROM WILLIAM I. KAUFMAN, *THE "I LOVE PEANUT BUTTER" COOKBOOK* (GARDEN CITY, N.Y.: DOUBLEDAY, 1965). REPRINTED WITH PERMISSION OF JACQUELINE KAUFMAN AND IVA KAUFMAN.

that it bothered me there was no direct human intercession in this brave new peanut butter world. He tried to reassure me.

"The decision making, the choice of what peanuts to use, the picking of ingredients from among our suppliers, the testing—all of that has human intervention," he said. "We test the peanut butter constantly, to make sure that everything is in the proper sequence and all of the ingredients are in the proper ratio. Once you get the product flowing, for sanitary reasons and consistency reasons, you want to keep it running. Anytime a system goes up and down, you put in potential quality problems and variability problems."[12]

While no human being touches the peanuts, 200 employees go to the plant every day to keep it running properly. As is the case with most other peanut butter plants, though, peanut butter fans shouldn't think of stopping by to say howdy. "Despite the friendly smell, [the] big red-brick

FIGURE 9.1 MODERN JIF PLANT

The entrance to the Jif plant in Lexington, Kentucky, now owned by Smuckers. After multiple renovations and expansions, it's the largest peanut butter plant in the world in terms of productivity. (Courtesy of Ron Garrison. Photo: *Lexington Herald-Leader*)

building looks intimidating—as inaccessible as a fortress," the *Lexington Herald-Leader* has noted. "There are few windows, no spacious parking lots along the street, no welcome mat" (figure 9.1).[13]

But, at least under Procter & Gamble, Jif did reach out to customers. "If there was ever a consumer comment within 150 miles of the plant, we would visit the consumer personally, whether it was a positive comment or a critical one," Paul Kiely says. "Everyone in leadership, including myself, went up to the 800-number offices in Cincinnati at the time and trained and took calls on Jif peanut butter."[14]

One reason peanut butter plants are not eager to entertain visitors is that you never know when something will go wrong. David Guin, who managed the Lexington plant from 1967 through 1987, says there were three or four roaster fires during his tenure.[15] And several would follow, including one in October 1990.

It isn't clear what caused that last fire, although peanut skins are a possible culprit. Cheryl Taylor, who served as plant safety officer, has poetically noted that peanut skins fly everywhere around the nut preparation area "like little parachutes."[16] But those parachutes don't always ensure a happy landing: Rita Keys, who has also been plant safety officer, points out the skins are highly flammable. Another possible culprit was the roaster vents, which have to be cleaned regularly to avoid a buildup of peanut oil residue. Whatever the cause, the sprinkler system in the roasting area was triggered, but the introduction of water into the extremely hot and highly confined space caused a pressure buildup of steam, and several panels from a peanut roaster were blown away.[17] One worker received burns on his upper body, and another was treated for smoke inhalation at a local hospital and released. Two of the plant's four roasters were damaged,[18] and the plant was out of commission for two weeks.[19]

"Thank God that there was never a roaster fire in the time I was there," says Paul Kiely. "I'll always remember going to a Rotary meeting when I was training with Dave [Guin, who preceded him as plant manager]. We were driving back and he said, "I always look in the sky and make sure that there isn't a plume of smoke coming up from the direction of the Jif plant."[20]

★★★

When Jif hit the market in 1958, it lagged far behind Skippy and Peter Pan. By the mid-1960s, it was still a distant third, and Procter & Gamble decided to change the advertising smoke signals it was sending to the public. About 1965 P&G linked up with Grey Advertising, which has given the world such advertising slogans as "Leave the driving to us" for Greyhound, "Ford has a better idea," and "Easy, breezy, beautiful Cover Girl." Grey decided that the Jiferoo, the peanut-butter-loving kangaroo that came with the slogan "You gotta jump for Jif," needed to hop off to the Outback. Its replacement would debut in November 1966.

Neil Kreisberg started at Grey in early 1966, rising to a variety of executive positions, including Jif account executive and supervisor. "Even though the vast majority of peanut butter was consumed by children, we decided we would talk to the mothers as the gatekeepers," he says, recounting Grey's first TV ad with cheerful gruffness.

"It started with a woman in a supermarket agonizing over something, lettuce or tomatoes. A woman's voice basically asks, 'What the hell are you doing?' She says, 'I want to get the best for my family.' And then they point to the horrible brand [of peanut butter] in the supermarket cart and say, 'Then what the hell is that doing there?' She says, 'Well, they're all the same.' And then the woman's voice says, 'No, tomatoes are different and peanut butter is different.' That led to Jif really does taste more like fresh peanuts and choosy mothers choose Jif."[21]

Hunter Yager, who would also become Jif account executive and supervisor, remembers the success the campaign had in test markets. "We created the campaign, the client bought it, and we put it on the air with this meager budget," he says. "But we said, 'Let's do a test market somewhere where we increase the advertising budget by a sizable amount, say double.' [The 'Choosy Mothers' campaign] leveraged Grey's reputation with Procter & Gamble to no end. Because with a very limited budget, no change in the product, and no change in packaging, the brand started to grow, and where the advertising was heavier, it grew even more."[22]

Getting people to switch brands, though, would not be easy, especially with peanut butter. "Peanut butter is a product that people are brand-loyal to, more than many others," says Ted Woehrle, who served as P&G's assistant brand manager and brand manager for Jif in the late 1980s and early 1990s. "Foods are important to people and they make strong emotional connections, a lot of times based on the food that their mother fed them, what they were raised on. So it's really hard to convert someone who was raised on Skippy peanut butter to something else."[23]

I can attest to this. When I was growing up in the Park Slope section of Brooklyn in the late 1950s and early 1960s, the only peanut butter in my home was Skippy—to me, the Greenwich Meridian of peanut butter, as emblematic as Campbell was of soup and Kleenex of tissues. When I started researching this book, I was astonished to learn it had long since been displaced as number one by Jif. But those are just the kangaroo people, I thought (okay, I'd been out of touch). I don't even eat much hydrogenated peanut butter anymore, but my sense of brand loyalty was still offended.

Even "Choosy Mothers" had a hard time shaking the brand loyalty of kids and grown-ups. "Jif didn't take a lot of business at the expense of Skippy's and Peter Pan's market share," says Ted Woehrle. "They slowly converted people who were using local and regional peanut butters and private labels [that is, store house brands]. If you were to look at a chart, it's almost a share point a year. Back in the mid-sixties, [Jif had] an 8 or 9 percent share. When I left the brand [in 1992], it was in the low thirties. Twenty-five years later, it was almost twenty-five points higher. In that time, Skippy's market share bounced between 19 and 22 percent. Peter

Pan probably bounced between 12 and 15. As Jif got bigger, it had more resources to put into advertising, fueling its growth. It was a classic Procter & Gamble growth story."[24]

Were there any local and regional brands of peanut butter the "Choosy Mothers" campaign killed off? Neil Kreisberg names a surprising victim: Big Top.

"One of the goals was to sell enough Jif so they could discontinue Big Top," he says. Why not just discontinue it? "We had to use up plant capacity. They had to keep the plant going all the time, and until we could sell enough Jif, they had to keep making Big Top," he adds. "The joke, when I started at Grey, was that the low man on the totem pole became executive vice president in charge of Big Top. That was my first title. We did nothing for them."[25] Big Top was discontinued in August 1972.

Grey Advertising was responsible for the slogan "Choosy Mothers Choose Jif," but who at Grey was responsible for the slogan? Memories vary. Hunter Yager says it was a copywriter named Sandy Wilson. Edward Meyer, later the head of Grey Advertising, was Grey's executive vice president in charge of the Procter & Gamble account in the mid-1960s. "Meyer did not think the word 'choosy' was appropriate," Yager, who served as Meyer's lieutenant, recalls. "And we, Sandy particularly, broke his head trying to come up with another word. [We couldn't] sell Meyer on 'choosy,' but he gave in because I guess he couldn't think of another word either."[26]

But that's not how Meyer remembers it. "The campaign was invented by Bernie Kahn, a creative director at Grey," he says. "We were on a plane back from Cincinnati, where we had been meeting on Jif copy, trying to figure out a way to distinguish the brand. Bernie and I were talking about mothers shopping for produce, the ones who insisted on the fresh peaches, and would it be plausible that those kinds of mothers would exercise the same amount of thought about peanut butter. Bernie wrote the line 'Choosy Mothers Choose Jif' on the plane and said to me, 'What do you think?' and I said, 'I think it's exactly the right idea.' I remember the flight vividly. It was a little unusual for the creative director to literally invent the campaign, but in this case, Bernie did."[27]

With gradual, point-a-year growth, Jif passed Skippy to become number one around the time of the peanut butter crisis of 1980 (figure 9.2). There it remained, until its market-leader status was threatened by a de-

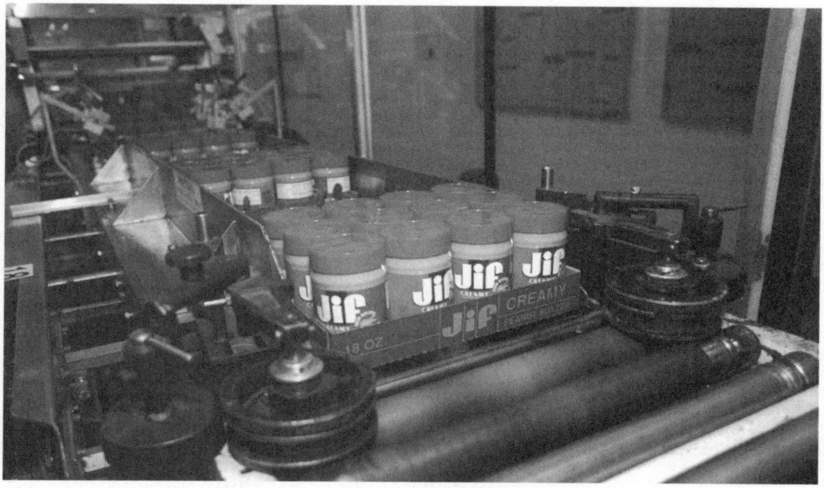

FIGURE 9.2 ASSEMBLY LINE

Jars of Jif coming down the assembly line. Since 1980 Jif has been the best-selling brand of peanut butter in the United States. (Courtesy of Ron Garrison. Photo: *Lexington Herald-Leader*)

cision on the part of P&G and Grey to change advertising campaigns. Around 1985 or 1986, Jif dispensed with "Choosy Mothers" and switched to "Taste the Jifference." "The brand and agency were concerned that the notion of 'Choosy Mothers Choose Jif' was becoming dated," says Ted Woehrle. "So Jif started a new campaign called 'Taste the Jifference.' "[28] It may have seemed like a better idea, but it wasn't.

"People get tired of things, particularly when you work on them day in and day out," says Neil Kreisberg. "We thought 'Taste the Jifference' was fresh and hip. [But] we put it on the air and business really got softer. We had a summit at Camelback in Arizona and spent three days figuring out the damn obvious, which was that all the elements of the 'Choosy Mothers Choose Jif' campaign were still relevant. We just had to execute it in a little fresher, more modern way."[29]

In 1988 the slogan was restored, but with a change. Instead of "Choosy Mothers Choose Jif," the selling line was now "Choosy Moms Choose Jif." "The change of the word 'mothers' to 'moms' was quite a big deal in the halls of Procter & Gamble, and several members of senior management weighed in on the risks associated with it," says Ted Woehrle, chuckling. "But they finally chose to say 'Choosy Moms Choose Jif,' went back to the campaign, and the growth continued. It was a small thing, but it shows you the P&G culture, the careful nature they have, worrying about changing from 'Choosy Mothers' to 'Choosy Moms.' "[30]

★ ★ ★

Despite Jif's market dominance in the United States, Procter & Gamble increasingly felt a product wasn't worthwhile unless it could conquer the world. In an effort to give Jif that kind of preeminence, it introduced Smooth Sensations in 1999. There were three kinds: peanut butter flavored with a berry blend, with apple cinnamon, and with chocolate silk (which meant they were actually peanut spreads, not peanut butters).

According to the *Lexington Herald-Leader*, Jif saw Smooth Sensations as a way to increase peanut butter sales by expanding the times of day when one might eat peanut butter beyond lunchtime; for example, an ad for the apple cinnamon variety showed it being spread on waffles at breakfast.[31] But Rita Keys, who worked at Jif for almost thirty years, says it was also P&G's attempt to make Jif palatable in the international marketplace. "Jif was never a global product," she says. "That might have been an attempt to try and go global. People in Europe just don't like peanut butter."[32]

Smooth Sensations was not the first attempt to sell flavored peanut spreads, nor would it be the last. In 1975 Kraft had introduced Koogle, which had cinnamon, banana, chocolate, and vanilla flavors. According to *Consumer Reports*, it was only about 60 percent peanuts and contained three times the sodium of peanut butter.[33] The cinnamon, *Consumer Reports* felt, was too hot and the vanilla too sweet. Subsequently, companies such as Peanut Butter and Co., based in New York's Greenwich Village, P. B. Loco of St. Paul, Minnesota, and others have purveyed a wide array of peanut spreads that include chocolate (both white and chocolate chocolate), banana (smooth and crunchy), raspberry, hot sauce, honey cinnamon, cinnamon raisin, caramel apple, chocolate-chip cookie dough, Asian curry, sun-dried tomato, maple, and honey. Many of them are tasty, but peanut butter purists demur.

The world apparently demurred at the prospect of Smooth Sensations, though, and by 2002 it was gone. Procter & Gamble started to look for a way to get rid of Jif.

As early as April 2001, it had decided to focus on its global brands such as Crest toothpaste, Pampers diapers, and Tide laundry detergent, as well as Folgers coffee, Hawaiian Punch, and Pringles potato chips, so North America–centric Jif and Crisco would have to go. P&G announced it wanted to either sell or trade the Jif factory in Lexington (the Portsmouth plant had stopped making Jif in 1993).[34] Jif was the number-one brand of peanut butter in the world, with $1 billion in annual sales. But the overwhelming majority of that was in the United States. "It's not thought likely that the billions of residents of China, India and Russia will suddenly develop a yen for spreadable goobers," the *Lexington Herald-Leader* noted. "To P&G, with more than 300 brands, 110,000 employees, and $40 billion in annual sales in 140 countries, Jif is peanuts."[35]

On October 10, 2001, Procter & Gamble sold Jif and Crisco to the J. M. Smucker Company.[36] Just as P&G had done when it bought W. T. Young Foods and Big Top peanut butter in 1955, it was an all-stock deal. Unlike that transaction, the deal was worth $1 billion. Some people wondered how Jif would make the transition from huge P&G, with its 110,000 employees, to the company headquartered on Strawberry Lane in Orrville, Ohio, which had only 2,000 workers. But Jif and Smuckers were not such strange breadfellows: Smuckers had tried to buy Jif in the mid-1970s. And *Fortune* approved of the sale, asking "What could be better than peanut butter marrying jelly?"[37]

Well known for its legendary advertising slogan, "With a name like Smuckers, it has to be good," the J. M. Smucker Company was founded in 1897 by Jerome Monroe Smucker, who sold apple butter from the back of a horse-drawn wagon. The company, which has been family-run for four generations, was incorporated in 1921. Its product line includes jellies, jams, preserves, and many other foods, including "Uncrustables," freezable peanut butter and honey sandwiches with the crusts removed, and Goober Grape, an appallingly sludgy concoction of peanut butter and jelly for those who lack the enterprise to open two different jars and spread the contents on a piece of bread.

The sale came just as the dot-com bust of the late 1990s and early 2000s was unwinding, and the business press took consolation in the fact that at least they could tell what products were involved. "At a time when investors are squinting to see true value in the likes of Tyco International, the value of Smuckers' simple businesses are easily understood," *Business Week* said.[38] (Tyco, a conglomerate, run in the 1990s by Dennis Kozlowski, acquired more than 1,000 companies in a diverse array of fields and became embroiled in financial scandal when Kozlowski received $81 million in unauthorized bonuses.[39] He later received an eight- to twenty-four-year prison sentence.)[40]

For Jif employees, the sale to Smuckers was both good and bad news. In 2003 *Fortune* declared J. M. Smucker the best company to work for in the United States, and P&G employees who acquired Smuckers stock did well. The *Lexington Herald-Leader* noted, "Unlike companies that offer employees free dry cleaning or on-site massages, Smucker's skips the frills in favor of a 'family' feel.'"[41] But apparently one of those skipped frills was profit sharing, which Procter & Gamble offered and Smuckers didn't.[42]

The sale helped to revitalize the peanut butter industry. According to Don Koehler, executive director of the Georgia Peanut Commission, P&G didn't have its heart in food. "For whatever reason, there were a lot of things that Procter & Gamble liked to do more than deal with peanut butter," he says. "When they sold the brand, it might have been the best thing that happened to us in the industry, because Smuckers is a food company and they have a vision for being a food company." Noting that Smuckers is the largest purchaser in the world of peanuts for roasting, he says it promotes its brands with a vigor P&G didn't show. "It really brought some excitement back to the peanut butter market again," he says. "They're advertising again, doing things near and dear to me." Citing a new fillip to the "Choosy Mothers" campaign, he adds, "I have three grandsons, so 'Choosy grandpas choose Jif'—I can relate to that real well."[43]

Koehler also likes the fact that Smuckers is family-owned. "Dealing with families is a nice way to do business," he says. "The Smucker family still is involved with their business, and the people who work with the J. M. Smucker Company don't want to beat folks out of something. They understand that everybody's got to have some profit to be able to survive, that it's all business, and it's business all the way back to the farmer. It's really been a breath of fresh air to go from dealing with these stockholder corporations back to a family-owned company."[44] Koehler says that his favorite peanut butter is Jif extra crunchy. I'm surprised when he tells me this—it feels like a mother saying, "I like little Johnny best of all," but he feels comfortable sharing his thoughts.

★★★

Smuckers shows that peanut butter is more important to it than it was to Procter & Gamble through its extensive involvement with natural or old-fashioned peanut butter, producing four brands at its plant in New Bethlehem, Pennsylvania: Smuckers Natural, Laura Scudder's, Adams, and Santa Cruz Organic. New Bethlehem is about sixty miles north of Pittsburgh, and every September the town holds a peanut butter festival that includes, oddly enough, a chicken barbecue and, more appropriately, the crowning of the Peanut Butter Queen.[45] For whatever reason, Smuckers is very low-profile about its New Bethlehem plant and the festival. Although the plant cosponsors the festival, the Smuckers Company in Orrville, Ohio, does no publicity for it, and, according to the *Pittsburgh Post-Gazette,* few people in the town of Clarion, only eighteen miles away, are even aware of the festival.

The reason Smuckers has a separate plant for its old-fashioned peanut butters is because the production demands of natural and stabilized are so different. Charles Smith, who managed Skippy's Little Rock plant in the 1980s, said it didn't bother him that the plant didn't produce old-fashioned peanut butter at the time. "It's harder to clean up," he said.[46] According to Skippy's Larry Shearon, "The whole point of stabilization is to keep the product uniform over time. Without stabilization, the oil separates from the solids, playing havoc with pumping. It requires constant agitation."[47]

Reflecting Procter & Gamble's attitude toward natural-style peanut butter, Billie Jean Gibbons, executive secretary to the manager of Jif's Lexington plant in the 1970s and 1980s, says, "You can't just eat natural peanut butter on the spur of the moment. You have to take it out of the refrigerator and let it sit. I call it 'pre-meditated peanut butter.'"[48] That attitude helps to explain why stabilized peanut butter is about 80 percent of the market, while natural or old-fashioned is only 17 percent.[49]

In the early twenty-first century, Jif maintains market dominance in the United States. In 2005–2006, it had a 34 percent share of the creamy market, as opposed to 20 percent for Skippy and 12 percent for Peter Pan. It was a closer race among crunchies, where Jif had 27 percent to Skippy super chunk's 23 percent and Peter Pan crunchy's 9 percent.[50]

Smuckers helps maintain Jif's preeminence with publicity ploys such as the Jif most-creative peanut butter sandwich contest. Among the winners have been Crunchy Chinese Fortune Cookie Sandwiches, small sandwiches in the shape of fortune cookies served with an Asian-style dipping sauce of creamy peanut butter, coconut milk, soy sauce, brown sugar, lemon juice, sesame oil, and chili powder (the 2008 winner) and the Louisiana-Bayou-meets-Philly-themed Po' Boy Peanut Butter Chicken Cheesesteak Sandwich, featuring a sauce made of Jif peanut butter, Worcestershire sauce, honey, and honey mustard (the 2009 winner). Inasmuch as the contest winners range in age from seven to twelve years old, it's possible some of them receive help from their parents, but perhaps that's being ungenerous to the winners.

Peanut butter inspires Americans' creativity in other ways: In "Joey Green's Wacky Uses for Jif Peanut Butter," Green notes that 1964 Republican presidential candidate Barry Goldwater once shaved with peanut butter on a camping trip. We don't know what brand he used, but Green helpfully cautions, "For best results, avoid shaving with Jif extra crunchy."[51] Going even further afield is the Web page "2000 Uses for Peanut Butter . . . and Then Some!," up to 3,500 uses the last time I checked. Use number 57: "New Olympic event: PB swimming." Use number 2,703: "Mix with lightning bugs and make your peanut butter glow in the dark." And for these troubled times, use number 3,369: "Control terrorists in flight by throwing the switch and filling the plane with peanut butter."[52]

Although Procter & Gamble no longer makes Jif, the various ways P&G chose to get creative with it have defined the experience of peanut butter for most Americans today. Its generous apportioning of hydrogenated vegetable oils to Jif when it debuted led to the peanut butter standard of identity. Popular tastes gravitated toward sweeter peanut butter as a result of Jif's sweeter formulation, and Skippy and Peter Pan found themselves forced to follow suit. As a result, the peanut butter most people eat today tastes the way it does and has the composition it has because a U.S.-based multinational soap maker thought that was the way to do it.

PEANUT BUTTER GOES INTERNATIONAL

Although peanut butter is regarded as a uniquely American food, it has taken root in foreign soil, even if not enough to suit Procter & Gamble.

Peanut butter got its start in the 1890s, at the same time as the American empire, which would eventually spread it around the world. Although countries such as Haiti and the Netherlands have their own distinctive peanut butter traditions, it's mainly found overseas wherever there are American expatriates, the American military, and locals who deal with them. Germany, which is top-heavy with U.S. military bases, is the number-two importer of U.S. peanut butter.[1] Of people in India who eat peanut butter, 75 percent are from the United States, 24 percent from other countries, and only 1 percent from India.[2] "The impulse to eat *my own food* is so powerful that gastronomic imperialism has left as much of a mark on the world map as its military counterpart," according to *The Meaning of Food*, a companion volume to the 2005 PBS series of the same name.[3]

Today it's difficult to find peanut butter outside the United States; in the past, it was all but impossible. "Peanut butter is almost unknown in many overseas markets and largely unappreciated in most others," Jasper Woodroof, a professor of food science at the University of Georgia, has written.[4]

Brian Sternthal, a marketing professor at Northwestern University, agrees. "Despite its American popularity and longevity, peanut butter remains primarily a North American phenomenon," he writes. "In many parts of the world, peanut butter is regarded as an unpalatable American curiosity."[5]

American writer Norbert Blei experienced this firsthand when he lived in the Greek islands with his two children in the early 1970s:

> Greek kids do not run around yelling, "I want a peanut butter sandwich."
>
> Greek kids are satisfied with a piece of fresh bread and a hunk of feta cheese. . . .
>
> One day, after two or three months on the island of Rhodes, I walked into an expensive self-service shop in the old marketplace of Rhodes City, and there on the shelf I found one tiny, dusty 6-ounce jar of Skippy Peanut Butter. . . . I took it back to our village, wrapped it carefully, and hid it in the closet.
>
> A few weeks later, my daughter had her fifth birthday. Toys and such being rather scarce, I took her to Rhodes City, sat her down at a cafe on the Mandraki, bought her chocolates and ice cream . . . and then gave her the gift of peanut butter. She carried that tiny jar with her for months, on four other islands and into two other countries.[6]

Further emphasizing the North American nature of peanut butter, Canada is far and away the largest export market for the U.S. peanut butter industry. Between 2004 and 2009, Canada imported 54,742 metric tons of peanut butter, 42 percent of U.S. exports. It was followed by Germany (13,956 tons, 11 percent), Mexico (7,606 tons, 6 percent), Japan (6,809 tons, 5 percent), Saudi Arabia (6,492 tons, also 5 percent), and South Korea (4,423 tons, 3 percent). The United Kingdom (3,014 tons), Hong Kong (2,627 tons), Singapore (2,578 tons), and the United Arab Emirates (2,518 tons) each accounted for 2 percent of American exports, with the UAE's intake rising the most rapidly: from 2006 to 2009, its consumption nearly doubled.[7]

Because the American peanut butter market is so competitive, some food brands that are well known here have abandoned the U.S. market, preferring to try their luck with peanut butter abroad. Walt Albritton is technical services manager at Kroger's Tara Foods plant, which makes peanut butter and other foods in Albany, Georgia. "Planters goes all over the world," he notes. "But [its peanut butter is] not domestic, even though they have a very high name recognition in the United States." (That changed in the spring of 2011, when Planters relaunched its peanut butter in the United States for the first time in thirty years.) Kraft is one of the leading brands of peanut butter in Canada (where it's been sold since 1960) and Australia (since 1931), but you won't find it on grocery shelves in the United States. "It's a tight market to get into from a shelf-space standpoint in a grocery chain," Albritton adds. "For Kroger to introduce a new peanut butter item, we almost have to cut one out to get it on the shelf."[8]

★★★

Although Americans like to think of ourselves as the center of the peanut-butter-eating world, Canadians consume peanut butter even more zealously than we do. "Canadians eat a little more per capita than Americans," says Patrick Archer, president of the American Peanut Council, a trade organization representing all segments of the American peanut industry.[9] "They like it for breakfast, especially on toast," he adds, an observation evoking this couplet from the Olympics' early 1960s doo-wop classic "Peanut Butter": "All my friends tell me that they dig it the most/Early in the morning when they spread it on toast." Peanut butter also shows up in Canadian literature. "Cooking lunch was no big deal," Margaret Atwood writes in "Death by Landscape," a short story about a group of girls on a life-changing summer-camp canoe trip, "it was just unwrapping the cheese and getting out the bread and peanut butter."[10]

Canadian peanut butter sold as far west as British Columbia is bilingual on its labels, marked either "smooth/*cremeux*" or "crunchy/*croquant*." Although it's no longer in business, Squirrel, a traditional Canadian brand, was made from 1980 to 2000 by Best Foods. When you opened the jar, there was a peanut nestled on top. After Best Foods was acquired by Unilever, makers of Skippy, in 2000, Squirrel was discontinued and Skippy was renamed "Skippy the Squirrel" in Canada, although the peanut on top was discontinued. In a ruthless corporate purge, the squirrel was then eliminated from the brand name, although today in Canada, Skippy peanut butter features a squirrel on its label and freshness seal.[11]

In Mexico the most popular brand is Aladino (Spanish for "Aladdin"). It contains a whopping 13 percent sugar, substantially more than American brands are allowed. Well-to-do Mexicans who have traveled to the United States have developed a taste for peanut butter and apparently have quite a sweet tooth as well.

Surprisingly, the world's oldest brand of peanut butter is not American, but Australian. Sanitarium, first made on January 28, 1898, was started by Edward Halsey, a Seventh-Day Adventist who had worked with John Harvey Kellogg at the Western Health Reform Institute in Battle Creek, Michigan. First produced in a small Melbourne bakery, it's now made in Berkeley Vale, about an hour north of Sydney.[12] In 2008 an acquaintance who lives in Australia sent me a jar. It contains no salt or sugar and is stabilized with about 1 percent of hydrogenated sunflower-seed oil, as opposed to the soy, canola, and cottonseed oils used in the United States. It is remarkably bland, probably the dullest peanut butter I tasted of the many I sampled for this book. I asked a company representative if the company steams its peanuts, as the Kelloggs supposedly did, instead of roasting them. Nope, she said: it roasts.[13]

Peanut butter is livelier in Haiti, where it's known as *mamba*; one variety is flavored with hot pepper.[14] Haiti is one of the few countries whose peanut butter traditions didn't originate in the United States. Peanut butter making in Haiti supposedly dates to the Spanish occupation of 1697,[15] although Spaniards have no peanut butter tradition of their own. In addition to being sold in jars, it's also sold by street vendors; most neighborhoods in the capital of Port-au-Prince have their own peanut butter vendor. Shelled peanuts, raw or roasted, are pounded into a pulp with a mortar and pestle and spooned out to customers at street-side stands, either alone, on bread, or with casaba, a honeydew-like melon. Four days after the 7.0 Haitian earthquake of January 2010, Haitian street vendors, including peanut butter vendors, were back at work, plying their wares well before international food aid arrived.[16]

One of the purveyors of that aid was Early County 2055, a nonprofit based in Blakely, Georgia, that organized a shipment of stabilized peanut butter to Haiti. Within ten days of the quake, it had overseen the loading of 75,000 pounds of peanut butter onto the Navy cargo ship USS *Sacagawea* bound for Port-au-Prince.[17] But Haitians, while grateful, were understandably wary: Regine Zamor, a Haitian American film producer and blogger, notes, "Free American rice slowed down our rice production and put lots of farmers out of business. It's important that another healthy Haitian industry doesn't get exploited."[18]

★★★

In Europe, the Germans import more American peanut butter than the Dutch by a factor of ten, but the Dutch are the biggest consumers on a per capita basis;[19] like the Canadians, they even exceed Americans in this regard. The Dutch have their own thriving peanut butter industry. But don't call it peanut butter there: in the Netherlands, peanut butter isn't peanut butter (*pindaboter*) but peanut cheese (*pindakaas*). Apparently, the dairy farmers have a strong union and don't want anything but butter to be called butter.

"The popularity of *pindakaas* goes with the fact that we are a bread-eating nation," a Dutch friend tells me. "Popular combinations are *pindakaas* with slices of cucumber, and *pindakaas* and jam (your peanut butter and jelly sandwich) or *pindakaas* and sugar. It's also used to make *pindasaus* (satay sauce) to go with Indonesian food, especially satay: *Pindakaas* is mixed together with coconut milk, soy sauce, garlic, chili pepper, ginger, or other spices and heated almost to the boiling point."

Imported brands such as Jif and Skippy are available. But the Dutch prefer their own brands, both for the taste and because imported brands are expensive and the Dutch are thrifty. Perhaps the most popular domestic Dutch brand is Calve Pindakaas. It's one of the tastiest stabilized peanut butters I sampled, perhaps because it's one of the sweetest (the crunchy variety has only 88 percent peanuts, leaving a lot of room for dextrose).

Despite its flavor and preeminence, Calve Pindakaas has been losing market share to supermarket house brands in the Netherlands, which play as rough as the Dutch soccer team did in the 2010 World Cup. Dutch store brands go as far as is legally possible to make the labels of their house brands resemble Calve, so that shoppers in a hurry might pick up a jar by mistake and not realize their error until they get home. Supermarkets also stock Calve in what are known as hernia or slipped-disc locations, low shelves where you have to bend far over to pick it up. "All's fair in love and *pindakaas*," my Dutch friend observes.

Peanut butter is popular in Germany because of all the U.S. servicemen and women stationed there since World War II: today the U.S. military has more than 50,000 military personnel at more than twenty German bases. One of the most popular brands is the American-made Lucky Joe, a name with roots in World War II. American soldiers used to give away or trade their peanut butter. The nickname for an American soldier was G.I. Joe, and the name caught on. But it's not just German people who like peanut butter. In 2008 Toto, a six-year-old male kangaroo, escaped from a wildlife park near Hanover and spent two weeks on the lam. Zookeepers exploited his fondness for peanut butter by smearing it on bushes and trees in areas where he had been sighted in an effort to recapture him.[20]

Some countries, however, resist the charms of peanut butter. "We want everyone to agree with us that it's excellent but haven't been successful with the French and Italians," says Leslie Wagner of the Southern Peanut Growers, a trade group devoted to promoting peanuts and peanut butter.[21] Rita Keys, who worked in human resources for Jif, sounds a similar note. "Italians love pasta and marinara, the French have their haute cuisine, but [Americans are] on the move, and [peanut butter is] more convenient and nutritious," she says.[22] During the 1999 Tour de France, Frankie Andreu of the U.S. Postal Service team complained he and his teammates couldn't find peanut butter anywhere. Procter & Gamble sent the team a supply of Smooth Sensations, its short-lived flavored peanut spreads.[23]

But peanut butter has made some beachheads in France: in the early 1960s, Marvin Rosefield, son of Skippy founder Joseph Rosefield, was talking to a waitress in Paris and mentioned he was in the peanut butter business. The waitress said she had some in her pantry at home. "What brand?" Rosefield asked her. "Skee-pee," she replied to Rosefield's delight.[24]

Although peanut butter doesn't have deep roots in eastern Europe, American influence has given it a foothold there as well. "There's a market for peanut butter in Poland right now," says Don Koehler, executive director of the Georgia Peanut Commission. "After Communism fell in Poland, a lot of the people who had come to this country fleeing Communism went back. And when they went back, they took a little peanut butter with them."[25]

Russia has proved a tougher nut to crack for peanut butter. In 1922, after the five-year civil war between Bolsheviks and pro-Czarist forces following the Russian Revolution, starvation was rampant. American business leaders called for the inclusion of peanut butter in relief shipments to the Soviet Union.[26] By 1992 the Soviet Union no longer existed, but the United States was still trying to get peanut butter into Russia.

"Of the many things Russia lacks, peanut butter is one," Celestine Bohlen wrote that year from Moscow in the *New York Times*. "To be sure, no one here knew they were missing it. But this week, in a gesture of self-interested humanitarian aid, the National Peanut Council of America [now the American Peanut Council] presented this hungry nation with its first peanut butter and jelly sandwich." A delegation of American farmers, shellers, and producers came bearing thirty tons of peanut butter and another one-and-a-half tons to be test-marketed in Moscow stores. A formal tasting took place at the Exhibition of National Economic Achievements, known by its Russian acronym VDNX.[27] The first verdict by a troupe from the Moscow Children's Theater was that the peanut butter—*arakhisovoye maslo*—was on the salty side, but no one complained about it sticking to the roof of their mouth.

★★★

In the Middle East, peanut butter is increasingly popular in Saudi Arabia. Patrick Archer cites the influence of Aramco, an acronym for the Arabian-American Oil Company, which was drilling for oil by the 1940s and 1950s. "As I understand it," he says, "Aramco brought it over for its workers, and that's how it got started there."[28] Most peanut butter in Saudi Arabia is imported from the United States. Its consumers are mainly Westerners and Asians, although Saudi children are becoming increasingly fond of it.[29] As early as 1980, the *New York Times* noted that the Saudis were purchasing 155 times more American peanut butter than they had in 1973. It suggested using it as a trade weapon against the Saudis if they ever threatened us again with an oil embargo.[30]

Several West African countries use ground and mashed-up peanuts in soups and sauces. The peanut-growing areas of West Africa overlap extensively with slave-trading regions, which is why peanuts are now a staple crop in the United States. In Nigeria, as in Haiti, shelled peanuts are pounded into a pulp using electrical grinders or, where there's no electricity, manual grinders;[31] traditionally, residents of both countries used a mortar and pestle. Containing both peanut hearts and skins, the pulp is made from raw or roasted peanuts and sold to customers on the street. The similarity of this custom may stem from Nigerians having been forcibly transported to Haiti to work on plantations during the slave trade, according to Marc Prou, a Haiti specialist in the Africana Studies Department at the University of Massachusetts–Boston.[32] Farther south, South Africa's Black Cat peanut butter has been made since 1926 (figure 10.1).[33]

Peanut butter, or sauces and stews based on ground-up peanuts, can be found throughout Southeast Asia. Peanut butter is a staple in the Philippines, which was occupied by the United States after the Spanish-American War. *Los Angeles Times* food writer Charles Perry notes that peanut-based satay sauce is a signature food of Indonesia. "One of the most famous Indonesian dishes is satay, little skewers of grilled meat served with mildly spicy sweet-sour sauces made with peanut butter, chiles, coconut milk, and fish sauce," he writes. "There's even a salad, *gado-gado*, with a rich satay-style peanut sauce."[34] Indonesia was a Dutch colony for several

FIGURE 10.1 PEANUT BUTTERS FROM AUSTRALIA, SOUTH AFRICA, AND SPAIN

Australia's Sanitarium, first made in 1898, is the world's oldest brand of peanut butter. South Africa's Black Cat, dating to 1926, is older than Peter Pan, Skippy, and Jif. The label of Spain's Capitan Mani emphasizes its all-American nature. (Courtesy of Allan Dean Walker)

Satay

Satay is an Indonesian dish which has attained worldwide popularity.

1½ pounds sirloin steak, cut into 16 strips (about ¼ inch thick) against the grain*
¼ cup plus 1 tablespoon peanut oil
1 teaspoon ground cinnamon
1 teaspoon ground coriander
1 teaspoon ground ginger
1 teaspoon dry mustard
½ teaspoon garlic powder
½ teaspoon freshly ground black pepper
½ cup creamy natural peanut butter
6 tablespoons soy sauce, preferably reduced-sodium soy sauce
¼ cup rice vinegar (or white wine vinegar or sherry vinegar: easier to find than rice vinegar, but has a less sharp taste)
2 teaspoons sugar
Sixteen 10-inch bamboo skewers, soaked in water for 20 minutes

Place the steak strips in a large bowl. Pour in 1 tablespoon peanut oil, then add the ground cinnamon, ground coriander, ground ginger, dry mustard, garlic powder, and ground black pepper. Toss well, cover, and place in the refrigerator to marinate at least 1 hour or up to 10 hours.

Whisk the peanut butter, soy sauce, rice vinegar, sugar, and the remaining ¼ cup peanut oil in a medium bowl until smooth; set aside as the dipping sauce for the satay.

Take one of the sirloin strips and thread it onto one of the skewers by weaving the skewer back and forth through the meat, starting at one short end and finishing at the other, thereby piercing the piece of meat three or four times with the skewer to keep it solidly attached. Keep the meat close to one end of the skewer so that the other end becomes a long handle for the satay. Set on a platter and repeat with all the skewers and steak strips.

Prepare the barbecue grill or preheat the broiler with the broiler pan about 4 inches from the heat source. You may want to wrap the exposed, long handles of the skewers in aluminum foil to protect them from the heat.

(continued)

Grill or broil the meat about 3 minutes, turning once, until medium-rare, juicy, still soft, and very fragrant. (The meat should feel like the lax skin between your thumb and index finger when pressed.) Unwrap the skewers if you've guarded them with aluminum foil and serve with the prepared peanut dipping sauce on the side.

* Cutting meat against the grain is fairly easy once you get the hang of it. Lay the steak on a clean cutting board and run your fingers across it, pressing down a bit. You'll eventually see which way the fibers are running, usually at an angle in the steak. Cut the steak at a 90-degree angle to these fibers so the pieces stay together in strips.

---

hundred years, helping to explain why the Netherlands is the number-one per capita consumer of peanut butter in Europe.

The farther away you get from Indonesia, Perry notes, the smaller the role peanuts play in the local cuisine. In Cambodia and Burma, they're chopped up and tossed into soups and salads, as in China. But Thailand is close enough to Indonesia that peanut sauce is an important part of its cuisine. Southern Thailand has peanut butter dishes such as *pra ram long song* (beef and spinach stewed in something like satay sauce) and *gai thua* (chicken in a peanut butter and coconut milk curry). A typical recipe for Thai peanut sauce is ground peanuts, red curry paste, sugar, a little vinegar, and vegetable oil. In Thailand, they grind peanuts to make it, but in the United States, Thai restaurants simply use peanut butter—it's convenient and people are accustomed to the taste.

Because peanut butter is so exotic overseas, manufacturers and importers take pains to let customers know what they're getting into. In Japan, Skippy has peanuts on the label, both blanched and unblanched, shelled and unshelled. The label of Japan's Blue Flag brand not only feature peanuts, but images of Snoopy from the comic strip "Peanuts" dancing his way around the jar.

★★★

Although Skippy is the second-leading brand in the United States, behind Jif, Skippy executive John Moorhead has claimed Skippy is the world's number-one-selling peanut butter by virtue of its export sales.[35] In addition to Japan, Skippy is sold in seventy-five countries, including Israel, South Africa, and Russia. One of the reasons Procter & Gamble sold Jif to Smuckers in 2002 is that it wasn't popular around the world, even with P&G's legendary marketing abilities.[36] Part of the problem may have been the name: in Europe, Jif is a brand of concentrated lemon juice, so the idea of its being a peanut butter, a food never popular there to begin with, strikes some Europeans as odd.

Peanut butter is more popular in the United States than almost anywhere else. But why? "I always wondered about that," says David Guin, who managed Jif's plant in Lexington, Kentucky, from 1967 though 1987. "Some of the good peanut-growing areas in Africa are where they've had real nutrition problems. Peanut butter is probably one of the most nutritious things you can eat. But people in Africa just didn't like the taste of peanut butter."[37]

Europeans aren't crazy about the taste of peanuts, either. The United States and Europe started importing peanuts from Gambia in the 1830s.[38] But while the Europeans used them to make cooking oil, Americans were, from the outset, abidingly fond of the taste of fresh-roasted peanuts, which is what gives peanut butter its flavor.

"Peanuts are more popular here than in other countries, particularly western Europe," says Andrew F. Smith, author of *Peanuts: The Illustrious History of the Goober Pea*. "Western Europe already has a nut, the almond. Virtually all European candies, if they have a nut in them, it's an almond. The Europeans just prefer that, and a peanut doesn't taste like an almond."[39]

Along with the taste, there's the texture. Americans grow up on peanut butter and children in other countries don't, establishing patterns for life. "If you grew up with peanut butter as a kid, you like it as an adult," says Patrick Archer. "People introduced to it as adults may not like the sticky texture."[40]

Don Taylor, who worked in quality control at Jif for more than thirty years, adds, "You'd think in Africa, it would be a food staple. From what I've read, it's the sticky consistency they don't like."[41] ("There's a food goin' round that's a sticky, sticky goo," the Olympics sing in "Peanut Butter." "Well it tastes real good, but it's so hard to chew.")

John Powell of the American Peanut Shellers Association theorizes Europeans don't like peanut butter because they associate it with the hard times following the devastation of World War II, when American CARE packages included peanut butter.[42] Working against this theory, however, is the popularity of Lucky Joe peanut butter in Germany.

The success of peanut butter in the United States can also be traced to our agricultural history: In the early part of the twentieth century, the boll weevil destroyed much of the southern cotton crop. Southern farmers turned to peanuts as a replacement cash crop and had to develop markets for it. While peanut butter enjoyed some popularity in the United States before World War I, the market was just a fraction of the size it is now.[43] "The need for a product of the peanut butter type became evident at the end of World War I in 1918," writes Jasper Woodroof, who was a professor of food science at the University of Georgia. "Farmers were seeking a market for the expanding peanut crop that was more lucrative than pig feed."[44]

Americans' passion for fast food also helps explain its popularity here. "Peanut butter is one of the original fast foods," says Dan Gorbet, a retired peanut breeder from the University of Florida. "You can combine a lot of things with peanut butter and make a flavorful, nutritious sandwich in a matter of minutes. You don't even have to turn the stove on."[45]

Finally, U.S. peanuts are of a higher quality than those grown in many Third World countries. "India and China primarily crush their peanuts for oil," says Leslie Wagner of the Southern Peanut Growers. "There are two reasons for that. One is the type of cooking they do, particularly in China. They tend to stir-fry. The other is that the quality of peanuts grown in India and China are mostly not edible. You don't have to have a good-quality peanut to crush it for oil; you can have pretty crummy peanuts. But if it's the meat you want, you need to have a sound, mature kernel. It's difficult to do that under the growing conditions in India and China.

Farming there tends to be less mechanized, more focused on smaller family farms worked by hand."

Wagner also notes that peanut butter in the United States is put to an array of gastronomic uses not accorded ground peanut paste elsewhere. "In other parts of the world, even if they have something we would recognize as peanut butter, they don't tend to eat it on a sandwich," she says.[46] "In Africa and Asian countries, they have peanut butter. But they use it as a base for sauce for a soup or stew. To them, it's only a savory base. Here, we know peanut butter can go in anything. It's a sweet! It's a savory! It's the main entrée! . . . So in terms of how we use and perceive peanut butter, I would say that's uniquely American."[47]

THE MUSIC OF PEANUT BUTTER

Because peanut butter is so distinctively American, songs about it are woven into American pop culture, as are songs about peanuts. The latter category includes "Goober Peas," the melodic Civil War–era invocation of camaraderie among Confederate soldiers, and Dizzy Gillespie's bebop-style "Salt Peanuts." "The Peanut Vendor" ("El Manisero"), a Cuban song in the rumba style, was popularized during the 1930s and 1940s by American musicians such as Stan Kenton. "Take Me Out to the Ballgame" encourages the listener to "buy me some peanuts and Cracker Jacks," and even "The Ballad of the Boll Weevil" obliquely evokes peanuts, as it was the weevil's destruction of the cotton crop that enabled the peanut to become a mainstay of southern agriculture.

Like the peanut from which it's derived, peanut butter has its own shelf of music. Interestingly, most of the standards about peanuts predate World War II, while peanut butter songs don't appear until afterward, a possible reflection of the fact that peanut butter did not attain a central role in our popular culture until baby boomers took a liking to it.

Perhaps the earliest peanut butter song is "Peanut Butter Blues" (1946), written by Peanuts Holland and recorded by Don Byas. A now-obscure but influential African American tenor saxophonist from Muskogee, Oklahoma, Byas moved to Europe after World War II. Oddly, the swing-style song, which appears on his albums *In Paris* and *1946*, makes no mention of peanut butter. The singer invites his girlfriend on a picnic, telling her:

> Run home and get your basket,
> Let's take a trip in the woods.
> We may not pick a lot of berries,
> But we'll sure come back feelin' good.

Maybe his inamorata packs peanut butter in her picnic basket. Gwen Guthrie's sultry, disco-flavored "Peanut Butter" (1983), recorded on her albums *Portrait* and *Padlock*, is also about feeling good: she invites her lover to "Come on, spread yourself on me like peanut butter."

The standard of peanut butter songs is the driving, rhythmic doo-wop classic "Peanut Butter" (1961), recorded by the Olympics:

> I went to a dinner and what did they eat?
> (Peanut, peanut butter)
> Well, I took a big bite and it stuck to my teeth.
> (Peanut, peanut butter)
> Now everybody looks like they got the mumps.
> (Peanut, peanut butter)
> Eatin' peanut butter in great big hunks.
> (Peanut, peanut butter)
> I like peanut butter—creamy peanut butter, chunky peanut butter, too.

The song's initial recording history is somewhat confused,[1] as it was recorded around the same time by the Marathons. Their version has an almost note-for-note similarity to the Olympics'. Even the groups' names are similar: the marathon is an Olympic event, after all. But the groups had different members. The Olympics, whose biggest hit was "Western Movies," were led by Walter Ward and featured tenor Charles Fizer, who was shot and killed during the Watts Riots in 1965. The Marathons, also known as the Vibrations, were led by Jimmy Johnson and had two tenors: Richard Owens and Carl Fisher. A twist version of "Peanut Butter" was recorded by Chubby Checker on his album *Let's Twist Again* (1962). It has some nice touches and there's a good sax solo on the bridge, but the backup band's perfunctory tone suggests they were eager to wrap the session up and get to lunch.

Jimmy Buffett's "Peanut Butter Conspiracy," on his album *A White Sport Coat and a Pink Crustacean* (1973), is clever, lively, and upbeat; it's also a morally dubious song in which the song's narrator recalls his early, struggling days as a musician. He and his friend worked minimum wage jobs, spent all their money on marijuana, and provided for their nutritional needs by stealing peanut butter from the local convenience store:

> Who's gonna steal the peanut butter?
> I'll get a can of sardines.
> Runnin' up and down the aisle of the mini-mart
> Stickin' food in our jeans.

The narrator assures his listeners he and his friend never took more than they needed and promised that if they ever became successful, they would pay the mini-mart back. But even as a success, the narrator still lifts the odd jar of peanut butter now and then, just in case hard times return.

The title of Buffett's song may be a musical hat tip to the short-lived late 1960s folk-rock group The Peanut Butter Conspiracy. Led by singer Barbara "Sandi" Robison, the Los Angeles–based quintet was most noted for the songs "It's a Happening Thing," which reflects the vitality and hope of the 1960s youth culture, and "Turn On a Friend (to the Good Life)." While they played off their name with album titles like *The Peanut Butter Conspiracy Is Spreading,* they never made any songs about peanut butter, although two of their titles were "Captain Sandwich" (about the danger of relying too much on authority figures) and "Peter Pan."

Garrison Keillor, creator of *A Prairie Home Companion,* has written a suitably woebegone (or Wobegon) song about peanut butter's consoling and redemptive powers, "The Ballad of Peanut Butter." One day a hapless boy fumbles a football, earning his playmates' derision. When he comes home, his mother serves him a peanut butter sandwich, something she'll do again whenever life goes badly for him, which is often. One day, however, he reads a book that convinces him cholesterol is the root of all dietary evil. (Stabilized peanut butter contains a minuscule amount of trans fat, but no cholesterol; however, consuming trans fats does raise cholesterol levels.) So the young man abandons peanut butter for health

Peanut Butter Crisscross Cookies

This is the classic peanut butter cookie.

1 cup shortening
1 cup peanut butter
1 cup granulated sugar
1 cup (packed) brown sugar
2 eggs
1 teaspoon vanilla
2½ cups all-purpose flour
1 teaspoon baking soda
Dash salt

Preheat oven to 400 degrees Fahrenheit.

Cream together shortening and peanut butter. Gradually add sugars, blending well. Add eggs, one at a time, beating until smooth. Add vanilla. Set aside.

Combine flour, baking soda, and salt. Stir into peanut butter mixture.

Using dampened hands, shape batter into 1-inch balls and place 2 inches apart on a greased cookie sheet. Flatten with a fork in a crisscross pattern, then bake for about 8 minutes.

★★★

Yield: approximately 6 dozen cookies

FROM LARRY ZISMAN AND HONEY ZISMAN, *THE GREAT AMERICAN PEANUT BUTTER BOOK* (NEW YORK: ST. MARTIN'S PRESS, 1985). REPRINTED WITH PERMISSION OF LARRY AND HONEY ZISMAN.

food—garden salads, whole wheat rolls, and green beans. But the dietary gods strike him down for his gastronomic perfidy—his dog dies, he smashes his pickup truck, his sweetheart leaves him, he loses his hair, his house catches fire, and he goes to prison. When his mother visits him there, she doesn't bring health food, but a peanut butter sandwich.

Because peanut butter is so popular among children, peanut butter songs are often children's songs. There's "Peanut Butter and Jelly," which tells you how to make a peanut butter and jelly sandwich. "First you take the peanuts and you dig them, you dig them," it begins. Then you take the shells and you crack them; you take the peanuts and you mash them; you pick the grapes and you squish them; you take the bread and you spread the peanut butter and jelly. Finally, you take the sandwich and you eat it. Each instruction is accompanied by pantomime gestures.

Then there's this brief rhyme:

A peanut sat on a railroad track
His heart was all aflutter.
A train came rollin' down the track,
Toot, toot, peanut butter.

Moving a little up the age and maturity scale, there's the wildly popular "It's Peanut Butter Jelly Time." Recorded in a frenetic hip-hop style by the Buckwheat Boyz and a staple on YouTube, the song features the animated image of a dancing banana while the singer basically repeats that it's peanut butter jelly time for one minute and forty-six seconds.

The song has insinuated itself into popular culture: One version has garnered nearly 5 million views on YouTube. On an episode of the animated TV show *Family Guy*, a man's dog attempts to cheer him up by dressing as the dancing banana and performing the song. When "professional" wrestler Alex Shelley enters the ring, his fans call out "It's Peanut Butter Shelley Time." And a contestant on a 2007 episode of *American Idol* donned a banana costume and performed the song, only to be disqualified within ten seconds.

No song, however, captures the irresistible nature of peanut butter quite like Shel Silverstein's spoken-word "Peanut Butter Sandwich." Silverstein was a versatile, talented, and successful beatnik-like poet ("I'm Being Swallowed by a Boa Constrictor"), singer-songwriter ("One's on the Way," for Loretta Lynn, and "Sylvia's Mother," for Dr. Hook & the Medicine Show), composer, cartoonist, screenwriter, and author of children's books (*A Light in the Attic* and *Where the Sidewalk Ends*).

"Peanut Butter Sandwich" tells the story of a young king so devoted to peanut butter sandwiches that he eats nothing else; he issues a royal decree that the only thing his subjects may learn is how to make them.

Disaster strikes one day when, after eating an especially sticky peanut butter sandwich, the king's jaws lock and he's unable to open them. Dentists, the royal plumber, a carpenter, a telephone lineman, and firemen are unable to open the king's jaws.

For years, the young king is saddled with his peanut butter lockjaw. Finally, his subjects hook grappling chains to his jaws and pull with all their might. Slowly, gradually, inexorably, they pry his jaws open. His first barely audible, hoarse words: "How about a peanut butter sandwich?"

DISCOGRAPHY

"Goober Peas" (1866): First published by A. E. Blackmar of New Orleans, who puckishly listed A. Pindar as the lyricist and P. Nutt as the composer. One of the best versions on YouTube is by the Ninety-seventh Regimental String Band. Available at http://www.creamyandcrunchy.com/.

"Take Me Out to the Ballgame" (1908): Written by Jack Norworth and Albert von Tilzer. Among the most distinctive versions on YouTube is one that features Jerry Lee Lewis and Neil Sedaka performing it over the closing credits of the mid-1960s television show *Shindig*, with the Shindig dancers dressed up as ball girls.

"The Peanut Vendor" ("El Manisero") (1920s): Written by Moises Simons. First recorded by Rita Montaner in 1927 or 1928; the best-selling version was recorded by Don Azpiazu and his Havana Casino Orchestra in 1930. Also recorded by Stan Kenton, Xavier Cugat, Perez Prado, Judy Garland, and many others. The Anita O'Day version is available at http://www.creamyandcrunchy.com/.

"The Ballad of the Boll Weevil": Traditional. Leadbelly's version was recorded by folklorist Alan Lomax in 1934. The best-known version was recorded by Brook Benton in 1961.

"Salt Peanuts" (1942): Written by Dizzy Gillespie and Kenny Clarke. Videos of Gillespie playing this, from 1947 and the 1970s, are available on YouTube. Also available at http://www.creamyandcrunchy.com/.

"Peanut Butter Blues" (1946): Written by Peanuts Holland. It's on two Don Byas albums, *In Paris* and *1946*, both very rare, although I was able to download it from Amazon for 89 cents.

"Peanut Butter" (1961): Written by Fred Smith, Cliff Goldsmith, H. B. Barnum, and Marty Cooper. It's on the CD *The Very Best of the Olympics*.

The Marathons' version, also from 1961, was released as a single by ArVee Records and is available on YouTube and at http://www.creamyandcrunchy.com/. Chubby Checker's version is on his album *Let's Twist Again* (1962).

Peanut Butter Conspiracy (the group) was founded in 1966 and broke up in 1970.

"Peanut Butter Conspiracy" (1973): Written by Jimmy Buffett. It's on his album *A White Sport Coat and a Pink Crustacean*. Available at http://www.creamyandcrunchy.com/.

"Peanut Butter Sandwich" (1983): Written by Shel Silverstein. It's on the audio version of his book *Where the Sidewalk Ends*.

"Peanut Butter" (1983): On two Gwen Guthrie albums: *Portrait* and *Padlock*. It's also difficult to obtain: I contacted eight record stores, and the only one that could locate a copy for me was Canterbury Records on Colorado Boulevard in Pasadena; it had to order the album from Europe.

"It's Peanut Butter Jelly Time" (early 2000s): It's on The Buckwheat Boyz's CD *The Buckwheat Boyz* and on YouTube. Available at http://www.creamyandcrunchy.com/.

"The Ballad of Peanut Butter" (2005): Written by Garrison Keillor.

"A peanut sat on a railroad track . . .": Available at http://www.creamyandcrunchy.com/.

There are several versions of "Peanut Butter and Jelly" on YouTube (including one by Barney the Dinosaur under the heading "Song About How to Make a PB&J Sandwich").

DEAF SMITH

WHAT'S OLD-FASHIONED IS NEW AGAIN

In the early 1970s, the clean-cut, conservative High Plains residents of Deaf Smith County in the Texas Panhandle were treated to the sight of Volkswagen buses filled with hippies turning off Interstate 40 and heading straight for the county seat of Hereford. The town was named for the breed of cattle first brought to the area in 1898, but these visitors weren't there for beef: they were looking for a start-up company called Arrowhead Mills and the organic foods it made, notably Deaf Smith peanut butter.

"We had hippies from New York and California coming to see the great guru Frank Ford," said Ford, who bought the company in 1960 and built it into a natural-foods powerhouse. "I think there were twenty-three of them there at one time. And guess what? I was a Republican. I had short hair. And here I was, their hero."[1]

Phil Rogers was one of the young travelers who made the pilgrimage to Hereford, on his way from Los Angeles to Michigan in the fall of 1971. "The town smelled like a slaughterhouse, the little Mexican cafeteria we ate at was incredible, and the peanut butter lasted at least until Thanksgiving," he later recalled, "even though we ate it in gobs."[2]

Arrowhead Mills' first products were whole wheat flour and cornmeal, which Ford ground with a stone mill and delivered to local stores from the back of his pickup truck (figure 12.1). In 1970 he added a peanut butter that was both natural (unstabilized) and organic (made from peanuts

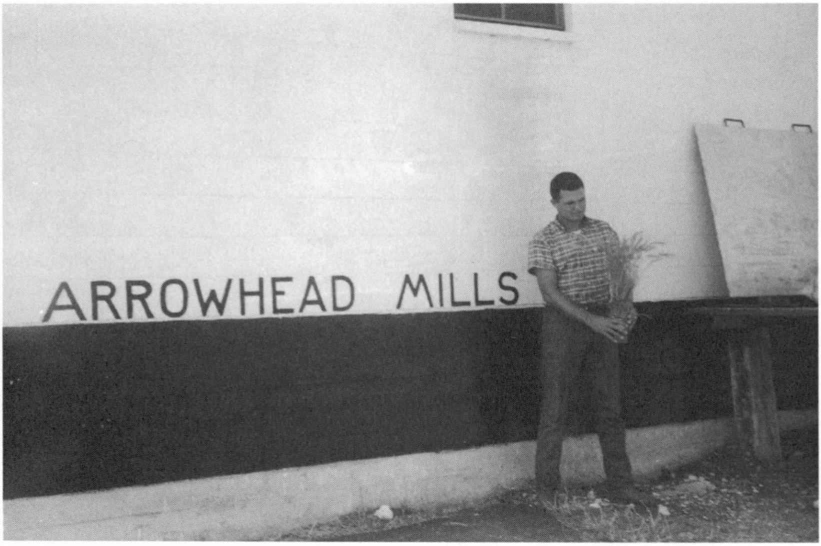

FIGURE 12.1 FRANK FORD

Frank Ford, whose sweat equity built Arrowhead Mills into a natural-foods powerhouse, holds a wheat plant at the Arrowhead Mills factory about 1960, ten years before he launched Deaf Smith peanut butter. (Bill and Marcella Bradly Collection, Deaf Smith County Historical Society)

grown without chemicals) to his product line. Locals raised their eyebrows, but with growing ecological awareness and the rise of the counterculture and back-to-the-land movements, Ford would prove to be uniquely emblematic of the spirit of the times.

"Our peanut butter, and Arrowhead Mills at the time, fit in very nicely with the hippy movement, the non-Establishment movement of the time," says Boyd Foster, Ford's chief lieutenant, who became the company's president. "Young people were quite willing to do something different than their parents, and eating wholesome, natural foods that had no additives and were not processed extensively fit very well into their way of thinking.

"So during the early seventies, a good part of our customers and clientele were hippy people," he adds. "Thank goodness a lot of those people have retained their thinking about eating healthy and wholesome food into their adulthood, when they have given up most of their other hippy ways."[3]

Those hippy ways were not second nature in Deaf Smith County in the early 1970s. In addition to having a county seat named after a steer, it contained part of the famous Old West XIT cattle ranch. But Foster says there was never any trouble between members of the local culture and the counterculture, although he adds, "We were regarded by some of the old-timers in town as being rather weird and strange. They didn't fully accept what we were doing, because they were accustomed to eating their usual foods and were not ready to adapt to a simpler way of eating."[4]

The man who put Arrowhead Mills on the map and became a leader of the burgeoning organic-food movement was the son of a county agricultural agent in Hereford. Frank Ford had worked since he was eleven years old. He went to Texas A&M, which had such a strong military tradition that it had more officers in World War II than West Point. After graduating, Ford became a second lieutenant and was stationed at Fort Lewis, Washington, from 1956 to 1958. He was a battery commander with the Army's Fourth Division, the first Army division to have nuclear weapons.

"I was commanding a captain's job, with a nuclear warhead, a rocket. It was called an Honest John rocket," he says. "We also trained with 155-millimeter howitzers. I think they probably chose me because I was idiot enough to sign for all that equipment."[5] Once out of the military, he returned to Hereford, and went to work for Arrowhead Mills, which he bought from founder Henry Turner. He worked hard to build the business, including the company's plant. His sweat equity on the project was such that he went from 195 to 170 pounds during construction, although he had been all muscle when he got out of the army.

Idealistic, religious, and dedicated to healthy living, Ford was many things, but not a shrinking violet. "He's a bit flamboyant—always has plenty to say and considers himself an expert on most everything," says Boyd Foster. "A born promoter who was very good at promoting Arrowhead Mills and its products. A very good speaker. He was sort of a magnet to our company."[6]

He also served as a leader in several national-level political fights: against President Carter's efforts to put mobile MX antiballistic missiles in the Texas Panhandle, against President Reagan's efforts to put a nuclear waste dump in Deaf Smith County (which Ford argued would poison the

Ogallala Aquifer, which supplies much of the area's irrigation water), and against the first President Bush's efforts to require prescriptions for herbs and vitamins. Although outgunned politically and financially, Ford and his allies won every fight. And Ford had another historically significant involvement with American politics.

"George Bush the First, when I was a Republican hotshot, sent his baby boy, who was running for Congress, to my desk," said Ford, who was active in Campus Crusade for Christ. "I did share Jesus with George W. for about an hour and he listened. He gave up women and other things that we won't mention, and met his wife, and seven years later, she made him give up alcohol. George W. was a cocky brat, but he did marry a wonderful lady."[7]

Ordinarily charming and gracious, Ford could also be a bit ornery. A proponent of natural peanut butter, he decried hydrogenation, saying it makes it harder to digest food (in fact, it makes it a bit easier, but it does pose other problems). When asked to expand on that, though, he expostulated, "I'm not a scientist. Do your own danged research."[8]

★★★

With his company starting to grow in the early 1970s, Ford needed help running it (figure 12.2). Boyd Foster was then a local farmer working on an MBA. He took a summer job at Arrowhead Mills in 1971 and wound up staying for twenty-five years, the last eighteen as president. George Speck, general manager at Portales Valley Mills, the New Mexico–based company that produced Deaf Smith peanut butter for Arrowhead Mills, says Foster was a crucial part of the rise of Arrowhead Mills. "Frank was the energy behind it," Speck says. "But when it came to running the business and making the business decisions, the one that really knew about how to do it was Boyd Foster."[9]

But the decision to name the peanut butter Deaf Smith was Ford's, and it was a good one. Unlike the synthetically cheerful names of corporate heavyweights Jif, Skippy, and Peter Pan, it had a funky, offbeat, countercultural resonance, even though its founder was a former military officer with a crew cut.

Although he was the county's namesake, Deaf Smith the man never set foot in Deaf Smith County. A hero of the Texas war for independence against Mexico, he was a native of upstate New York. Although he suffered

FIGURE 12.2 ARROWHEAD MILLS

The Arrowhead Mills plant in Hereford, Texas, in the early 1970s. New-age devotees of natural foods from around the country descended on the plant, drawn by Arrowhead Mills' natural products, including Deaf Smith peanut butter. Deaf Smith was actually made for Arrowhead Mills in nearby Portales, New Mexico. (Bill and Marcella Bradly Collection, Deaf Smith County Historical Society)

from partial hearing loss, he compensated by being extremely observant, and served as a scout and spy for Sam Houston. Deaf Smith fought in the battle of San Jacinto and was the first American to reach the Alamo after it fell.[10] He married a Tejana, a Spanish-speaking native of Texas, and moved freely among the Anglo and Tejano societies, just as Frank Ford would later move freely among the traditional culture and the counterculture.

Frank Ford also made another important decision: to make Deaf Smith out of Valencia peanuts (figure 12.3). Small and sweet, Valencias have been called "the Vidalia onions of peanuts."[11] They had never been used in peanut butter. A little more than 1 percent of the American peanut crop, Valencias are more difficult to grow than other varieties. But Paul Hawken of Erewhon Foods, another pioneer in the organic-food movement, told Ford that farmers grew the Valencia just over the border in New Mexico and recommended it to him.[12]

Valencias flourish in hot, dry weather and require a shorter growing season than runners and Virginias, which is fortunate, because eastern

FIGURE 12.3 DEAF SMITH JAR

A thick slice of whole wheat bread rests on a cutting board next to a jar of Deaf Smith peanut butter. Emblematic of the counterculture of the late 1960s and early 1970s, Deaf Smith sparked a revival of old-fashioned or natural peanut butter. It was the first peanut butter to use Valencia peanuts. (Courtesy of Juan [Jae] Gaytan and Arrowhead Mills)

New Mexico, at an elevation of 4,000-plus feet, has a shorter growing season than the Deep South. The area's low nighttime temperatures result in fewer plant diseases; so there's less of a need for herbicides and pesticides, making it easier to grow organic peanuts there. Valencias are planted in May and early June and harvested in October. After harvesting, the peanuts dry in the sun for seven to ten days. The farmers have to worry about rain during this period, as well as wind, which can blow the peanuts out of their rows and cut crop yield.

Ford linked up with Portales Valley Mills, in Portales, New Mexico, seventy-five miles down the road from Hereford. Owned by former New Mexico governor John Burroughs and run by his son-in-law, Herb Marchman, it processed Valencias into a full range of peanut products.

Although southeastern New Mexico is a good place to grow organic peanuts, local farmers needed some convincing. "It was quite a challenge to get the farmers to grow the product for [Arrowhead Mills]," Marchman says. "They were not used to not using herbicides and pesticides and special fertilizers, and thought it was going to be a loss of volume and money, so we had to pay some pretty good premiums to get the growers to consider it. The first couple of years, they were very skeptical about whether they were losing money or not. But the environmental climate changed, and people understood some of the risks of the chemicals that were used."[13]

As the organic crop became successful, the need to pay the farmers extra didn't fade, Marchman notes. "We always had to pay a premium. You had to manually weed the fields, use compost-type fertilizers, and have smaller areas. It was just more expensive to do."

Even when it's not grown organically, the Valencia peanut poses challenges to farmers that other varieties don't. "They're a lot of work," says Verla Brown, wife of Delbert Brown, who used to grow Valencias in the Portales area and calls them the trickiest crop they ever grew. "You've got to water them right, fertilize them right, and plow them right."[14]

Jimmie Shearer, head of Sunland, Inc., which processes Valencia peanuts and peanut butter in Portales, agrees. "The Valencia is the hardest of the four varieties to grow," he says. "They tend to break off more easily when pulled from the ground. The stem that connects the peanut to the vine is extremely weak, so you have to handle them very gently or they come loose. And if they come loose from the vine [that is, the peanut plant], there's no way to get them in the truck. With Virginias, they have to use saws to cut the stem off, it's so darn tough."[15]

Another distinctive characteristic of Valencias is that they can come three, four, or even five to a shell. For years, Delbert Brown collected five-peanut Valencias and stored them in a jar, hoping to use them as the prototype for developing a strain of Valencias that would consistently produce five-seeded pods. But one day, a hungry farmhand, not realizing what he was doing, turned Brown's genetic stock into a snack, and that was that.[16]

The majority of Valencia growers use a Pearman brand digger. With Pearmans, no machinery touches the peanuts as they're dug out of the field. The diggers have two chains that grab hold of the peanut plants, gently pull them out of the ground, and turn them upside down to sit in windrows in the field—all without making contact with the peanuts. The KMC diggers typically used to harvest other varieties have a chain the peanuts ride on.

Valencias not only are more trouble to grow than other peanuts, but also are less prolific. A typical runner or Virginia peanut plant will have forty peanuts on it, but Valencias, like Spanish peanuts, have only twenty or so because the peanuts cluster around the plant's taproot. On runners and Virginias, the peanuts grow on the roots branching out from the taproot, providing more spaces for the peanuts. Because Valencias, especially organic Valencias, are more difficult to grow and less abundant than other varieties, peanut butter made from Valencias tends to be more expensive.

The complexity of dealing with Valencias may help explain why they constitute only 1 to 2 percent of the U.S. peanut crop, and why peanut breeders are less interested in dealing with them. There are at least fifteen runner varieties farmers can choose from, but only two main types of Valencias—Valencia A and Valencia C, both released for production by the agriculture experiment station at New Mexico State University in the 1970s. About 90 percent of Valencias are grown in southeastern New Mexico, mostly in Roosevelt County, whose county seat is Portales. Valencias are also grown in the adjoining counties of the Texas Panhandle. Farmers and processors of runner and Virginia peanuts speak with a southern accent, but Valencia people have a distinctive western twang.

Frank Ford felt the sweetness and tastiness of the Valencia was worth the trouble, though. As the first peanut butter to use Valencias, Deaf Smith blazed a trail whose followers would include Trader Joe's, Sunland, MaraNatha, Once Again Nut Butters, Joseph's Sugar-Free, and Kirkland, the house brand of Costco. Deaf Smith was also the first organic peanut butter and may have been the first to use unblanched peanuts (i.e., including the peanut skins in the butter). Most peanut butters remove the skins, which are reputed to be somewhat bitter, but the natural sweetness of Valencias offsets this, and some peanut butter connoisseurs value the taste of skins the same way some chocolate fanciers prefer bittersweet to milk chocolate.

Deaf Smith was not the first natural peanut butter: originally, all peanut butter was unstabilized. But by 1970 young people had no experience of growing up with it, and Deaf Smith was a revelation to them. (And to critics as well: in its 1978 peanut butter survey, *Consumer Reports* noted Deaf Smith had more peanut flavor and aroma than most brands, although it faulted it for being slightly bitter and astringent and having a peanut-skin flavor.)[17]

Deaf Smith would spark a rebirth of natural or old-fashioned peanut butter. In the early 1970s, it was probably no more than 2 or 3 percent of the market. While there's still much less of it than stabilized, natural is now as much as 17 percent of the market.[18]

Granola Goodness Mix

The late 1960s and early 1970s saw the flourishing of the counterculture and its devotion to healthy eating. No snack is more emblematic of that zeitgeist than granola.

⅔ cup creamy peanut butter
⅔ cup honey
½ teaspoon ground cinnamon
1 teaspoon vanilla
4 cups granola
1 cup raisins
¼ cup chopped dates
¼ cup chopped figs
1 cup peanuts

Preheat oven to 300 degrees Fahrenheit.

Combine peanut butter, honey, and cinnamon in a saucepan and heat until mixture is smooth and creamy. Remove from heat and stir in vanilla and granola.

Spoon mixture into a greased 9 x 13-inch pan. Bake for 35 to 40 minutes, stirring occasionally.

Turn oven off. Mix in raisins, dates, figs, and peanuts. Let stand in unlit oven for about 1½ hours, stirring occasionally, until dry.

★ ★ ★

Store in a covered container.

Yield: approximately 8 cups of mix.

FROM LARRY ZISMAN AND HONEY ZISMAN, *THE GREAT AMERICAN PEANUT BUTTER BOOK* (NEW YORK: ST. MARTIN'S PRESS, 1985). REPRINTED WITH PERMISSION OF LARRY AND HONEY ZISMAN.

In a harbinger of that growth, sales of Deaf Smith rose quickly: from a modest start, Frank Ford would later remember selling perhaps $15 million worth of Deaf Smith in the 1970s.[19] At Portales Valley Mills, George Speck recalls this growth in terms of shipping. "In the mid-seventies, we produced maybe half a truckload a week," he says. "Then, by 1980, we were making a truck a week. Then finally two trucks a week."[20] Portales Valley Mills president Herb Marchman remembers it in terms of production machinery. "We had some equipment that had been used to make peanut butter in small batches for a candy operation at one time," he says. "We used that to start on a small scale and quickly found out it was not enough. Through the years, we continued to increase capacity and upgrade equipment to handle the increased volume."[21] Health-food stores that carried Deaf Smith peanut butter before supermarkets caught on were instrumental in its growing sales.

★★★

One of those who discovered Deaf Smith in the early 1970s was writer Norbert Blei. Eating it with his children also helped to teach him a fundamental truth: kids, especially kids accustomed to stabilized peanut butter, do not like unstabilized unless they get a lot of encouragement. In 1974 Blei wrote:

> I can vaguely remember, in my peanut-butter youth, an oily sort of peanut butter. But then we threw it out because it was too messy or old-fashioned or something. Or maybe the oil just magically disappeared from the jar one day, like the cream from the top of the old glass milk bottle.
>
> But entering a health-food store a few weeks ago, I came up with a two-pound jar of old-fashioned peanut butter ("Creamy, unhydrogenated . . . from sunshine-dried peanuts, grown on composted soil without herbicides or pesticides. Ingredients: organically grown Valencia peanuts") and with the brand name of Deaf Smith. Deaf Smith! Now that alone makes it a peanut-butter freak's sort of peanut butter.
>
> So I bring it home and try it out on the kids. "WE WANT SKIPPY!" they're yelling. "Hush, hush. Give Deaf Smith a chance."

I gently unscrew the top and there it is . . . the richest, darkest-looking peanut butter I have ever seen. It kind of floats there in an oily mirage. The incense spreads. A time for reverence. I take some and pass the jar around. It is gritty and super-sticky and loose and bubbly and deeply satisfying. No time now for peanut-butter artistry, recipes, or even bread. And we go at it the only way true peanut-butter people understand, a fingerful at a time. We are back in peanut-butterdom.

"Who is Deaf Smith?" a child unsticks his mouth and asks in peanut-butter breath.

"Well," I begin, using all the peanut butter put-on I can spread, "he's probably a distant relation of George Washington Carver, who invented peanut butter years ago. Not much is known about old Deaf Smith except that he makes a helluva real peanut butter. I imagine everybody keeps asking him, 'What's the secret, Old Deaf Smith? Why is your peanut butter so great?' But old Deaf Smith just smiles and never answers."

"Why"

"Because he's deaf. Furthermore, real peanut-butter people tend to be rather close-mouthed, keeping the happiness and meaning within them."[22]

★ ★ ★

Until the late 1980s, Deaf Smith was manufactured at Portales Valley Mills. But when that company was sold, production was moved to American Nut in Lewisville, Texas, a former subsidiary of Portales Valley Mills. Problems developed, though: a 1987 *Consumer Reports* article rated Deaf Smith as below average, complaining of raw nut flavor in the creamy and little roasted-nut flavor in the crunchy.[23] In 1989 production of Deaf Smith was moved back to Portales, where it would now be made by Sunland.

That wasn't the only transition for Deaf Smith peanut butter: Ford and Foster had been trying to change its name to Arrowhead Mills, to provide uniformity to its growing product line of natural foods. But Deaf Smith fans dug in their heels. "We wanted to promote Arrowhead Mills as our primary brand name," Foster recalls. "We started putting both names on the label, with the idea that we would eventually phase out Deaf Smith. But a lot of our early consumers always wanted to call it Deaf Smith and did not accept Arrowhead Mills. So we retained 'Deaf Smith' in small print for a time."[24] By 1995, though, Deaf Smith the peanut butter had joined Deaf Smith the man in the mists of history. It became Arrowhead Mills Organic Valencia, then Arrowhead Mills Creamy Organic.

In 1998 the Hain Food Group (now Hain Celestial), one of the largest health-food companies in the United States, bought Arrowhead Mills.[25] Former Portales Valley Mills general manager George Speck, who has also worked for Sunland, says there is one difference between Deaf Smith and what's now Arrowhead Mills Creamy Organic: the latter still uses the peanut skins, but not as many. "When Frank Ford and Boyd Foster were making it, they wanted as many of the skins left on as possible," he says. "Now, the [loose] skins are allowed to fall off."[26] So Deaf Smith would have been slightly more bitter than its descendant.

After leaving Hereford, Frank Ford lived in northern San Diego County in Southern California with his second wife, Jane Hahn, until his death in early 2011 (figure 12.4). He proudly noted the multicultural nature of his family. "My wife is Chinese, my son-in-law is Latino, and my daughter-

FIGURE 12.4 FRANK FORD

Frank Ford in 2009. Reminiscing on the early days of Deaf Smith, he said, "We had hippies from New York and California coming to see the great guru Frank Ford. And guess what? I was a Republican. I had short hair. And here I was, their hero." (Courtesy of Ingrid Hahn Chen)

in-law is black," he said. "We've got a little United Nations."[27] He insisted he was in good health, despite having leukemia, which he felt was the result of contact with the nuclear warhead under his command in the 1950s. "I'm feeling fine and don't take any drugs, not even aspirin," he said. "Never have." To the end, Ford was emblematic of both the traditional culture and the counterculture. He remained active with Campus Crusade for Christ and its offshoot Athletes in Action, but ended a telephone conversation by telling his interviewer to "keep on truckin'."

For many Americans, Deaf Smith was their first encounter with natural peanut butter and so retains a special place in their affections. The Seattle-based "City Comforts" blog is devoted to issues of architecture and urban design. But one of the Web site's most popular entries was about site founder David Sucher's nostalgia for Deaf Smith. He posted an entry in the summer of 2004 and four years later was surprised to still be getting new posts about it.[28]

One poster said, "In college I baked my own bread. Nothing can match warm oatmeal bread with Deaf Smith peanut butter and hot apple cider on a cold winter day in Wisconsin."[29]

A second found her insomnia cured by conjuring the name Deaf Smith. "I woke up at 3 A.M. this morning thinking of that delicious peanut butter I used to love back in the late 1970s, but unable to remember the name. . . . Google led me to your site and the name. . . . Thank you—I can go back to sleep now."[30]

A third, not realizing that Deaf Smith had been reincarnated as Arrowhead Mills Creamy Organic, clearly wished he was back on the road again, part of the legion that had descended on Hereford in their Volkswagen buses. "It has vanished into the modern world of convenience and quick food pleasures," he wrote. "It was made in Texas, that's all I ever knew. Perhaps it's time for a road trip to locate its source—any takers?"[31]

THE RISE AND FALL OF THE FLORUNNER

In July 1970, Robert Choate Jr. told a Senate subcommittee that most breakfast cereals were nutritionally worthless.[1] The observations of Choate, who two years earlier had helped to set up a White House conference on food, nutrition, and health, caused observers to muse that a peanut butter and jelly sandwich might make a better breakfast for children. That December, the U.S. Supreme Court effectively ended a twelve-year battle between the Food and Drug Administration and the peanut butter industry when it declined to reject the FDA standard that peanut butter had to contain at least 90 percent peanuts. A year earlier, a largely unnoticed but no less significant landmark in the history of peanut butter occurred: the debut of the Florunner.

Since the 1890s, peanut butter had been made from a combination of Spanish peanuts, whose high oil content made them especially flavorful, and Virginias, whose low oil content kept the butter from getting too oily and which contributed a distinctive, subtle taste of their own (figure 13.1). As recently as 1959, *Consumer Bulletin* had said, "Any variety of peanut may be used for butter, although usually commercially made peanut butter is a mixture of Virginia and Spanish peanuts."[2]

But a new runner variety developed at the University of Florida and released in 1969 would change the very nature of peanut butter. The Flo-

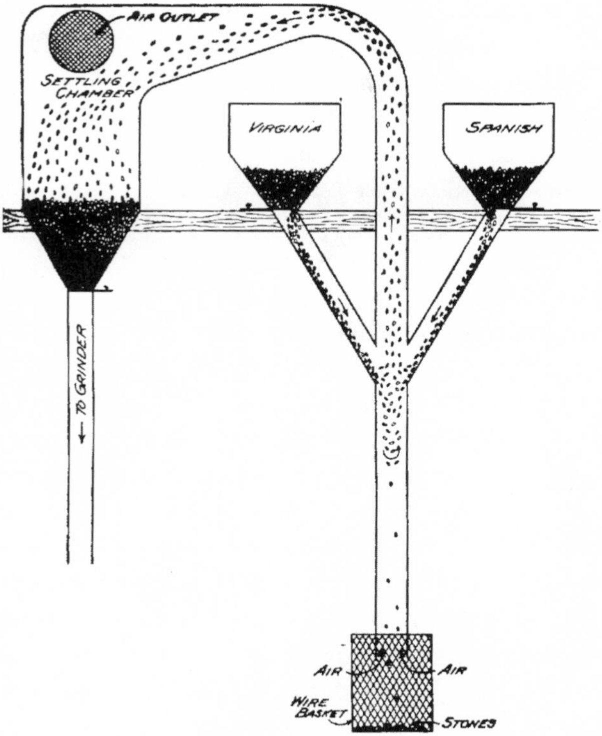

FIGURE 13.1 1912 PEANUT DE-STONER

A 1912 diagram showing how stones were removed from peanuts before being ground into peanut butter features Spanish and Virginia peanuts, then the industry standard. From its earliest days in the mid-1890s until about 1970, peanut butter was typically made from a blend of Spanish and Virginias. Because of the improved taste and prolific nature of the Florunner, the peanut butter industry switched to runners starting in the early 1970s. (Bureau of Plant Industry, U.S. Department of Agriculture)

runner, named after the state it was created in and the type of peanut it was made from, was developed by Al Norden, a peanut breeder and professor of agronomy at the university's main campus in Gainesville.[3] Dan Gorbet worked with Norden starting in 1970 from the university's Marianna Research Center. He puts the birth of the Florunner in context.

"Runners historically were thought of more as a hog peanut. A lot of them were planted just for feeding hogs," he says. "They didn't consider them of quite the same quality as Spanish, which had a sweeter taste. So they thought that was the most desirable thing to put in peanut butter and other products. But when Florunner came on the scene, there was a significant improvement in the oil chemistry and flavor, as well as the yield and grade aspects."[4]

The improvement in the Florunner's oil chemistry, from the peanut butter industry's point of view, was that it had a higher percentage of oleic acid than Spanish peanuts. Oleic acid is one of the two main fatty acids in peanut oil. Linoleic acid is polyunsaturated, which is considered heart-healthy, as is monounsaturated oleic acid. But oleic acid is more stable, which means longer shelf life and greater industry profits.

Florunners also had a higher percentage of peanut to shell, which meant that farmers earned more for a ton of them than they did for a ton of Spanish peanuts. Shellers received more money from peanut butter manufacturers and the manufacturers got more peanuts per ton. Then there was the flavor. "The Florunner was an awfully good-tasting peanut," says retired farmer Stanley Pittman.[5] And Florunners, like runner peanuts in general, had another advantage over Spanish: they had fresh seed dormancy, meaning farmers didn't have to worry about them sprouting in the field and ruining the crop, which Spanish peanuts can do if the harvest is delayed.

But what amazed everyone in the peanut industry about the Florunner (and helped reduce Spanish peanuts to a marginal niche in the American peanut market) was how prolific they were. Skippy's Frank Delfino says the Florunner produced two to three times the yield per acre compared with previous runners,[6] an assessment seconded by Stanley Pittman.[7] Dan Gorbet says that's an exaggeration, but an understandable one.

"It increased yields by 25 percent," he says. "But that's still an unheard-of change. We had a very fortunate situation, with new fungicides becoming available to control leaf spot [a peanut-plant disease]. There were new center-pivot irrigation systems. There were new herbicides and new harvesting equipment like the inverter [which allowed farmers to mechanically turn the peanut plants upside down into windrows in the fields, letting them dry more quickly]."[8] It was the combination of these new farming techniques with the Florunner's yield increase that caused the spurt in productivity.

When they learned how productive the Florunner was, peanut farmers were eager to grow it, even in places it wasn't fully adapted to. Farmers in Texas were warned by agricultural extension agents and researchers that what worked in Georgia and the Florida Panhandle might not work there, because the Florunner was a later-maturing peanut than the Spanish, and Texas has higher elevations and earlier winters. "The growers said, 'To heck with it—it does so good, we're going to grow it anyhow,'" Dan Gorbet laughs. "It was not a problem in southern and central Texas, but some years they had a little trouble in the High Plains and north-central area" as the crop was still in the field when the first frosts came.[9]

While farmers were enthusiastic about the Florunner, peanut butter manufacturers were understandably skittish at changing the basis of their product.

"The first year, one of the manufacturers said, 'We'll put 15 percent [Florunners] in and see if we have any problems with consumer complaints,'" says Don Koehler, executive director of the Georgia Peanut Commission. Koehler isn't sure, but thinks it may have been Jif. "That was a time when folks wrote letters if they had a problem. They didn't have 800 numbers or things like that. They didn't get any letters from folks complaining about it. So they started increasing [the percentage of Florunners] and found that still nobody complained."[10] Al Norden also went on tour in defense of his brainchild, meeting with farmers, shellers, and peanut butter manufacturers, telling them they didn't need Spanish peanuts: they could use the Florunner and still have a good peanut butter.[11]

"It's kept peanut butter affordable," Koehler adds. "The farmer can't make the yield on [less prolific] Spanish peanuts. So the price would have had to go up. We had a peanut that yielded better and shelled out better. So the industry all of a sudden figured out, 'Wait a minute—We're buying a ton of peanuts and we get more kernels.' That's really kept peanut butter affordable. Peanut butter is one of the few things that has been anti-inflationary over time."[12]

Despite the cruel and abusive remarks directed at runners by partisans of Spanish, Virginia, and Valencia peanuts, the Florunner and runner varieties that followed in its wake would increasingly become the stuff peanut butter is made of. Today 99 percent of the peanuts grown in Georgia, the peanut-growingest state, are runners. "The market in the Southeast was much more diverse [before the Florunner]," Dan Gorbet says. "It just kind of wiped the board clean. Prior to Florunner, we were growing Spanish, Virginias, runners, and some Valencias. When Florunner came on board, in less than five years it was the only variety grown."[13] For anyone over fifty who thinks peanut butter tasted different when you were growing up, you're not a rank sentimentalist—you're right. Like me, you may recall the rich, evocative taste of Spanish peanuts. But the world moves on, and for major U.S. peanut butter manufacturers, that means runners.

But the Florunner, having dispatched Spanish and Virginias from most jars of peanut butter, would eventually wind up on the ash heap of peanut butter history itself. As Stanley Pittman notes, "It began to disease up on us a little bit."[14] The disease was tomato spotted wilt virus, which produces yellow splotches on the leaves of the peanut plant, while the peanuts develop mottled, cracked skins that are red and brown instead of light pink. By the early 1990s, Florunners were gone; the dominant variety replacing them was the Georgia Green, a descendant of the Florunner. It became the most popular variety until 2010, when it was replaced by several new runner varieties.

The fact that Florunners were grown in virtual monoculture may have contributed to their demise, much as cotton was done in by the boll weevil three generations earlier. Although new runner varieties have followed in the Florunner's footsteps, the peanut butter industry still recalls the Florunner with special fondness. "The manufacturers complain about the varieties we've put out in recent times because they're not exactly like Florunner," says Dan Gorbet. "The industry took a rather dramatic leap forward with that variety."[15]

In 1970, just as the Florunner made its debut, Ernest Hemingway's *Islands in the Stream* was published posthumously. Written in 1950 and 1951, it features Thomas Hudson, a Hemingway-like character sailing the Caribbean on his fishing boat. In one passage, Hudson instructs a crewman:

> "Well, go down to the galley and see if that bottle of tea is cold and bring it up. Antonio's butchering the fish. So make a sandwich, will you, please?"
>
> "Sure. What kind of sandwich?"

> "Peanut butter and onion if there's plenty of onion."
> "Peanut butter and onion it is, sir."[16]

Soon afterward, the crewman returns with the iced tea and sandwich:

> He handed a sandwich, wrapped in a paper towel segment, to Thomas Hudson and said, "One of the highest points in the sandwich-maker's art. We call it the Mount Everest Special. For commanders only."[17]

When Hemingway wrote this, Hudson's peanut butter sandwich was probably made from Spanish and Virginias. But from now on, literary characters would scale the heights of the sandwich kingdom with Florunners and their descendants.

As the 1970s unfolded, another celebrity's fondness for peanut butter would contribute to his downfall. As Elvis Presley increasingly turned into the bloated, rhinestone-studded King of later years, he gave free rein to his passion for peanut butter (and other goodies). In February 1976, Presley and members of his entourage flew on his private jet from Memphis to Denver to dine on Fool's Gold Loaves, Brobdingnagian sandwiches made by the Colorado Gold Mine Company restaurant. They consisted of loaves of bread hollowed out, spread thickly with peanut butter and blueberry jelly, and filled with a pound of crisp fried bacon. Presley and his friends ordered twenty-two of them, a case of champagne, and Perrier for Elvis and the other nondrinkers aboard. They didn't even get off the plane for a little exercise: the order was delivered to them on the tarmac at Denver Airport. The cost of this excursion: a mere $16,000.[18] A year and a half later, Presley was dead.

Better publicity for peanuts and peanut butter came from the 1976 presidential campaign. Governor Jimmy Carter of Georgia, the first peanut farmer since Thomas Jefferson to run for president, adroitly used his connection to America's beloved food to bolster his public image. An article in the *New York Times* said Carter had already accomplished what countless public relations experts and millions of dollars had been struggling to do for decades: rescuing the peanut from obscurity. "A casual observer wouldn't guess that a sticky sandwich filler, a tasteless oil, and a free bar snack could add up to the nation's fifth largest commodity, a major business that provides as much as $200 million a year in income to

Elvis Spread

This is an interesting variation on the theme of the Elvis sandwich.

6 strips thick-cut bacon
1¼ cups creamy standard peanut butter
2 ripe medium bananas, peeled and cut into 2-inch sections
1 tablespoon unsalted butter, at room temperature
1 tablespoon honey*

Fry the bacon in a nonstick skillet set over medium-high heat until the strips are very crispy, about 4 minutes, turning occasionally. Transfer the bacon slices to a paper-towel-lined plate and blot the strips dry with more paper towels. Set aside.

Place the peanut butter, bananas, butter, and honey in a food processor fitted with the chopping blade. Process until very smooth, scraping down the sides of the bowl as necessary.

Chop the bacon, then add it to the food processor and pulse two or three times to get it evenly distributed in the mixture. Scoop the bread into a bowl or container, cover tightly, and store in the refrigerator for up to 4 days; bring the spread to room temperature before using.

★★★

Yield: 2 cups.

---

* BRUCE WEINSTEIN AND MARK SCARBROUGH ARE PARTIAL TO STAR THISTLE HONEY.

FROM BRUCE WEINSTEIN AND MARK SCARBROUGH, *THE ULTIMATE PEANUT BUTTER BOOK* (NEW YORK: HARPERCOLLINS, 2005). © 2005. REPRINTED WITH PERMISSION FROM HARPERCOLLINS PUBLISHERS.

64,000 farmers," reporter Steven Rattner wrote. "But peanuts are big business, and bolstered by the most famous peanut grower in history, the peanut people have gone on the attack."[19]

When they had to, the peanut people showed they could play defense as well. The Democratic Party asked Planters if the party could use its Mr. Peanut character as a mascot at their convention; Planters' response was "Nuts." "Mr. Peanut is an apolitical figure," said Roy H. Fishman, division vice president for public relations. "He is a trademark associated with Planters and Standard Brands."[20] Carter would have better luck with Baskin-Robbins: after his election victory on November 2, the ice cream maker created a new flavor in his honor, Peanut Butter 'n Chocolate.

THE PEANUT BUTTER CRISIS OF 1980

In the fall of 2011, severe drought conditions across the South (coupled with the decision of farmers to plant more cotton) produced an unusually small peanut crop. This caused the price of peanut butter to spike. "Time to open the Strategic National Peanut Butter Reserve," one wag posted on the Internet. For peanut industry veterans, it brought to mind another dark year in peanut butter annals—1980.

In late August of that year, Roger Knapp trudged through the sun-baked peanut fields of southern Georgia. Normally that late in the growing season, peanut plants from different rows would have merged into a solid sea of green.[1] But individual rows were still visible to the thirty-seven-year-old director of commodity purchasing for the company that owned Skippy; the plants were stark and stunted. The year 1980 was the worst one for peanut farmers in two generations.

It wasn't just the peanut crop that suffered: That summer, the drought suffocated hens in Georgia and produced cotton bolls the size of bumblebees in Mississippi and beans the size of BBs in Arkansas.[2] The temperature in Dallas reached 100 degrees for forty-two consecutive days, and the National Oceanic and Atmospheric Administration would eventually put total crop losses across the South at between $13 and $16 billion.[3]

By mid-October, the U.S. Department of Agriculture predicted a 21 percent drop in peanut production for the current crop year, and the *New*

York Times noted there was a good chance prices could shoot up, especially if exporters shipped out 30 percent of the American crop, as they usually did.[4] Peanut butter manufacturers and other peanut processors could not expect much help from overseas, as the United States had a restrictive import quota of 1.7 million pounds.

Jim Andrews, who grew peanuts on his farm near Sylvester, Georgia, normally harvested 900 tons of peanuts from his 400 acres; in 1980 his crop was 100 tons. "I didn't even make enough peanuts to pay the rent," he said, projecting a loss of $300,000 for the year. "It seems like I'm about wiped out."[5]

Total losses for Georgia peanut farmers were estimated at $150 million, and Raymond Singletary, who ran a peanut-shelling company in Blakely, Georgia, said, "I've been in peanuts for fifty years. This is the roughest year by far."[6]

With the peanut crop in ruins, the peanut butter industry looked to the White House, where former peanut farmer Jimmy Carter was in charge (figure 14.1). But although the industry sought immediate relief from restrictive U.S. peanut import quotas, the *New York Times* reported on October 13 that the Carter administration was resisting its efforts. The Peanut Butter and Nut Processors Association had asked Secretary of Agriculture Bob Bergland two weeks earlier to lift those quotas, but USDA officials merely said the request was under study, and no one expected a decision before the November 4 election.[7]

A quick decision could have helped President Carter, who was running behind in his race for reelection with former California governor Ronald Reagan. An ample supply of peanuts could have earned Carter immense goodwill throughout the peanut-producing states of the South, but he refused to act before the election. Why? Albert Nason, an archivist at the Jimmy Carter Library and Museum, surmises that Carter didn't want to be seen as trying to buy support.[8] He could have used the help: in the 1980 Reagan landslide, the only peanut-producing state Carter carried was his native Georgia.

Earlier in the season, prices of 30 to 40 cents a pound had been quoted for peanuts.[9] By the first week of December, the price had risen to as high as $1.50 a pound, four times the usual cost—when peanuts could be found at all. The shortfall in the U.S. peanut crop was now pegged at a staggering 42 percent and would eventually rise to 46 percent,[10] almost

FIGURE 14.1 JIMMY CARTER

Jimmy Carter, the first peanut farmer elected president since Thomas Jefferson, in a 1976 campaign photo. His 1980 reelection bid was damaged by his principled refusal to increase peanut import quotas, which peanut and peanut butter companies were clamoring for, until after the election. In part as a result, the only southern state he carried was his native Georgia. (Courtesy of Charles Rafshoon)

half the crop. And because the carcinogenic mold aflatoxin that afflicts peanuts flourishes in dry weather, about 15 percent of the surviving peanut crop was affected, instead of the normal 2 percent.[11] Richie Seaton, a commodities specialist for the Georgia Department of Agriculture, wryly observed, "You won't be getting peanuts for peanuts."[12]

On December 4, when it was too late to do President Carter any good, the Department of Agriculture recommended importing 200 million pounds of peanuts.[13] The next day Reuben Askew, President Carter's special trade representative, ordered the lifting of import quotas in line with that recommendation.[14]

Jimmy Carter's Peanut Butter Pie

Despite his status as the first peanut farmer to become president since Thomas Jefferson, Jimmy Carter's 1980 reelection bid was undone in part by his not moving in a timely manner to raise peanut import quotas in the face of that year's drought and peanut shortage. That didn't stop him from contributing this recipe to *The Great American Peanut Butter Book*.

1 package (8 ounces) cream cheese
1 cup of 4x sugar
¼ cup crunchy peanut butter
½ cup milk
¼ cup of peanuts (halves)
1 container (9 ounces) Cool Whip

Whip cream cheese until soft and fluffy, beat in peanut butter and sugar, slowly add milk, fold in Cool Whip.

Put into graham cracker pie crusts, sprinkle tops with peanuts, then freeze.

★★★

Yield: 2 pies.

LARRY ZISMAN AND HONEY ZISMAN, *THE GREAT AMERICAN PEANUT BUTTER BOOK* (NEW YORK: ST. MARTIN'S PRESS, 1985). REPRINTED WITH PERMISSION OF LARRY AND HONEY ZISMAN.

But there was no immediate relief. Even zookeepers found themselves worrying about the peanut shortfall. On December 14, a warehouseman at the Woodland Park Zoo in Seattle told the Associated Press the zoo had exhausted its supply of peanuts the week before. "How do you explain a peanut shortage to an anxious elephant or a lethargic orangutan?" the AP asked. "Don't even try, says Hank Klein, assistant curator of education at Woodland Park. Instead, he advises slipping the elephant a plump banana and tossing some raisins or walnuts into the orangutan's cage."

Zoos that didn't feed peanuts to the animals fretted about the lack of peanuts in the vending machines for their human visitors.[15]

On January 6, 1981, the U.S. International Trade Commission voted to raise the peanut import quota again, setting the new limit at 400 million pounds of unshelled peanuts, about 340 million pounds' worth when shelled. A commission report questioned whether extra supplies could be found in China, India, and the other main producing countries, though, because of shortages and domestic requirements there. India had experienced a major shortfall of its own and decided not to export any peanuts, while Chinese peanuts were even more expensive than those grown in the United States.[16]

Other countries weren't lining up to help, either. For years, the United States had virtually closed its ports to peanut imports while American growers competed fiercely overseas. Now that the tables were turned, American efforts to buy peanuts abroad were met with reactions ranging from amusement to outright hostility.[17] For American peanut butter companies, there was another problem: other countries grew different kinds of peanuts and had different quality standards.

By December the price of Skippy had been raised by 10 to 15 percent. "When supplies are this far down, the price, in effect, rations the product," said Skippy's Roger Knapp.[18] Nor was it the only form of rationing: with peanut butter manufacturers operating at less than 85 percent of capacity, companies like CPC International, which owned Skippy, allocated shipments of peanut butter to supermarkets, which then imposed limits on how much customers could buy.[19] Some stores set a limit of one or two jars per customer, and people started hoarding "I'll bet there are houses in this town with fifty jars of peanut butter stored away," Jake Bender, manager of a supermarket in Dubuque, Iowa, told *Newsweek*.[20] At New York City's Pathmark chain, which received only three-quarters of what it got the previous year, there had already been a run on peanut butter at some of its stores, even though the price had climbed by 20 percent in December.[21]

Around New York City, peanut butter selection was limited. While no stores were completely sold out, some brands, as well as the standard 28-ounce size across the board, were in short supply, with prices at least double those of September. Consumers puzzled over those high prices, since most of the year's peanuts had been sold at traditional support prices before the drought destroyed much of the crop. They were told it was the result of supply and demand. (Interestingly, in health-food stores, where 18-ounce jars of natural peanut butter sold for $3.50 and up, as opposed to $2.50 for stabilized peanut butter in supermarkets, *New York Times* reporter Florence Fabricant found shelves well stocked.)[22]

With prices up in some areas by as much as 75 percent, the U.S. Department of Agriculture stopped buying peanut butter for sandwiches in its school lunch program and switched to cheese. Consumers cut back as well, with twenty-three-year-old Sue Lanoue of Boston saying, "We'll just eat eggs until the price goes down."[23] Florence Fabricant suggested consumers could extend their precious peanut butter supply by mixing it in a blender with tofu, or by stirring it in with plain yogurt at a ratio of one part yogurt to two parts peanut butter. She also suggested mixing creamy peanut butter with an unsugared cereal such as bran flakes for that crunchy effect.[24]

Doug Rauch, head of product development for Trader Joe's and Pronto markets in Los Angeles, came up with All-American Nut Butter, a spread made from organically grown cotton kernels mixed with 15 percent peanut oil, which sold for two-thirds the price of peanut butter. Another alternative was inexpensive sunflower spread.

Time was not amused: "In addition to roasted sunflower seeds, ingredients include hydrogenated rapeseed, which is commonly fed to birds and is said not to stick to beaks," it noted. "As for the flavor, both cottonseed and sunflower spreads compare to the real thing like, say, California sauternes to Chateau d'Yquem."[25]

But Rauch, who later went on to become president of Trader Joe's, defended his innovation. "If you put it on bread with jelly," he insisted, "you can't tell the difference."[26]

The difference between 1980 and previous years was all too obvious to people in the peanut industry, though. In 1979, peanuts had gone for $455 a ton, but in late January 1981, peanut butter companies were bidding $1,510 a ton for quality peanuts from the 1980 crop, if they could find any.[27] Losses for nearly 60,000 peanut farmers, mostly in the Southeast, were extensive. The peanut-processing season was shortened by up to three months, costing many seasonal workers substantial pay. Aggravating matters, by February 1, fewer than 7 million pounds of the 400 million peanuts approved for import had reached our shores.

"You couldn't get peanuts," John Gretz, then an engineer with Jif, recalls.[28] For Skippy executive Carl Bleier, that spring was an endless hunt for goobers. "They had a war room in Englewood Cliffs," he says of the New Jersey headquarters of CPC's Best Foods division. "They were looking for peanuts in Egypt, Africa, India, China. There were all these ships floating across the Atlantic." Crews had to be hired and trucks scheduled to meet the ships. The trucks were routed to temporary distribution centers in Savannah, Macon, and other southern cities, where crews unloaded them, placed them in cold storage, and sent them to Skippy's Little Rock plant as quickly as they could be processed. In one eighteen-week period, Bleier logged 167 flights, going from one distribution center to another in Georgia, Alabama, and northern Florida.[29]

As the spring wore on, peanuts started to flow in from overseas. "The great peanut crisis has been slightly eased with the arrival in May of additional imports from China and India," the *New York* Times reported on June 10, 1981.[30] It isn't clear if the Indians had a better crop than expected, the Chinese price came down, or beleaguered peanut butter companies simply agreed to meet their price. Even when the peanuts arrived, though, there were still problems.

"The hard part was that we had very high quality standards," says Larry Shearon, then plant engineer at Skippy's Little Rock plant. "We were not going to get the same quality peanuts and we were not going to get the same blend—we used to do Florunners [then the main runner variety] and Spanish from Texas." On top of that, Shearon says, there were mischievous surprises from the Chinese workers who loaded the peanuts. "For some odd reason, the Chinese would put 'gifts' in with the peanuts," he says. "There were little dolls. . . . One joker actually put in some firecrackers. We'd find them on the screens and pull them out. There were enough of these things that you had to look for them."[31]

At least one Chinese American was happy to see peanuts from her native land, though. Rita Keys, who worked a variety of managerial jobs at Jif's plant in Lexington, Kentucky, was taking a Chinese cooking class that year. "When I told Jane Wong Yang, my teacher, that we were getting some peanuts from China, she was excited and asked if I could get her a few," Keys recalls. "So I got her a pound of peanuts from China, and in return I got a dozen egg rolls."[32]

Although peanut butter prices didn't come down, consumers were assured of a supply until the fall 1981 peanut crop came in. But there was no guarantee that was going to be a good crop year, either. As early as February 1, Russell Schools, executive director of the Virginia Peanut Growers Association, cautioned, "People should be warned that we're in the driest winter in more than twenty years. If we don't get a lot of rain soon, we'll be facing another drought year."[33] And in June, the *New York Times* reported, "Abnormally dry conditions still prevailed this week in several of the peanut states, including Georgia, which produces the most."[34]

Talk like this apparently made executives at Swift nervous. Fearing a second year's shortfall for its Peter Pan brand, they toured southern Texas peanut-buying points with a warehouseman from northeastern Texas and offered to buy 15 million pounds of the 1981 crop at substantially above-market prices (figure 14.2). According to *Texas Monthly*, Swift deposited $13 million in the warehouseman's bank account, and he began entering into contracts with farmers.[35]

But then the weather turned. In its first appraisal of the 1981 peanut crop, the USDA foresaw a crop of 3.69 billion pounds, which would restore

FIGURE 14.2 *TEXAS MONTHLY* PETER PAN ILLUSTRATION

When it appeared that 1981 would be another year of epic drought, Swift's Peter Pan agreed to buy peanuts from southern Texas farmers at above-market prices. But when the prospect of a drought evaporated, so did Swift's agreements with the farmers, causing several to go broke and sue Swift. In this *Texas Monthly* drawing, Peter Pan is the Pied Piper, leading peanut farmers astray. (Courtesy of John Cuneo)

U.S. peanut output to pre-drought levels.[36] Swift told the warehouseman it was no longer going to be "in the banking business"[37] and decided not to buy peanuts through him even though he had already authorized $3 million in payments with money he expected to receive from Swift. The warehouseman apparently stayed in the banking business longer than he should have, according to lawsuits filed by southern Texas farmers, in some cases writing checks for peanuts on insufficient funds, and in others either refusing to take delivery or doing so and then not paying.[38]

More than 250 Texas peanut farmers filed suits against Swift, which sued the warehouseman, who sued Swift. Clayton Lacy, then a peanut farmer in Frio County, Texas, and today a member of the Texas Peanut Producers Board, says the farmers who sued generally got some money from Swift, although not as much as they had hoped for.[39]

The 1981 peanut crop turned out even better than the USDA estimated: 3.98 billion pounds, rebounding from 1980's 2.3 billion pounds.[40] It was business as usual again in the peanut fields, but there was a landmark change in the peanut butter industry: Jif passed Skippy to become number one and has never looked back. "Skippy and Peter Pan were having trouble getting peanuts," former Jif engineer John Gretz says. "I think our buyers managed to secure foreign peanuts in the quantities we needed. There were shortages on the store shelves at the time, and Jif managed to keep their supply up. People transitioned—they bought what was available."[41] The drought was ephemeral, but Jif's market leadership has proved enduring.

"YOU MEAN IT'S NOT GOOD FOR ME?"

In the late 1980s, peanut butter's abiding popularity was demonstrated by the appearance of stores exclusively devoted to selling peanut-butter-related products. There was Peanut Butter Fantasies in Boston's historic Fanueil Hall, Peanut Butter and Jelly, Inc., and Goin' Nuts in New York City, and Trombley's in Woburn, Massachusetts. But as Americans grew increasingly health conscious, there were dark clouds on the horizon for peanut butter, with increasing public worry about aflatoxin, peanut allergies, fat, trans fats, and even choking. People began to say, "You mean it's not good for me?" and peanut butter sales fell off.

Consumer Reports had been assessing peanut butter since 1943, but in 1972 it began testing it for carcinogenic aflatoxin, produced by *Aspergillus flavus*, a mold that grows on peanut shells. If a peanut's shell is cracked, *Aspergillus* may contaminate the peanut. Eaten in sufficient concentrations over a long enough period of time, it can cause liver cancer, although this rarely happens in the United States or most industrialized countries. Still, an ounce of prevention is worth a pound of cure. In 1976 more than 19,000 jars of Pantry Pride and Sweetlife peanut butter were recalled from Pantry Pride supermarkets in East Coast states because of aflatoxin contamination.[1] Four years later, Deep South Products of Lake City, Florida, had to destroy more than 1,000 cases of peanut butter for the same reason.[2] Of the Big Three, Jif would take the lead in fighting aflatoxin in the peanut fields.

"When Procter & Gamble was making peanut butter, they were probably a little more advanced technically than the competition," says John Gretz, who worked in engineering at the Jif plant in Lexington. "They did a lot of work in controlling aflatoxin. Not only did they work in the plant to control it, they did substantial work with the farmers." I mentioned to him that former Jif plant manager Paul Kiely had told me that Jif had wanted farmers to keep their fields irrigated. "That was it," Gretz said. "That was the breakthrough. They found it was the stress caused by dry weather that really instigated the problem of aflatoxin."[3] (Paradoxically, damp conditions when peanuts are stored can also promote the growth of aflatoxin.)

In 1965 the U.S. Food and Drug Administration established 30 parts per billion (ppb) of aflatoxin as the acceptable limit in food; in 1969 the limit was lowered to 20 ppb. In 1972 *Consumer Reports* wrote that the FDA was expected to lower the limit to 5 ppb.[4] In 1978 a reduction to 15 ppb was under consideration.[5] Possibly because of pressure from the food industry, the limit has remained at 20. As a rule, though, the peanut butter industry does a good job of screening out aflatoxin at every step of the production cycle.

In the fall of 2008, I visited the Dellwood buying point in Greenwood, in the panhandle of Florida, with retired farmer Stanley Pittman. A buying point has two sides: a private side, run like a business, where farmers are paid for their peanuts based on their quality, and a government side, where state and federal inspectors first determine that quality, including the extent to which the peanuts are contaminated by aflatoxin. One inspector pulled a contaminated peanut out of a drawer to show me, saying it was one of only two she had seen so far that season—the previous year, a drought year, she had seen a lot more. Under the microscope the aflatoxin looked like a dandelion after it's flowered, with a stem topped by whitish, seed-bearing parachutes in the shape of a ball.

I then visited a Birdsong shelling plant in Sylvester, Georgia. Birdsong Peanuts is one of the two major shellers in the United States, along with the Golden Peanut Company. Birdsong analyzes peanuts more thoroughly than federal and state inspectors do at buying points, using a vertical mill test to perform a chemical analysis rather than just a visual inspection.

Finally, I went to Tara Foods in Albany, Georgia, where technical services manager Walt Albritton gave me a tour of the plant. Although it makes other foods, Tara is one of the largest manufacturers of peanut butter outside of the Big Three; it processes 80 million pounds of peanut butter a year. (Jif, the world's largest, is estimated to process 190 million pounds.) It uses the same kind of technology Birdsong does. "The USDA limit is 20 parts per billion," Albritton told me. "We don't accept any peanuts in this plant higher than 15. We basically disregard the USDA official readings on a load of peanuts for aflatoxin and do our own testing. We pay extra to do a vertical mill test. It's a more sophisticated way of grinding up the sample to test for aflatoxin. If there's any toxin there, we're going to know it."[6]

How much aflatoxin is there in peanut butter? It depends on the kind you buy. Although the large stabilized brands are routinely shunned by health-food advocates, they'll be surprised to learn that those are the healthiest when it comes to aflatoxin. Ned Groth is the head of Groth Consulting Services, a company specializing in environmental health policy risk communication. He spent twenty-five years in the laboratory at Consumers Union, the parent firm of *Consumer Reports,* many of them as technical director.

"The big brands always have minimal levels, meaning 2 or 3 parts per billion," he says. "They have all kinds of quality-control measures. You can't get it down to zero—peanuts are grown outside and mold is present in the fields. With the big companies, 3 or 4 ppb is a bad year and 1 or 2 ppb is a good year." The most worrisome peanut butter for aflatoxin, he says, is the stuff you grind yourself at the corner health-food store. "If you go out to natural-food stores and health-food stores and get peanut butter that is ground on-site, you can find some pretty whopping high levels, like 50 ppb," he adds. "The small operators don't have the intense risk-management strategies in place that the big processors do."[7]

How do the various natural and old-fashioned peanut butters rate on aflatoxin? Groth says it depends on their quality control, noting that some naturals are made by the big manufacturers, just marketed differently. For example, Smuckers Natural, Laura Scudder's, Adams, and Santa Cruz Organic are all made by Smuckers, the maker of Jif.

How dangerous is aflatoxin? If you live in the Third World, very.

The Cornell University Department of Animal Science notes that aflatoxin, especially the B1 variety, is a potent carcinogen, with possible adverse effects from long-term exposure to even low levels. Although these cases resulted from heavily contaminated food, acute aflatoxicosis in India, Taiwan, and Uganda have caused vomiting, abdominal pain, convulsions, coma, and even death. In a cautionary comment about the "regulation be damned" attitude prevalent in the United States in recent years, the Department of Animal Science notes that lack of regulatory systems for aflatoxin monitoring and control is one of the factors that increases the likelihood of acute aflatoxicosis.[8]

Things are better in the United States. Tim Sanders is a research leader and research plant physiologist with the U.S. Department of Agriculture's Agricultural Research Service in Raleigh, North Carolina. "In my opinion, it's not a health issue in the United States," he says, noting that the industry does a good job of screening it out. "It occurs so rarely and at such a low level and we have such a good diet, that the level of aflatoxin [found in peanut butter] is not going to impact our health. If you're in Africa and you're eating a few parts per million [of aflatoxin] every day and have a horrible diet, the potential is there for it [to be a problem]."[9] But the idea, he adds, is to keep it out of our food supply as much as possible. "How much aflatoxin do I want my children to eat?" Sanders asks. "None."

Ned Groth highlights the lack of aflatoxin risk to Americans another way. "If you were born in America in the last couple of generations, your odds of dying of cancer are about 25 percent," he says. "The risk of getting liver cancer from aflatoxin in peanut butter is somewhere in the neighborhood of 10 to 15 to 20 cases of cancer per million exposed consumers. Suppose you eat a lot of peanut butter. Let's round up your odds to 100 in a million, or 1 in 10,000. Then you're increasing your cancer risk from .25 to .2501, which is not very noticeable in the run of things."[10]

Ironically, while the risk of aflatoxin to American consumers is low, Groth says it's higher than the risk from pesticides. While the risk from aflatoxin is between ten and twenty cases of cancer per million exposed consumers, Groth notes the EPA tries to keep carcinogenic pesticide residues at levels below the risk of one in a million. He explains this disparity in terms of "hazard and outrage," a term coined by Peter Sandman, an expert on risk communication. "Hazard is the part of risk that will make you sick or kill you," Groth says. "Outrage makes you afraid or mad. Different risks have different outrage components. One thing that makes a risk less outrageous is if it's naturally occurring. It's not like some farmer went out and sprayed something on his crops for money, and you have to eat the residue. That's considered more outrageous. So one reason consumers are more willing to accept aflatoxin, I think, is that it's natural. You can't eliminate it."[11]

While the ability to test for aflatoxin has improved because of new equipment and methods, one has to hope things haven't gotten worse because of Bush-era laxness toward product safety and corporate accountability. *Consumer Reports,* which runs an article on peanut butter every few years, hasn't tested peanut butter for aflatoxin since 2002. "We had a guy at Consumers Union who was the head of the chemical department," Groth says. "He said, 'You should test peanut butter every year and keep a data base.' I thought that was a great idea, but the people who made up test-project budgets didn't think they had the money for it."[12] The companies themselves are not going to share the information, so it's hard to tell if things are getting better or not.

★★★

"Arachibutyrophobia" is the ten-dollar word for the fear of peanut butter sticking to the roof of your mouth. But although there's apparently no word for it, people are better advised to worry about its getting stuck in their throat.

"Sometimes it's so sticky I can barely breathe—I have to get some cold water," says screenwriter and playwright Roger O. Hirson. "There's a moment there where you think you've had it—what a terrible way to die."[13] It's not a groundless fear. In 1981 Dr. Henry Heimlich, inventor of the Heimlich maneuver, wrote to the *New York Times.* An article had appeared on how to avoid overeating during the Christmas holidays, suggesting a tablespoon or two of peanut butter before heading out on the party circuit. That didn't go down well with Dr. Heimlich.

"We have records of persons choking to death after eating peanut butter off a spoon. The problem is that the thick substance becomes lodged in the throat or spreads through the lungs and cannot be removed by any means," he wrote. "If one chooses to eat peanut butter, put it on a piece of bread. In reports of choking incidents, it has been proved that the Heimlich maneuver has expelled peanut-buttered bread from the throats of choking victims and saved their lives."[14]

★ ★ ★

Around 1991 the infant daughter of Anne Munoz-Furlong and her husband, Terry Furlong, was diagnosed with milk and egg allergies. The Furlongs weren't alone, as food allergies, peanut allergies in particular, were starting to spike. The doctors to whom they took their daughter didn't know much about food allergies, as allergies weren't as pervasive as they are now.[15] Having the means to do so, the Furlongs quit their full-time jobs and founded the Food Allergy & Anaphylaxis Network (FAAN) in Fairfax, Virginia.

The work of doctors Scott Sicherer and Hugh Sampson provides a window into how rapidly peanut allergies have increased. Dr. Sicherer is a professor of pediatrics at the Jaffe Food Allergy Institute at Mount Sinai School of Medicine in New York City, while Dr. Sampson is a professor of pediatrics, allergy, and immunology there. Over a little more than a decade, they called more than 3,500 households around the United States that had been randomly selected and asked if their children under eighteen had peanut allergies. In 1997, 0.4 percent of the respondents said yes. In 2002, it was 0.8 percent, and in 2008, 1.4 percent.[16] In an eleven-year period, the reported rate of peanut allergies among children in this study more than tripled. Doctors Sicherer and Sampson call it an apparent epidemic.[17]

The results of their study track with studies conducted in Canada, Australia, and the United Kingdom. A 2007 British study revealed an even higher self-reported rate of peanut allergy among children: 1.8 percent.[18] For adults in the United States, the rate is 0.6 percent.[19]

In October 2008, the Centers for Disease Control came out with a study on food allergies for those under the age of eighteen. Between 1997 and 2007, the CDC found food allergies among the young up 18 percent.[20] The CDC used a different methodology than Sicherer and Sampson's study, so one can't automatically conclude the rate of peanut allergy is rising more quickly than for food allergies in general, although that would seem to be the case. Overall, according to FAAN, about 12 million

Americans have food allergies,[21] with peanuts and tree nuts among the most common food allergens.

Why is peanut allergy increasing so rapidly? One theory is that it's caused by high use of pesticides, fungicides, and herbicides, as well as pollution and environmental degradation. A few springs ago, I was talking to a woman in her early forties at the Ritmo Latino music store on Broadway in downtown Los Angeles while waiting to get tickets for the *Los Angeles Times* Book Festival. As a child, she had had three food allergies; she now had thirty. She used to be able to eat peanut butter and jelly; she no longer could. The problem, she said, is that there's so much junk in the air and water now, with residual pesticides on foods and cleaning oil still on processing plant machinery.[22]

Another theory says things aren't too dirty; they're too clean. The "hygiene hypothesis" holds that children in the Western world are coddled and protected, not exposed to things as they were in the past; consequently, they don't build up an immunity to them.[23] "My grandmother used to say, 'For a child to be healthy, they need to eat a peck of dirt before they grow up,'" says Don Koehler, executive director of the Georgia Peanut Commission. "The thing we may be finding is that we're not letting our children eat that peck of dirt."[24] Two other theories are that doctors are simply diagnosing more allergies than in the past, or that antibiotics used to combat childhood infections may play a role.[25]

The way a peanut is prepared for consumption can affect how allergenic it is. Dr. Sicherer says that roasting peanuts changes their sugars so that the immune system can "see" their proteins more clearly,[26] proteins being what trigger allergic reactions. In Asia, people boil or fry peanuts; in the United States, we ordinarily roast them for peanut butter. The woman who runs my local Thai restaurant says that in Thailand, people make peanut sauce by grinding peanuts; Thai restaurants in the United States use peanut butter, as it's less labor-intensive and Americans like it. Unlike American children, Thai children have only a negligible rate of peanut allergy.[27] Is the explanation to be found in grinding fresh peanuts instead of roasting them?

In its severest form, peanut allergy can be deadly, and it doesn't take much to trigger an attack. Greg Jackson, a student at Indiana University, is highly sensitive to peanuts. Once, as he grabbed a toothpick from the back of a cupboard, it brushed against a single shelled peanut on the pantry shelf. After he put the toothpick in his mouth, his skin turned red and he started vomiting. He had to be taken to the emergency room.[28]

Dr. Alan Greene, a pediatrician at the Stanford University School of Medicine, notes two ways people can die from food allergies. The first is laryngospasm: as food is swallowed, it produces immediate swelling that spreads to the vocal chords. If the vocal chords swell shut, a person can't breathe and dies with terrifying swiftness. The second mechanism is anaphylactic shock, in which a person goes into shock as long as two hours after eating the food to which he or she is allergic and dies.[29]

Author Dan Brown used anaphylactic shock as a murder weapon in *The Da Vinci Code*. Needing a way to kill an allergic henchman who knows too much, the bad guy toasts him with cognac laced with dust from the bottom of a can of peanuts.[30] While this was fiction, the deadly effects of peanut and other food allergies are all too real. On the Web site Food Allergy Support, the "Reactions and Stories: In Memory" forum is a kind of virtual Vietnam Veterans Memorial; its accounts of young people who died of food allergies provide a haunting last look at those who have passed before their time.[31]

In an effort to protect their children, many parents keep them away from peanut butter and peanut products. Andrew F. Smith, author of *Peanuts: The Illustrious History of the Goober Pea*, advised his daughter not to give her children peanuts or peanut butter until they were five years old.[32] But studies suggest that, in some cases, the opposite approach may work better. A 2007 British study found the rate of peanut allergy to be ten times higher among British Jews than Israeli Jews.[33] The study theorized that because Israeli children are fed peanut snacks at an early age, they build up their immunity. In parts of Africa where peanuts are made into a soup for weaning, the problem of peanut allergy doesn't exist.

Because peanut allergy is a life-and-death issue for some children, schools have turned into a battleground on the issue. The Food Allergy & Anaphylaxis Network does not support a peanut ban in schools; FAAN vice president of advocacy and government relations Christopher Weiss says "ban" is one of his least favorite words in the English language. "The vast majority of schools still serve peanut in some form—whether it's peanut butter or whatever. And that's fine," he says. "Because we've found you don't need to get rid of peanuts at school to keep kids with peanut allergies safe. Now, some schools have gotten rid of it—that's fine, too. It seems to work for them. But the schools that have done that are definitely in the minority."

Asked why FAAN is so agnostic about peanut bans in schools, he says, "Part of the function of schools is to prepare kids for adulthood. When kids leave elementary school, they're not going to go into a peanut-free world. Couple that with the medical aspect—the science is telling us that you don't need to prohibit peanuts at school in order to keep these kids safe."[34]

While Weiss can reason his way through this contentious issue, not everyone can. In April 2007, Lisa Searles asked the board of education at her son's elementary school in Seymour, Connecticut, to ban peanut butter at the school. She was astonished by how angry parents who opposed the idea became. "People were extremely rude," she said. "They just thought it was a ridiculous request." People left nasty posts on local message boards; one online writer even suggested putting all allergic children in a room together and feeding them peanuts.[35]

The other main battleground has been airplanes, but FAAN's Weiss says this one has been largely settled, as most airlines have stopped handing out bags of peanuts. Published studies looking at allergic reactions on airlines note that some were serious, but that the serious incidents were the result of somebody directly eating peanuts. "The airborne reactions all seemed to involve the flight crew handing out bags of peanuts, where peanut was the only ingredient," Weiss says. "It wasn't trail mix or a candy bar. You had a person surrounded by other people, and all of a sudden, they all open up the bags of peanuts. That seemed to release enough peanut dust to trigger a reaction. None of the airborne reactions were severe. But you can't overlook the fact they occurred.

"A few airlines still hand out peanuts, specifically Delta and Southwest," Weiss continues. "With Southwest, if you have a peanut allergy and call them in advance and let them know, they'll serve something different on your flight. Delta is arguably the problematic airline. They'll offer a buffer zone if you notify them in advance. They'll try not to hand out bags of peanuts within three rows from where you're sitting.

"In theory, I guess that should work and keep you safe, but the problem we've encountered with Delta is that the buffer zone is often not enforced properly. A flight crew will forget about it, or there'll be some miscommunication between personnel—it just ends up being a mess. The buffer zone is probably not the smartest approach that an airline can take; how much longer Delta will do that, I don't know."[36]

The U.S. Department of Transportation considered formally implementing a peanut ban on airplanes in 1998, or at least establishing peanut-free zones. But Congress passed an appropriations bill threatening to cut DOT's funding unless it first commissioned a scientific study that clearly identified risks from peanuts to airline passengers with peanut allergies. FAAN has offered on several occasions to help DOT conduct such a study, but DOT has never responded.[37]

In 1998, as the Department of Transportation mulled what to do about the in-flight risks peanuts posed to allergic passengers, the *New York Times* noted that in the struggle over peanut allergies those who felt peanuts were being unfairly stigmatized were starting to push back. "There have been signs of a pro-peanut backlash," it said that September. "Slate, the on-line magazine, posted an article last week headlined 'Nuttiness: How Far Can Peanut Hysteria Go?' Slate poked fun at the Transportation Department, speculating that the future would bring government-funded clinics that distribute cashews to 'peanut abusers' and napalm strikes on Georgia and South Carolina to 'fight peanuts at their source.' "[38]

In a less satirical vein is the complaint of Martin Kanan, CEO of King Nut Companies in Ohio, which packages peanut snacks for airlines. "The peanut is such a great snack and such an American snack," he says. "What's next? Is it banning peanuts in ballparks?"[39] Well, yes, in part: at the Seattle Mariners' stadium, "peanut-controlled" sections have been set aside for two or three games every year. They are thoroughly cleaned before each game, and peanuts aren't sold at nearby concession stands.[40] The St. Louis Cardinals and Minnesota Twins have also had "peanut-free" sections, and minor league teams such as New Hampshire's Nashua Pride and Alabama's Birmingham Barons have gone even further, not selling peanuts at all in their parks for an entire season.[41]

Several methods of fighting peanut allergy are being investigated: one is oral immunotherapy, in which children are fed small amounts of the substance to which they are allergic. The dose is then gradually increased in the hope children will acclimate to it. National Jewish Health, a leading research institute in Denver, is experimenting with a peanut-allergy patch that would be worn on the skin, like the patches used by people trying to quit smoking.[42] Medical researchers are also conducting studies with vaccines and even Chinese herbal medicine; a concoction of nine herbs completely blocked anaphylactic symptoms in mice. Human trials are pending.

In the meantime, the best course of action for children with peanut or other food allergies is to avoid the food to which they're allergic, read food labels carefully, and carry an epinephrine pen with which to inject themselves if they are exposed, as this helps to reverse or halt the anaphylactic reaction and can save their lives by giving them time to get to the emergency room. Some parents have even trained sniffer dogs to detect the presence of peanuts or other foods to which their child is allergic. While these precautions can complicate children's lives, Dr. Sicherer says the children are otherwise typical kids, noting, "Children with a food allergy can do everything other children can do, except eat the food to which they are allergic."[43]

★★★

In the mid-1990s, the public got the erroneous impression that the partially hydrogenated oils used to stabilize peanut butter were high in trans fats.[44] Trans fats, the unhealthiest kind of fats, increase the risk of coronary heart disease by raising levels of "bad" (LDL) cholesterol and lowering levels of "good" (HDL) cholesterol. But ordinarily they are found in hydrogenated peanut butter at very low levels, about .0032 gram per two-tablespoon serving.[45] You would need to multiply that by 156 times to get to the point where standards set by the FDA even require their presence to be noted on the jar label. Public concern about trans fats is legitimate, but misplaced with regard to peanut butter. (For a more thorough discussion of hydrogenation and trans fats, see chapter 4.)

★★★

The health problem that would give the peanut and peanut butter industries the biggest headache, though, was fat. Peanuts, being half oil, are half fat, and if you eat too many, you'll get fat. Even Don Koehler, executive director of the Georgia Peanut Commission, acknowledges this. "In Atlanta, at one of the Hilton hotels, there was a chef who had a sandwich on

Peanut Butter Meatballs

What better recipe to include in a chapter about health concerns than one for meatballs?

½ cup peanut butter
½ pound ground beef
¼ cup finely chopped onion
2 tablespoons chili sauce
1 teaspoon salt
⅛ teaspoon pepper
1 egg, beaten
2 tablespoons peanut oil
2 cups seasoned tomato sauce

Mix peanut butter lightly with beef, onion, chili sauce, salt, pepper, and egg.

Form into 12 meatballs. Brown in hot peanut oil. Add tomato sauce, cover, and simmer about 30 minutes.

Serve with cooked rice or spaghetti.

★★★

Yield: 4 servings.

WILLIAM I. KAUFMAN, *THE "I LOVE PEANUT BUTTER" COOKBOOK* (GARDEN CITY, N.Y.: DOUBLEDAY, 1965). REPRINTED WITH PERMISSION OF JACQUELINE KAUFMAN AND IVA KAUFMAN.

the menu called JB's Favorite," he says. "He took peanut butter, cheddar cheese, bacon, and sourdough bread and grilled it like a grilled cheese sandwich. It was delicious enough that I wouldn't mind eating one every day, but I wasn't going to, because I don't need to weigh 500 pounds."[46]

In the late 1980s and early 1990s, it seemed everyone was worried about weighing too much. "Peanut Butter: Health Food or Diet Disaster?" asked

Glamour magazine,[47] while *Family Circle* gave peanuts a "Do Not Eat" designation, along with butter and lard.[48] More than 10 percent of American peanut consumers stopped eating them, and millions more decreased their consumption.[49] Sales of peanut butter fell off dramatically: in 1991–1992, Americans ate nearly 900 million pounds of peanut butter. By 1994–1995, it was just over 700 million pounds, a decline of nearly 25 percent.[50]

As they had done when Jimmy Carter was running for president, the peanut people went on the attack. In 1996 the American Peanut Shellers Association established the Peanut Institute, with APSA executive director John Powell serving as its president, and Pat Kearney of PMK & Associates, a consulting firm specializing in nutrition communications, as program director. The institute's dual mission was to sponsor nutrition research about peanuts at some of America's leading universities and to publicize good nutritional news about peanuts and peanut butter gleaned from that research or elsewhere.

The campaign against fat in the early 1990s, the Peanut Institute noted, failed to make distinctions between the different kinds of fats: polyunsaturated and monounsaturated fat are healthy; saturated fats are bad for you; and trans fats, prominent in doughnuts, probably do in as many policemen as shoot-outs.

"Everybody started to ask, 'What foods are high in fat?'" Kearney recalls. "People would say, 'Don't eat nuts, eat pretzels.' People didn't cut their calories—they just started eating more refined carbohydrate foods. It's called the Snackwell Syndrome."[51]

Snackwells are devil's-food cookies made by Nabisco. Fat-free, they nonetheless have 50 calories each because of such calorie-rich carbohydrates as high-fructose corn syrup. If you eat a box of 12 Snackwells, you've eaten no fat but have still consumed 600 calories, 24 more than you'll get from a Big Mac. Snackwells aren't a heart attack on a plate like the Big Mac, 60 percent of whose 292 calories from fat are saturated, but you'll still get fat eating them and get none of the nutritional virtues of peanut butter.

Among the good nutritional news about peanuts and peanut butter the Peanut Institute put forward:

- They contain resveratrol, also found in wine and grapes, which is believed to be heart-healthy.

- They contain beta-sitosterol, which inhibits cancer growth and protects against heart disease.
- Peanut butter has a lot of protein, fiber, zinc, and vitamin E.
- Peanuts contain mostly, but not all, unsaturated fat. An ounce of dry-roasted salted peanuts has 13.5 grams of fat, of which 7 grams, or 52 percent, are monounsaturated; 4.5 grams, or 33 percent, are polyunsaturated; and 2 grams, or 15 percent, are saturated.[52]

Still, in the end, even good fat is fat. As Marion Nestle, the Paulette Goddard Professor of Nutrition, Food Studies, and Public Health at New York University, notes in her book *What to Eat*: "All fats —no exceptions— are mixtures of saturated, monounsaturated, and polyunsaturated fats."[53]

By the early 2000s, the industry's counterattack had revived the fortunes of peanuts and peanut butter. In May 2002 *Oxygen* magazine put peanut butter on a list of "Bad foods gone good," while in October 2003, the *Los Angeles Times* observed, "Reviled in the low-fat '90's, peanuts and nuts are back on science's good side as a snack that doesn't pack on pounds and may lower cholesterol and the risk of heart disease."[54]

The most extraordinary aspect of the peanut butter revival was the peanut butter diet. Although it sounds highly counterintuitive, it's based on the fact that peanut butter, if not consumed in Elvis-like quantities, is a stick-to-your-ribs food that can help suppress your appetite. The diet first appeared as an article in the March 2001 issue of *Prevention* magazine and was then expanded into a book published that August. It has placed as high as seventh on Amazon.com's best-seller list.[55] Peanut butter: a dietetic food. Who knew?

In 1994 peanut butter bottomed out at 710 million pounds eaten by American consumers. In 1996, when the Peanut Institute was founded, the total was still at 728 million pounds. Over the next four or five years, the total bounced back and forth in the 740- to 770-million-pound range, but then steadily increased, hitting 1.2 billion pounds in 2010–2011.[56] Americans had resumed their love affair with peanut butter.

THE SHORT, HAPPY LIFE OF SORRELLS PICKARD

In Hollywood, film and TV actors often say, "But I really want to direct." Herb Dow, a successful film editor and executive with an easygoing, no-nonsense manner and the cherubic face of a 1950s TV-sitcom dad, had a different dream: He really wanted to have his own peanut butter company. His dream came true, but not in the way he probably imagined.

In the early 1980s, Dow and his wife ate dinner on Friday nights at the Magic Pan, part of a chain of restaurants specializing in crepes, in Woodland Hills in the San Fernando Valley of Los Angeles. "We were sitting in the bar, having a drink or two before dinner, back when you used to do that," he says. "I brought up peanut butter one night with the bartender. And all of a sudden, like fifteen people were talking about peanut butter. 'Well, I know someone who eats it this way . . . ' The next week I brought it up on purpose and got the same reaction. When you ask somebody if they like peanut butter, eighty percent will say, 'I love peanut butter!' If you ask them if they like chicken, they don't say, 'I love chicken.' "[1]

A few years later, a film editor from Georgia told Dow, "You have to meet my friend Sorrells Pickard." Pickard, whose real name was Jimmy Bazzell, was a charismatic and accomplished country-and-western musician whose credits include playing guitar with Ringo Starr on *Beaucoups of Blues* and writing three of that album's songs. He had also done some movie acting. A native of Jacksonville, Florida, Pickard came from a family that not only featured a lot of peanut farmers but had its own peanut butter recipe. Like Dow, he was an enthusiast. The men met and hit it off, and Dow decided to turn his dream into reality, with himself as the company's chairman and Pickard as its public image (figures 16.1 and 16.2).

Given the vagaries of fund-raising, developing a business plan, hiring staff, and finding time, it would be eighteen years from that night in the Magic Pan until the company Herb Dow envisioned became a reality. Even after the first business plan was written in early 1998, the company underwent several major changes. Originally, it was conceived as a chain of kiosks in shopping malls that sold peanut butter sandwiches such as the Elvis (grilled peanut butter and bananas) and the J. Edgar Hoover (peanut butter, onions, and mayonnaise, with the coy suggestion that customers could dress it the way they liked it).

But Dow and Bryan Corlett, whom he hired as the company's president, had a gastronomic epiphany when they attended a gourmet food trade show in San Francisco: there were 400 kinds of gourmet jelly, but not a single gourmet peanut butter. They decided to fill this niche, and the Sorrells Pickard brand became the Grey Poupon of the peanut butter world. Since more than half of the $800 million Americans then spent on peanut butter was consumed by adults, this approach had its logic.

Kiosks were out and Sorrells Pickard Gourmet Peanut Butter (SPGPB) was in. Dow abandoned his original plan to make SPGPB natural or unstabilized after learning that natural was just a fraction of the peanut butter market. Based in Irvine, a bastion of high technology and higher education in Orange County forty-five miles south of Los Angeles, SPGPB was set up as a marketing company, not a manufacturer, so it

FIGURE 16.1 HERB DOW

Film editor and executive Herb Dow fulfilled a lifelong dream by starting his own peanut butter company. It turned out a remarkably good product but was undone by business decisions and a stock market crash. (Courtesy of Tony Schmitz)

FIGURE 16.2 SORRELLS PICKARD

Sorrells Pickard on the porch of his ancestral family home in Jackson County, Florida. An accomplished country musician who wrote several of the songs and performed on Ringo Starr's *Beaucoups of Blues* album, he was the public face of Sorrells Pickard Gourmet Peanut Butter. (Courtesy of Herb Dow)

owned no plant or equipment. Its peanut butter would be manufactured at the Sessions Company, a small independent peanut butter factory in Enterprise, Alabama.

Enterprise is at the heart of the southern peanut-growing belt, concentrated in southwest Georgia, southeast Alabama, and the central Florida Panhandle. The leading landmark in the town of 24,000 is a statue to the boll weevil, honoring the pestilential insect that laid waste to cotton around the time of World War I but provided the basis for the South's agricultural revival through peanuts. The circular road around Enterprise is Boll Weevil Circle, and a local radio station, WVVL, markets itself as Weevil 101. It might be said that the people of Enterprise have learned to fear no weevil.

Sorrells Pickard had roots in the area, as his grand-uncle had farmed in Jackson County, Florida, just south of Enterprise. But he had been raised in Jacksonville, so his peanut-farming skills and knowledge were rusty. To buttress them, he turned to his cousin Stanley Pittman. Pittman had started peanut farming in Jackson County with his father as a teenager in the 1950s, when peanuts were harvested by mule-drawn plows and left in the field to dry around stack poles for months. Now huge, modern, and expensive digger-shaker-inverters pulled peanut plants from the ground, shook the dirt off them, and turned them upside down in windrows so the peanuts could be fully exposed to the sun for two or three days before being separated from the peanut plant by combines.

Pittman had his own 3,000-acre farm. Hard-working, good-natured, and helpful, he was getting close to retirement; his leonine beard signaled his status as a kind of village elder. If Bascom, the town of 106 he lived in, were large enough to have a city council, he'd be on it; if it were an Indian tribe, he'd be the chief. (Despite its village status, Bascom has a few big-city claims to fame: it's the birthplace of actress Faye Dunaway, born in a sharecropper's shack down the road from Pittman's home; she occasionally comes home incognito. And the county seat, Marianna, is the birthplace of 1960s singer-songwriter Bobby Goldsboro.)

Stanley Pittman not only built the house he and his wife lived in for more than forty years, but also helped to build the Lovedale Baptist Church down the road. Jackson County, where Pittman had lived all his life, is one of the most rural counties in Florida, with a population density of 50 people per square mile (Manhattan, by way of contrast, has about 70,000 people per square mile). Its crossroads consist of general stores and sometimes-abandoned gas stations. Three-quarters of its 46,000 people are white, the other quarter black. Its weather is warm and humid, and daytime drivers along its back roads are often rewarded with vistas of billowing cathedral-in-the-sky cumulus-cloud formations, followed by blood-red sunsets framed by live oaks draped in Spanish moss. At night during harvest season, the slightly pungent and agreeable aroma of peanuts drying in windrows in the fields wafts through the air, and you need to keep an eye out for deer that might dart across the road.

Because of its soil, climate, and peanut-farming tradition, no county in Florida grows more peanuts than Jackson County. This made Stanley Pittman the go-to guy for peanuts as far as Sorrells Pickard was concerned. "I was the one they looked to for guidance and development on different varieties that allowed us to make larger yields on peanuts," Pittman says. "And disease-resistant peanuts. All this came into play—things most people wouldn't even think about."[2]

Pittman in turn was helped by Dan Gorbet, a genial, portly peanut breeder and professor of agriculture at the University of Florida Marianna Agricultural Experiment Station, a few miles from Pittman's place and just down the road from a recently rehabilitated Greek Revival mansion that dwarfs Tara from *Gone with the Wind*. Gorbet and his colleagues developed different kinds of peanut varieties, as well as trying out various chemicals to protect peanut plants against disease. Gorbet was a pioneer of high-oleic peanuts, which have a higher-than-usual concentration of healthy monounsaturated fats. Gorbet recommended that Sorrells Pickard Gourmet Peanut Butter be made with the Sun Oleic 97R peanut, one of the first high oleics to come out of the Marianna Experiment Station. Not only would its appealing flavor characteristics make SPGPB tastier, but its oleic oil would make it healthier.

On the advice of Dan Gorbet, Stanley Pittman recommended the Sun Oleic 97R to Herb Dow, but it turned out to be susceptible to tomato spotted wilt virus, a condition that causes peanuts to develop red splotchy cracks and makes them commercially useless. "The growers said to me, 'We can't grow this,'" Gorbet recalls sadly, as if mourning the loss of a child. "And I had to agree with them."[3] Up against a production deadline, Herb Dow and his colleagues decided to go with the peanuts on hand at the Sessions Company.

In its first annual report in February 1998, the Sorrells Pickard Company boasted, "Our product line directly descends from the peanut butter recipe of Sorrells Pickard's grandmother, which family and friends have raved about for decades."[4] But not everyone did: Dave Hovet, a specialist in food product design in Enterprise who helped Dow and Pickard formulate their peanut butter for the mass market, was appalled. "We changed it from the original formulation," he later recalled. "The one thing they had in it that blew my mind was vinegar—powdered vinegar. That was the first damn thing I tasted in the back of my mouth."[5]

Vinegar in peanut butter is not unheard of: a 1920 pamphlet on peanut butter from the U.S. Department of Agriculture features a recipe for a "peanut butter sandwich cream" that includes two tablespoons of vinegar.[6] But these were different times, and the powdered vinegar was out. The final list of ingredients for Sorrells Pickard Gourmet Peanut Butter was fresh roasted peanuts, sugar, hydrogenated vegetable oils, molasses, salt, coconut, vanilla, lemon, cinnamon, and natural flavors.

Dixie French Toast

Unlike the Pickard family recipe for peanut butter, this doesn't include any vinegar.

½ cup Sorrells Pickard Gourmet Peanut Butter*
8 slices crisp bacon, crumbled
12 slices white bread
2 bananas
2 eggs
1 cup milk
¼ teaspoon salt

Combine the peanut butter and bacon and spread each slice of bread with about 1 tablespoon of the mixture.

Slice bananas and place on the prepared bread, using ⅓ banana per sandwich.

Close sandwiches. Beat eggs, milk, and salt together.

Dip closed sandwiches in the mixture and brown in a little hot cooking oil. Serve with strawberry jam.

★ ★ ★

Yield: 6 servings.

---

* SORRELLS PICKARD IS NO LONGER MADE, SO IT IS ACCEPTABLE TO SUBSTITUTE ANOTHER BRAND.

FROM *SORRELLS PICKARD WORLD'S GREATEST PEANUT BUTTER COOKBOOK* (A PROMOTIONAL PAMPHLET DISTRIBUTED BY SORRELLS PICKARD GOURMET PEANUT BUTTER). REPRINTED BY PERMISSION OF HERB DOW.

One of the signature characteristics of Sorrells Pickard was its creamy smoothness, which was accidental. "The first batch we made came out creamier than it should have," Dow recalls. "But everybody liked that, because it wouldn't tear bread or crumble matzoh. The next time we made it, we went through 15,000 jars getting it that creamy. When you're in production, you have to run for an hour—that's 5,000 jars. On the fourth pass, we finally got it creamy enough."[7] Dave Hovet later compared the consistency of Sorrells Pickard to the texture of a Dove ice cream bar. It had a rich, roasted peanut flavor and was sweet, but not too sweet, with a suggestion of lemon rind. Another distinctive aspect of SPGPB was its jar, which was square instead of round to emphasize its gourmet status (a status that made its 18-ounce jars cost $1 more than other brands [figure 16.3]). The label featured the beaming face of Sorrells Pickard, with his fedora and grizzled, well-trimmed beard. Unfortunately, peanut butter production lines are designed for round rather than square jars, and Dave Hovet later recalled this causing some problems. It also bedeviled consumers, who found it hard to scrape the last globs of peanut butter from the corners of the jar.

In the fall of 1998, Sorrells Pickard Gourmet Peanut Butter was test-marketed in Denver, kicked off by a high-profile party at the Denver Art

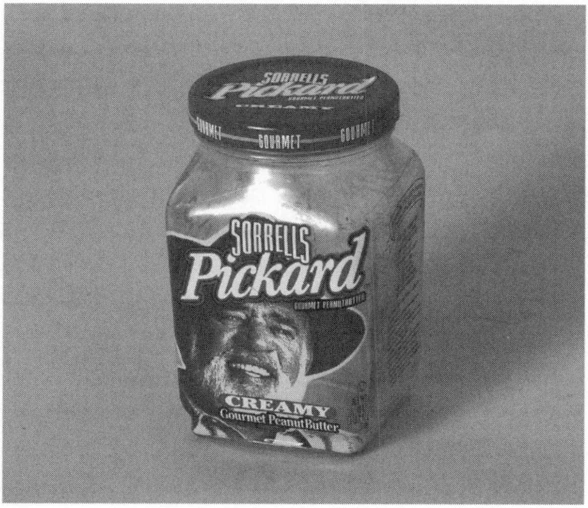

FIGURE 16.3 JAR OF SORRELLS PICKARD GOURMET PEANUT BUTTER

Sorrells Pickard's smiling face beams from a jar of his eponymous peanut butter. The square jar was designed to highlight its upscale appeal, but the unusual shape made it harder to fill jars at the factory and to scrape the last globs of peanut butter from the corners of the jar. (Courtesy of Allan Dean Walker)

Museum that featured a performance by Sorrells Pickard and his band. For the debut gala, a local microbrewery made peanut butter ale using SPGPB. Herb Dow says it was delicious, although it was hard to get the peanut butter to flow through the pipes used in making the beer. When Pickard did a promotional appearance on a local newscast, the weather lady couldn't stop eating the stuff.

She wasn't alone. From Denver, Sorrells Pickard fanned out across the West. Between November 1999 and June 2000, the company sold a million jars of peanut butter. A June 2000 article in the *Orange County Business Journal* noted that SPGPB's sales had been $500,000 the year before and were projected at $6 to $9 million for 2000.[8] Sorrells Pickard was in 6,000 supermarkets in eleven western states, including Vons, Safeway, Gelson's, Albertsons, and Ralphs. "To be in all the major chains in a one-year period is a great accomplishment," said Nate Franke, a retail analyst at Deloitte & Touche.[9]

The expansion of Sorrells Pickard was aided by a well-executed marketing and advertising campaign. In one TV commercial, an attractive woman smears peanut butter behind her ears and on her wrists and legs as if it were perfume, causing her to attract the attention of a man walking his dog down the street. A sixty-second radio spot featuring Sorrells Pickard singing the company's jingle was perhaps the only advertisement in the history of country music station KZLA in Los Angeles that had listeners calling in asking for it to be played again.

Because of Dow's connections in the entertainment industry, he was able to secure valuable product placements on TV shows such as *Friends, Dawson's Creek*, and *Dharma and Greg*, and in movies such as *Sweet November.* Rock music icon Little Richard was a fan.

But for Herb Dow, the high point was returning to his hometown of Colusa in Northern California as a successful peanut butter entrepreneur. It was part of a jar-signing tour that Dow and Pickard embarked upon: they rented a big Cadillac and drove from Los Angeles to Northern California and back, stopping at supermarkets so Pickard could sign jars.

As a boy, Dow had been something of a juvenile delinquent, getting in trouble for drinking and driving and blowing up mailboxes with pipe bombs. "My father was a county probation officer, and my older brother and I were total embarrassments to him," he recalls. "I remember one cop saying to me, 'I don't care who your father is—your brother used that excuse up a long time ago.'" But now, everything had changed. "To have my peanut butter on the shelves in Colusa . . . ," he says, his voice trailing off. "A woman came to see me who wouldn't date me in high school. It was an amazing experience."[10]

At the time, Jif had a 31 percent market share; Skippy, 20 percent; and Peter Pan, 12. Dow ambitiously set a goal of capturing 8 percent of national market share. "The financial objective," Sorrells Pickard's original business plan said, "is to expand rapidly, but prudently, in order to position ourselves for an initial public offering by 2002 or sooner."[11]

But while Sorrells Pickard's expansion was rapid, it turned out not to be prudent.

"We went from 250 supermarkets in Denver in November 1998 to every major supermarket in the eleven western states by June 1999," Dow says. "We were selling too much, and we were underfinanced."[12] Food product designer Dave Hovet agreed and felt there were other problems as well. "Sorrells Pickard was a wonderful product, but the marketing strategy was flawed," he said. "They were coming along well in Southern California and Colorado, but then they went north and kept advertising. Herb Dow brought a film crew in here—that had to be expensive. Also, they had too many people involved—too many chiefs and not enough Indians."[13]

These problems notwithstanding, it looked like Sorrells Pickard would get the financing it needed to overcome its rookie mistakes. But then came the dot-com crash. Two financiers from San Francisco had agreed to put up the $7.5 million that Sorrells Pickard needed to stay afloat. On Friday, March 24, 2000, Dow and company president Bryan Corlett went to a restaurant near Irvine where they had agreed to meet the financiers. The men never showed up.

"When we got back to the office, there was a message that their margin call had eaten them up because of the NASDAQ crash, and they were gone," Dow recalls.[14] He scurried to raise funds from other sources, but the money they had lost was needed immediately to pay outstanding bills. The bills got stamped past due, suppliers pulled out, and Sorrells Pickard Gourmet Peanut Butter collapsed.

Seven years after its demise, I ate what may have been the last jar of Sorrells Pickard Gourmet Peanut Butter. In the spring of 2007, a writers' group I belonged to was meeting at the home of one of our members, a food writer in West Los Angeles. She still had a partially eaten jar of SPGPB, which she gave to me. There were fork marks in it—surprising, as everyone knows the proper way to eat peanut butter from a jar is with a teaspoon (unless your girlfriend has just brutally dumped you, in which case a tablespoon is considered acceptable). In terms of both its smooth texture and its blend of spices, it was bewitching stuff. But it was too late for Herb Dow.

"It took me eighteen years to get to market from the original concept," he says. "All of my friends, family, and neighbors invested in it. If NASDAQ had crashed the next Monday instead of that Friday, we'd still be in business."

An even more bitter fate awaited Sorrells Pickard himself. A bit overweight, he went on the Atkins diet and rapidly lost thirty pounds. Then, on July 5, 2003, while getting up from a chair, he had a heart attack and died at age sixty-three. "His whole family lived to be 90, 100," Dow says. "He needed to lose weight, but he was healthy as a horse." Pickard's cousin Stanley Pittman has retired from farming. Neither of his sons has shown an interest in farming, so his younger second cousin, Jeffery, has taken over the farm and expanded it.

Dan Gorbet, who advised Sorrells Pickard on peanut selection, has also retired from his professorship at the University of Florida, although he still finds reasons to go to the office. And Herb Dow works as a consultant in the film industry and periodically tries to restart Sorrells Pickard Gourmet Peanut Butter. "I'm eating Skippy now," Dow says philosophically. "Aah—ya know?"

PEANUT CORPORATION OF AMERICA

"THERE WAS NO RED FLAG"

Shirley Almer owned a bowling alley in Wadena, Minnesota. A strong, resilient woman, the seventy-two-year-old Almer had beaten lung cancer and a brain tumor, fighting back to regain the use of her limbs and speech (figure 17.1). In December 2008 she entered a nursing home in nearby Brainerd to recover from a urinary tract infection.[1] While there, she started buying Christmas presents and was planning to get a puppy.

But during what was expected to be a quick and easy convalescence, she began complaining of stomach cramps and had diarrhea.[2] She went into a downward spiral, and on the day before she was originally scheduled for release, her family was stunned to learn doctors were giving her hours to live. She died on December 21 and is buried in Greenwood Cemetery in New York Mills, a small town in northwestern Minnesota.[3] While in the rehab facility, she had eaten toast with peanut butter distributed by the King Nut Company and made by the Peanut Corporation of America.[4] It was contaminated with *Salmonella*. "Cancer couldn't claim her," her son, Jeffrey, later told Congress. "But peanut butter did."[5]

Clifford Tousignant, seventy-eight, who lived in nearby Brainerd, also ate some PCA-made peanut butter in a rehab facility not far from Shirley Almer's.[6] A Korean War veteran with three Purple Hearts, he had spent twenty-two years in the military, then worked in the security department

FIGURE 17.1 SHIRLEY ALMER

Shirley Almer had beaten lung cancer and a brain tumor. "Cancer couldn't claim her," her son, Jeffrey, told a congressional subcommittee investigating the Peanut Corporation of America. "But peanut butter did." (Courtesy of Don Hoffman, Rex McDonald Studio)

of a shipyard in Superior, Wisconsin. A big, friendly teddy bear of a man, he had six children, fifteen grandchildren, and fourteen great-grandchildren (figure 17.2).

On December 28, 2008, he started to have diarrhea. Over the next two weeks, his diarrhea got worse, and he suffered from vomiting and increasingly agonizing stomach pains.[7] There were constant blood draws and medical tests. The skin around his anus caused constant pain and itching and eventually ulcerated. He went into an irreversible decline, dying on the morning of January 12, 2009. He is buried in Sunrise Memorial Park in Hermantown, a suburb of Duluth.[8]

Four days after his death, the Peanut Corporation of America announced a voluntary recall of products made in its Blakely, Georgia, plant since July 2008.[9] Twelve days later, the recall was expanded to include all products made there since January 1, 2007.[10]

Peanut butter and peanut paste made by PCA in Blakely and its plant in Plainview, Texas, would trigger the largest food-product recall in American history. Nine people died, and at least 700 were injured (and those are just the official statistics: William Marler, an attorney specializing in food-borne illness litigation, says that for every reported case, just over thirty-eight are unreported).[11] All the illnesses began between Septem-

FIGURE 17.2 CLIFFORD TOUSIGNANT

Clifford Tousignant was a Korean War veteran with three Purple Hearts who worked in the security department of a shipyard in Superior, Wisconsin. None of the nine deaths from Peanut Corporation of America peanut butter was one you'd want to experience, but his was particularly unpleasant. (Courtesy of Paul Tousignant)

ber 3 and December 29, 2008, with most people getting sick after October 1.[12]

Fifty-four companies had to recall 1,900 products,[13] among them Kellogg (Keebler and Famous Amos peanut butter cookies),[14] Walgreen's (chocolate candy with peanuts), Hain Celestial (frozen pad Thai dinners), high-end mail-order firm Harry and David (Olympia Delight Trail Mix products),[15] and Sara Lee (Chef Pierre Chocolate Peanut Butter Silk Pie).[16] Even man's best friend wasn't safe: peanut butter-flavored dog biscuits were recalled after a dog in Oregon came down with *Salmonella* poisoning.[17]

To go by the public image it projected, there was nothing to worry about at Peanut Corporation of America. On January 6, four days before news reports about the *Salmonella* outbreak began to surface, its Web site was all happy talk. "At Peanut Corporation of America, we know we need to shine so that you and your customers can be assured of consistent quality, safety, and dependability when you allow us to process your peanuts," it said. "We work constantly to maintain a clean environment so we can provide a clean, safe product."[18]

The truth was far grimmer. Workers in the Blakely plant saw roaches and rats scurry around the plant on a daily basis. The roof was so leaky that after a heavy rain, they had to step over puddles inside the building.[19]

David James, who worked in the shipping department, once opened a tote bag of peanuts to find baby mice in it. "It was filthy and nasty all around the place," he said. He also saw new stickers being put on out-of-date buckets of peanut paste, which was used as an ingredient in cookies, cakes, and other products. James Griffin, a cook in the plant, said, "I never ate the peanut butter, and I wouldn't allow my kids to eat it."[20]

When the U.S. Food and Drug Administration inspected the Blakely plant on January 9, 2009, it found not only foot-long gaps in the roof but mold on the ceilings and walls. Even after PCA discovered the *Salmonella* contamination, it didn't clean its equipment. The FDA inspectors who looked at the plant felt it should never have been making peanut butter in the first place, because it didn't provide enough separation between raw peanuts and finished peanut butter, a likely route for cross-contamination.[21]

Remarkably, although Georgia state inspectors had found rust that could flake into food and gaps in warehouse doors big enough for rodents to get in, Georgia assistant agricultural commissioner Oscar Garrison described the violations as "minor," saying, "there was really no red flag that gave us concern at the time."[22] But the FDA was able to access plant records state inspectors couldn't by invoking the 2002 Public Health Security and Bioterrorism Preparedness Response Act.[23] Those records indicated that PCA products had tested positive for *Salmonella* twelve times in 2007 and 2008.[24] PCA had those products retested, then sent them out to the public. The practice of initially obtaining a positive sample and subsequently getting a negative result without having cleaned up the plant was illegal, said Michael Rogers, director of the FDA's division field investigations.[25]

Officials in Texas had even less excuse than those in Georgia for failing to take action against PCA: Kenneth Kendrick, who served as assistant plant manager between July and November 2006, repeatedly told the Texas Department of Health about cases of rat infestation and feces in the product.[26] He also reported a roof leak that allowed rainwater contaminated with bird feces to drip onto the peanuts. The health department did nothing and did not even seem to be aware the plant was operating without a license.

In addition to discovering that PCA had failed to dispose of *Salmonella*-contaminated peanut butter and peanut paste, the FDA learned of a surprisingly callous attitude on the part of PCA management. In one e-mail to Blakely plant manager Sammy Lightsey, owner Stewart Parnell referred to a batch of product that had tested positive for *Salmonella* and then been retested and cleared (figure 17.3) (This is possible because *Salmonella* isn't uniformly distributed throughout the food it contaminates.) Although standard procedure in the industry is to destroy anything found to be contaminated, Parnell wasn't having any of it. "Turn them loose," he told Lightsey.[27] In other words: ship them to unsuspecting customers. Parnell also complained that tests identifying the dangerous *Salmonella* bacteria in his products were "costing us huge $$$$$."[28]

Parnell, fifty-four at the time of the outbreak, had taken over the business from his father. A tennis buff and member of the Oakwood Country Club in his hometown of Lynchburg, Parnell flew his own airplane and was a member of Life Flight Atlantic, an organization that matches airplane pilots with patients who need free medical transportation. However, as the *Atlanta Journal-Constitution* noted, Parnell's company and trouble weren't strangers. On several occasions in the early 1990s, PCA was sued by companies it had supplied with peanuts that had unacceptably high levels of aflatoxin, a carcinogenic mold that grows on peanuts under conditions of drought stress.[29]

FIGURE 17.3 STEWART PARNELL

Salmonella-contaminated peanut butter made by Stewart Parnell's Peanut Corporation of America killed 9 people, injured more than 700, and triggered the largest food recall in American history. Despite the existence of internal PCA documents showing it deliberately shipped defective product, there has never been a state or federal criminal investigation of PCA. (AP photo/Don Petersen)

The *Salmonella* outbreak had its ironies. The King Nut Company, supplied by PCA for its King Nut brand peanut butter, also distributed another brand called Parnell's Pride.[30] And as the crisis unfolded, it came out that Parnell was serving on an industry advisory board that helped the U.S. Department of Agriculture set quality standards for peanuts.[31] He had been appointed by Mike Johanns, secretary of agriculture under George W. Bush, and reappointed by Johanns to a second term. Almost as soon as Tom Vilsack was sworn in as President Obama's secretary of agriculture in January 2009, he booted Parnell off the board.[32]

This was the second case involving *Salmonella* contamination of peanut butter in two years, the first being the Peter Pan contamination of 2006–2007 (see chapter 5). In attorney William Marler's opinion, there's an important difference between the two cases, though. "ConAgra was just lazy," he says. "PCA knew they were shipping contaminated product and did so anyway."[33]

The PCA outbreak had a devastating effect on the peanut butter industry. By early February, panicky consumers were avoiding all brands of peanut butter, not just products associated with PCA. Peanut butter sales plunged by almost 25 percent compared with the year before.[34] In the Atlanta suburb of Douglasville, Stacey Newbern threw out her 6.5 pound jar of Skippy. "We chucked the whole tub. Better safe than sorry," the mother of eight boys said. "Peanut butter, once the great American comfort food, [now] makes us uncomfortable,"[35] reported the *Atlanta Journal-Constitution*.

The two *Salmonella* outbreaks weren't the only problems plaguing peanut butter; in May 2010, Minnesota-based Parker's Farm issued a recall for its peanut butter because it was contaminated with *Listeria monocytogenes*, a virulent food-borne bacteria.[36] And peanut butter wasn't the only trouble-prone food: other products recalled either during or shortly after George W. Bush's industry-friendly eight years in the White House included jalapeño and serrano peppers, lettuce, alfalfa sprouts, spinach, cantaloupes, ground beef patties, cookie dough, cream cheese, spreadable cheddar cheese, salsa, chicken pot pie, and frozen pizza. But the PCA recall touched a public nerve in the American psyche the others didn't. "What's more sacred than peanut butter?" asked Senator Tom Harkin (D-Iowa).[37]

Another victim of the PCA outbreak was the town of Blakely. Located in the piney woods of southwestern Georgia in the heart of peanut country, the town of 5,700 cherishes its peanut heritage. On the grounds of the county courthouse is a statue not of a Civil War general or a town father, but a peanut. Its base proclaims, "The people of Early County have erected this monument in tribute to the peanut, which is so largely responsible for our growth and prosperity." On the northeast side of Courthouse Square is a mural sponsored by Birdsong Peanuts, a large peanut-shelling company, featuring an image of traditional peanut farming, with peanuts being harvested by a mule-drawn plow and stacked in a field on stack poles to dry. Blakely was also the hometown of the father-in-law of William T. Young, whose Big Top Peanut Butter served as the precursor to Jif.

By January 22, 2009, all but three of the Blakely plant's forty-six employees were out of work.[38] It was the second blow in rapid succession to the area, as the nearby Georgia Pacific paper products plant had only days earlier scaled back its production and dismissed 100 workers. This one-two punch was especially hard for the town in the wake of the 2008 collapse of the U.S. economy. But it was boom times at McDonald's: Lawanda McGriff, who managed the Blakely McDonald's, said that when the PCA plant closed "we had approximately 50 people come down here trying to get hired."[39] (The janitor at PCA earned $6.55 an hour, so he might have done better at McDonald's.)[40] In the wake of the PCA scandal, Blakely would start Peanut Proud, a festival held every March designed to highlight positive aspects of the peanut industry.

On February 9, the FBI raided the Blakely plant, also executing a search warrant at PCA's headquarters, a converted garage behind the house of PCA owner Stewart Parnell in Lynchburg, Virginia.[41] Four days later, on Friday, February 13, PCA filed for bankruptcy.[42]

★★★

A sign of the extent to which corporations ruled the roost in Washington during the George W. Bush years was that before the FDA could publish a recall statement about PCA products, its wording had to be approved by the legal and public relations departments of PCA.[43] In the 1970s, the FDA had conducted 35,000 annual inspections, visiting every food plant in the country every other year. But in 2010, former FDA associate commissioner William Hubbard said, "Today, with fewer inspectors and far more food plants, the agency can realistically inspect only the 6,000 high-risk facilities out there."[44]

Inveighing against the corporate-inspired defunding of the FDA, an editorial in the *Providence Journal* asked, "Where were the regulators? Why did it take so long for suspect products to be recalled and consumers warned? The answer, as with previous food scares, lies in a timid, largely toothless and understaffed Food and Drug Administration." Noting that the FDA oversees 80 percent of the American food supply with only 2,000 inspectors, it said, "Congress must pass legislation giving the FDA more authority, including enforcement powers, and the resources it needs for meaningful oversight."[45] The satirical newspaper *The Onion* took a more sardonic approach. "FDA Approves *Salmonella*" was its banner headline, with the subhead "Pathogen 'Now Part of a Well-Balanced Diet.'" The article quoted an imaginary FDA official as beaming, "It's approved. Healthy, delicious Salmonella is finally approved."[46]

Would Congress heed the *Providence Journal*'s advice? On February 10, 2009, the Subcommittee on Oversight and Investigations of the House Energy and Commerce Committee, chaired by Bart Stupak (D-Mich.), held a hearing into the outbreak. Congressman Greg Walden (R-Ore.), the subcommittee's ranking Republican, was responsible for the hearing's two best moments of political theater (figure 17.4). During a panel featuring relatives of the victims of PCA peanut butter, he asked if Stewart Parnell was in the audience. There was silence. He repeated the question. More silence. "You know," he mused, "I would think that the least he could have done was be here to hear your comments." And when Parnell and Blakely plant manager Sammy Lightsey appeared before the subcommittee, Walden held up a large glass jar of PCA products wrapped in yellow crime-scene tape and offered Parnell and Lightsey the opportunity to sample their own products. Both declined.[47]

Although the hearing went on for almost four hours and fifteen minutes, Parnell's appearance lasted only six minutes. Other than identifying his lawyer, all he did was plead the Fifth. Sensing that it wasn't going to have a lively interchange with Parnell, the subcommittee quickly dismissed him, after which he was forced to run a gauntlet of jostling reporters who chased him for blocks.

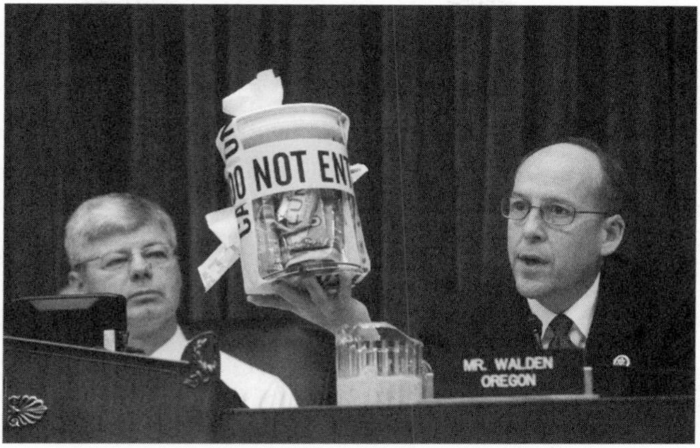

FIGURE 17.4 GREG WALDEN

Congressman Greg Walden (R-Ore.) challenges PCA owner Stewart Parnell and Sammy Lightsey, manager of PCA's plant in Blakely, Georgia, to sample their own products in a congressional subcommittee hearing on February 11, 2009, as committee chairman Bart Stupak (D-Mich.) looks on. Parnell and Lightsey declined Walden's invitation. (AP photo/ J. Scott Applewhite)

Charles Deibel, president of Deibel Laboratories, appeared before the subcommittee after Parnell. "It is not unusual for Deibel Labs or other food-testing laboratories to find that samples clients submit do test positive for *Salmonella* and other pathogens, nor is it unusual that clients request that samples be retested," Deibel said. "What is virtually unheard of is for an entity to disregard those results and place potentially contaminated products into the stream of commerce."[48]

The Food Safety Modernization Act overwhelmingly passed the House of Representatives in July 2009 and was reported out of the Senate Health, Education, Labor, and Pensions Committee that fall. But it didn't pass until December 2010. By that time, congressional Republicans, now in the House majority, blocked funding for its implementation,[49] in effect gutting the law Congress had passed to improve American food safety.

In May 2009, the Georgia state legislature passed Senate Bill 80, which was signed into law by Governor Sonny Perdue. It mandated new food-testing regulations, which went into effect in the spring of 2010.

Unfortunately, the law contained an amendment, adopted just before it passed, allowing companies to bypass testing if they submit a "food safety plan" to the state.[50]

Although there were 9 known deaths and more than 700 people injured, only 124 claims were filed against PCA; claimants split $12 million in insurance money based on severity of illness. Kellogg paid an additional undisclosed amount.[51] William Marler, who handled lawsuits for about forty-five victims in the case, says, "In 17 years of litigating every major food-borne illness outbreak in the U.S., I have not seen a clearer situation that demanded criminal prosecution."[52]

None has been forthcoming. The state of Georgia left it to the federal government to prosecute. On January 30, 2009, federal health officials announced the launch of a criminal investigation by the Department of Justice under provisions of the 1938 Federal Food, Drug, and Cosmetic Act.[53] But when I spoke almost two years later with Wyn Hornbuckle in the public affairs office of the Department of Justice's Environment and Natural Resources Division, he wouldn't even confirm the existence of such an investigation.[54]

In an effort to get Stewart Parnell's side of the story, I called him at home in Lynchburg, Virginia, in October 2010. His daughter Katie answered. She was charming and gracious, but the strain in her voice indicated this wasn't her favorite subject. She told me she'd get her father to call me back, and to my surprise he did, several hours later.

"Why did you send out peanut butter you knew was bad?" I asked him.

"That's not the real story," he said.

"What's the real story?" I asked.

He said that if his lawyer gave him the green light, he'd be happy to talk to me. (I called the lawyer and left a message but am still waiting to hear back from him.)[55]

Both in his hometown of Lynchburg and in the peanut industry, Stewart Parnell kept a low profile even before the PCA *Salmonella* outbreak. "I never saw him at nonprofit fund-raisers or social events," said Bert Dodson Jr., the vice mayor of Lynchburg, who played high school football with Parnell. And Patrick Archer, president of the American Peanut Council, said, "I wasn't even sure what he looked like when all this came up."[56]

Parnell and his wife still live in a large Cape Cod–style house in a comfortable suburban neighborhood of Lynchburg. They have a vacation home in Nags Head, on the Outer Banks of North Carolina near Kitty Hawk, and he's still a member of the Oakwood Country Club in Lynchburg.[57] In the truth-is-stranger-than-fiction category, Parnell has even been working in the peanut industry again as a consultant.[58] But Richard Stone, Parnell's longtime tennis partner, vigorously defends him. "I've never known him to lie, cheat or steal—ever," Stone says. "Most people are lax with the little things, but he's not."[59]

What will happen to Parnell? Probably nothing. William Marler says the federal investigation of PCA is rumored to be ongoing in Georgia, but its time frame—or whether it will ever materialize at all—is a matter of pure conjecture. The odds that Parnell or anyone connected with PCA will ever see the inside of a prison cell, he says, are less than 5 percent.[60]

PEANUT BUTTER SAVES THE WORLD

In the case of the Peanut Corporation of America, peanut butter took life. But for starving children in sub-Saharan Africa and elsewhere in the Third World, it represents a second chance at life.

Peanut-butter-based pastes, known as ready-to-use therapeutic foods (RUTFs), consist of peanut butter with milk and sugar powders and a bit of vegetable oil, enriched with vitamins and minerals. A three-ounce serving of Plumpy'Nut, the best-known of these pastes, has 500 calories and a lot of protein in addition to the vitamins and minerals.

Third World children starve because their mothers can't produce enough milk for them or afford to buy it. Even if they could, there's often no electricity in their villages and therefore no refrigeration. Powdered milk doesn't work because the water in these villages doesn't taste good and is often contaminated.[1] But African and Asian kids, like their American counterparts, love the taste of peanut butter, especially when combined with sugar. RUTFs don't need to be mixed with water, cooked, or refrigerated, and they keep for two years. Mothers—or children, if they're old enough—simply open the packet and squeeze the stuff out.

In 2007 Anderson Cooper and a team from *60 Minutes* went to Niger to watch Plumpy'Nut in action. On a United Nations list of developing countries, Niger ranks as the least developed—number 177 on a list of 177 countries.[2] It straddles the Sahara Desert in the north and the semi-arid grasslands of the Sahel in the south.

In a remote village twelve hours by car from the capital of Niger, Cooper and his team awoke at dawn, after sleeping outside under mosquito nets, to observe mothers emerging from the fields; many had walked for hours in the dark along rural paths infested with scorpions, spiders, and poisonous snakes. They were heading to a station where aid workers distributed Plumpy'Nut.

In Niger and other sub-Saharan countries, the need for therapeutic peanut paste is most acute during the "hunger season," just before the new harvest, when families have eaten most of the food from the previous year's crops. Often all they have left is millet, a basic grain. Millet alone doesn't have enough nutrients to keep children alive; in America it is used most commonly as birdseed.

Severe Acute Malnutrition is widespread and devastating. Every year in South Asia, sub-Saharan Africa, and elsewhere in the Third World, it kills more than twice as many children as HIV/AIDS, malaria, and tuberculosis combined. How effective is therapeutic peanut paste in combating starvation? In 2005 the region visited by *60 Minutes* had the highest rate of malnutrition in Niger; by 2007 it had the lowest. Experts can't find enough good things to say about ready-to-use therapeutic foods. *60 Minutes* says, "[They] may just be the most important advance ever to cure and prevent malnutrition," while Dr. Milton Tectonidis, chief nutritionist for Doctors Without Borders, calls the introduction of RUTFs "a revolution in nutritional affairs."[3] The peanut allergy problems that plague developed nations are rare in the Third World, so Plumpy'Nut and similar pastes pose no threat to starving children there. Asked about allergic reactions by African children to peanut products, Dr. Susan Shepherd, a pediatrician from Butte, Montana, then running Doctors Without Borders in Niger, told *60 Minutes*, "We just don't see it. In developing countries, food allergy is not nearly the problem that it is in industrialized countries."[4]

Plumpy'Nut was developed in 1999 by Andre Briend and Michel Lescanne (figure 18.1). Briend is a French scientist and pediatric nutritionist who then worked at the French Institute of Research for Development. Lescanne is the director of Nutriset, a family-owned food company based in Normandy.

FIGURE 18.1 PLUMPY'NUT

Package of Plumpy'Nut®, the most popular ready-to-use therapeutic food (RUTF) based on peanut paste. It was developed by Michel Lescanne, director of the French company Nutriset, and Andre Briend, a pediatric nutritionist. Nutriset has aggressively defended its patent for the product, causing a split among those who fight Third World hunger over whether lifesaving RUTFs should be patented. Nutriset maintains that voiding its patents will open the way for transnational food giants to enter the market, one it has so far dominated. (Photo Copyright © 2007 Nutriset S.A.S.)

Before therapeutic peanut pastes, the standard treatment for malnutrition was F100, a milk powder fortified with vitamins and minerals. But it had to be combined with clean drinking water, always a chancy prospect in remote Third World villages, and it promoted the growth of bacteria when left unrefrigerated. Plumpy'Nut and similar pastes contain less than 2 percent water, making it impossible for bacteria to grow in them.

Before settling on a peanut-based paste, Briend considered fortified pancakes and biscuits.[5] But he was inspired by Nutella, a sweet, hazelnut paste his children loved.[6] Lescanne played a key role in developing the taste, texture, and shelf life of Plumpy'Nut.[7] The two developers of Plumpy'Nut had differing motivations, which still has repercussions in the world of humanitarian famine control.

"Andre and I were all about this as a therapeutic opportunity and Michel was like 'This is an entrepreneurial opportunity,'" says Mark Manary, who conducted the first field tests of therapeutic peanut pastes.[8]

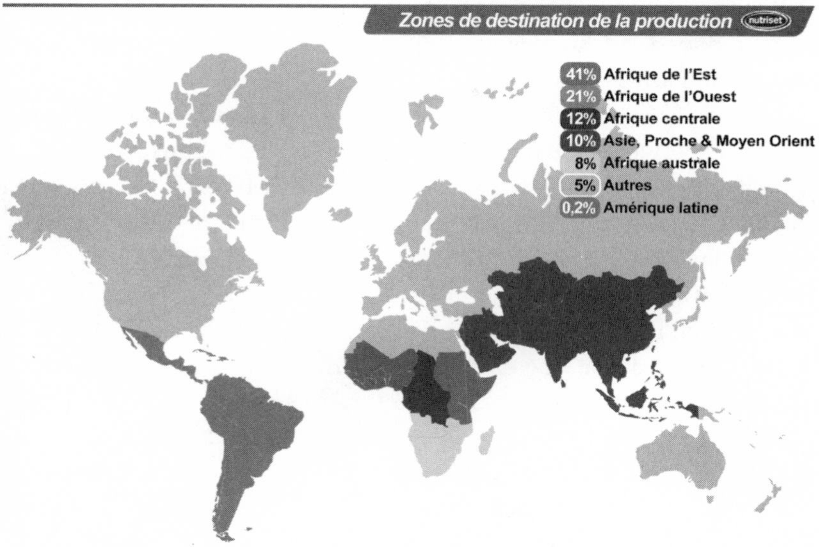

FIGURE 18.2 GLOBAL MAP OF RUTF CONSUMPTION

World map prepared by Nutriset showing regions where Plumpy'Nut® is used most extensively. Although consumed most heavily in Africa, ready-to-use therapeutic foods also combat hunger in Asia and Latin America. (Figure Copyright © 2009 Nutriset S.A.S.)

Business has been good. In 2009, sales of Plumpy'Nut were between $65 and $70 million-plus for 14,000 metric tons, most of it purchased by the United Nations Children's Fund.[9] Nutriset's shipments of Plumpy'Nut tripled between 2007 and 2008,[10] and UNICEF expected global production to rise to 50,000 tons a year by 2011 (figure 18.2).[11] The French Institute of Research for Development (IRD), where Briend worked, receives 1 percent of Nutriset sales; Briend himself has declined to assert any ownership interest.[12]

Manary, a pediatrician and nutrition scientist at Washington University in St. Louis, conducted the first field tests of therapeutic peanut pastes in Malawi during the 2000–2001 hunger season. He was working at a hospital that had a crowded malnutrition ward, with many children lying on mats. "These kids are deathly ill, you're doing whatever you can for them, and you think you're on the right track," Manary said. "Then you come in the next morning and four of them have died."[13] As the *New York Times* reported, he emptied out his ward and sent the starving children home with Plumpy'Nut.

As often happens with innovators, Manary's gamble provoked hostility. One expert told Manary at a conference, "You're killing children." But 95 percent of the children who went home with Plumpy'Nut recovered completely, a much better rate than in-patient treatment.[14] Doctors Without Borders was impressed with Manary's results, realizing RUTFs could be administered at home. This allowed poverty-stricken African mothers and children to avoid the long and expensive hospital stays that also exposed weakened, starving children to the diseases customarily found in Third World medical facilities.

Manary and his wife, Mardi, run Project Peanut Butter, a secular charity dedicated to both producing RUTFs and giving them away free of charge. It has ongoing operations in Malawi, is expanding into Sierra Leone, and plans to open clinics and food production facilities in at least three more countries in sub-Saharan Africa.[15] The Manarys emphasize local production; their pastes are produced in the countries where they're consumed. Project Peanut Butter's factory in Malawi also buys peanuts and other crops from 6,000 local farmers, thus helping to sustain the local economy.

They also assist other nongovernmental organizations working in this field. "We just helped a group of Catholic charity workers begin their own small-scale production and distribution of RUTFs to their patients in the Payates Tuberculosis Clinic, which is in a slum located on a garbage dump outside Manila" in the Philippines, Mardi Manary says. "We celebrate and support these small-scale production groups if they receive proper training—RUTFs must be made carefully to be effective and free of contaminants."[16]

Other religious charities engaged in this work include Mother-Administered Nutritive Aid (MANA), based in Charlotte, North Carolina, and Peanut Butter House, a joint effort between the First Presbyterian Church of Fort Collins, Colorado, and Hope Feeds, an international charity devoted to saving children with HIV and AIDS. (The partnership came about because the antiretroviral drugs that fight HIV/AIDS can't be taken without food and so are useless to starving children.)[17] For-profit companies making therapeutic peanut pastes in addition to Nutriset include Norwegian-based Compact and German firm MSI.

The field of RUTFs may soon expand from curing acute malnutrition to preventing it. Edesia Global Solutions of Providence, Rhode Island, is both a nonprofit and an independent licensed producer of Nutriset products; the *New York Times* says it "dances along the nebulous line between capitalism and charity."[18] According to Edesia spokeswoman Marie Wisecup, one of its goals is to prevent malnutrition in children aged six months to two years, a critical stage of development, and it is developing RUTFs for that purpose.[19]

Although feeding the hungry might seem like something everyone can agree on, it isn't. Nutriset, along with the IRD owns the patent to Plumpy'Nut and similar pastes. Aid organizations such as Doctors Without Borders are opposed to patents on important humanitarian products, but the patents held by Nutriset and the IRD last until 2018 and can be enforced in Europe, North America, and about thirty African countries. *Science* magazine notes that Nutriset has threatened lawsuits to keep companies such as Compact and MSI from selling similar pastes.[20]

The patent has triggered backlash in a variety of forms. Some producers ignore it, while India has imposed tight restrictions on Plumpy'Nut, calling it an unproven colonialist import.[21] "Poverty is a business," says Patricia Wolff, the founder of Meds & Foods for Kids, which produces RUTFs in Haiti. "There's money to be made, and there are people who have that way of thinking."[22]

In Malawi, Mark and Mardi Manary's Project Peanut Butter has been producing Chiponde, the local name for their RUTF, since 2002 (figure 18.3). They weren't even aware of the Plumpy'Nut patent until 2004, when Nutriset contacted them and granted them a license to produce Chiponde, even though it has a different formula.[23] Mardi Manary assumes they got the green light because of her husband's pioneering work on RUTFs. To avoid legal unpleasantness, the Manarys agreed to put the name Plumpy'Nut on their product as well as their own name, Chiponde.[24]

Adeline Lescanne, Michel's daughter and the deputy general manager of Nutriset, defends the patent, saying, "We are a bit afraid that big industrial companies will come."[25] These fears aren't groundless: PepsiCo has talked about bringing ready-to-use foods to needy populations, causing concerned nutritionists to muse that Pepsi-branded therapies could be "potent ambassadors for equivalently branded baby foods, cola drinks, and snack foods."[26] Today, lifesaving RUTFs; tomorrow, Cheetos.

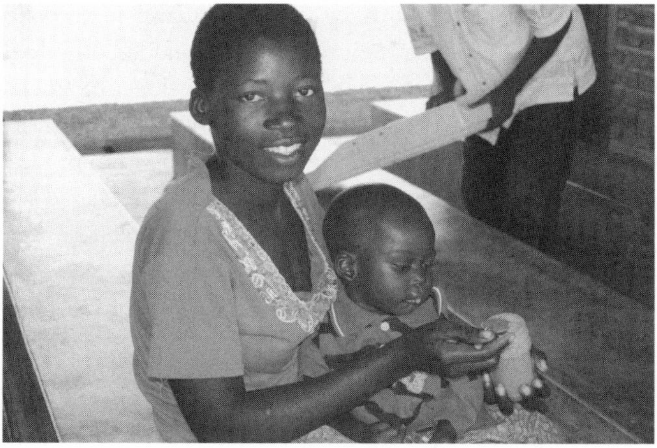

FIGURE 18.3 MADONNA WITH CHIPONDE

A young woman in Malawi feeds Chiponde, a ready-to-use therapeutic food based on peanut paste, to her son. Because of their protein-rich nature, tastiness, and ability to retain nutritional value for two years without refrigeration or the addition of water, RUTFs have proven a boon in fighting hunger in the Third World. (Courtesy of Project Peanut Butter)

Formula for Chiponde

This formula is for explanation purposes only. In the field, portions have to be weighed out carefully. Similarly, the conditions under which Chiponde is made must be supervised carefully for cleanliness.

21 percent vegetable oil
25 percent sugar
27 percent peanut paste
25 percent milk powder
1.6 percent vitamins and mineral powder

RECIPE PREPARED BY ZACHERY LINNEMAN, OF PROJECT PEANUT BUTTER, AT THE DIRECTION OF MARDI MANARY.

Andre Briend, co-creator of Plumpy'Nut, doesn't seem to think it's all that patentable. On one visit to Malawi, he whipped a batch up in a blender to show that Plumpy'Nut could be made almost anywhere. More worrisome for Nutriset, a lawsuit was filed in federal district court in Washington, D.C., in 2010 seeking to have the patent for Plumpy'Nut invalidated.[27] The plaintiffs were Breedlove Foods, a Texas-based food maker, and Mama Cares, the charitable arm of a snack-food maker in Carlsbad, California. While both entities are small nonprofits connected with Christian aid organizations, the American peanut lobby, which is not small, has a strong interest in the case, given the huge market potential involved.

★★★

Although UNICEF and Doctors Without Borders, both winners of the Nobel Peace Prize, strive to help the world's poor and disenfranchised, there are occasions when they inadvertently work against their interests. The delivery of RUTFs to Haiti in the wake of the 2010 earthquake there is a case study.

On January 12, a devastating 7.0 earthquake struck Haiti. Between 100,000 and 200,000 Haitians were killed, more than 300,000 were injured, and a million were made homeless. Many homes and commercial buildings either collapsed or were severely damaged.

The earthquake caused a massive humanitarian crisis and a pressing need to feed the newly homeless. Meds & Foods for Kids (MFK) was perfectly situated to help meet that need. A Haitian company established by Patricia Wolff, a pediatrician from St. Louis, is based in Cap Haitien, a city on Haiti's north coast. Located on the second floor of a white house along a bumpy road, it has about twenty workers who produce more than three tons a month of peanut paste or RUTF called Medika Mamba.

People needed therapeutic peanut paste in the wake of the earthquake. If it could be produced domestically, that would also boost the local economy. But MFK was unable to help because of screwups by UNICEF and Doctors Without Borders. In 2007, according to *Foreign Policy* magazine, MFK asked UNICEF for an audit, which it needed to order to sell to the UN and other major aid agencies.[28] UNICEF dragged its feet, then delegated responsibility for the audit to Doctors Without Borders.[29] During the audit, Doctors Without Borders underwent an internal reorganization, which delayed the process. Then the official who was supposed to conduct the audit left. MFK was audited by another organization, but neither UNICEF nor Doctors Without Borders was willing to accept the audit. Before things could be sorted out, the earthquake hit, and MFK was ineligible to sell to UNICEF and other major aid organizations.

"Whatever the rationale for not auditing MFK, the result was clear," *Foreign Policy* noted. "MFK became yet another Haitian producer unable to compete in the aid market. It's a contest that, to Haitian producers, often seems rigged"[30] (in favor of large American and European exporters). In the wake of the post-earthquake snafu, MFK decided that if it couldn't beat them, it would join them. It became a part of Nutriset, which then shut down a Plumpy'Nut production plant in the neighboring Dominican Republic.

★★★

Although Plumpy'Nut and ready-to-use therapeutic foods are a little more than ten years old, the first effort to create them dates back more than fifty years. According to former plant manager and engineer Frank Delfino, Skippy did pioneering work in RUTFs, but its efforts didn't fall on fertile ground.

"In the late 1950s and early 1960s, Skippy worked on and formulated a product that was essentially the same as this Plumpy'Nut," he says. "At Alameda, we manufactured 500 cases or something like that of this material, which consisted of peanuts, dehydrated milk powder, vitamins, and minerals and some peanut oil to lubricate it."[31]

The main problem, Delfino says, was that it was about 10 percent milk powder, which leached out the peanut butter, making it look anemic. Nonetheless, Skippy gave the product and its recipe to someone in Washington, probably at the U.S. Department of Agriculture. "They were looking for markets for peanuts," he says. "As far as I know, we never heard 'boo' out of them. And now, forty-five years later, somebody else is manufacturing it in Africa."[32]

Rather than envisioning it for use overseas, Delfino says, Skippy thought it might find a market in the federal food stamp or school lunch programs. But it never made it to market, awaiting the pioneering efforts of Andre Briend, Michel Lescanne, and Mark Manary two generations later. When John Harvey Kellogg took out the first patent on peanut butter in the mid-1890s, he thought of it as a health food. More than a century later, in ways he couldn't have imagined, it still is.

WHERE ARE THE PEANUT BUTTERS OF YESTERYEAR?

Today Jif, Skippy, and Peter Pan dominate a highly concentrated peanut butter market, with Smart Balance and Planters rounding out the top tier. Many brands have fallen by the wayside in the more than 100 years since peanut butter was first developed, including regional stalwarts Dr. Schindler's (Baltimore and Washington, D.C.), Robb Ross (Sioux City, Iowa), Toner's Radiant Roast (Denver), Meadors Old Timey (South Carolina), and even the namesake brand of peanut butter pioneer George Bayle (St. Louis).

Nine hundred million dollars' worth of peanut butter was sold in 2008,[1] with Americans eating 1.1 billion pounds of peanut butter in 2007–2008 alone.[2] And it has become thoroughly woven into the American lexicon. The handle of the peanut butter wrench (used by competitive bicyclists to tighten old 15-millimeter crank bolts) is exactly the right size for scooping peanut butter out of a jar. Berea College in Kentucky has a luncheon lecture series called "Peanut Butter and Gender." In 2010 Louisiana fisherman and oysterman Raleigh Lasseigne's 200 acres of oyster beds were devastated by the British Petroleum oil spill following the explosion of its Deepwater Horizon drilling platform in the Gulf of Mexico. The oil was so thick in shallow water, Lasseigne said, that "you could pick it up with a stick and it looked like peanut butter coming out of there."[3]

George W. Bush supposedly ate a peanut butter and jelly sandwich every day in the White House,[4] causing *New York Times* columnist Maureen Dowd to imagine the scene at the Oval Office in the fall of 2006 when public support for the war against Iraq cratered after the release of the Iraq Study Group's report. "Henry the K lumbers up to the door," she wrote, "and in a low, Teutonic rumble says, 'It's time we stopped taking *care* of you and started *caring* about you. Would you like a peanut butter and jelly sandwich?' "[5]

The varieties of peanut butter available have expanded in recent years. But the peanut butter industry, like many sectors of the American economy, has become more concentrated. The numbers of farmers, shellers, manufacturers, brands, and small independent factories have all declined.

In the 1940s, there were between 400,000 and 500,000 peanut farmers in the United States; today there are perhaps 7,000 or 8,000.[6] And the falloff in the number of black farmers has been even more precipitous than among whites. White farmers have declined by 33 percent since the 1970s, but during that time 80 percent of black farmers went out of business,[7] presumably because they lacked the business contacts available to whites. While 14 percent of farmers were black at the turn of the twentieth century,[8] that figure had shrunk to 1.4 percent by 2002.[9]

Wendell Williams, a black farmer in Jackson County, Florida, grows peanuts and other crops. "Are black farmers an endangered species?" I asked him in the fall of 2008. He laughed. "They past endangered," he said, laughing again. "They really are."[10]

Today there are also fewer companies that remove the shells from peanuts. John Powell is executive director of the American Peanut Shellers Association. "Right now, we have eight member companies," he says. "There are about fourteen shellers left in the United States."[11] Back in the 1970s there were seventy or eighty. Just two of the surviving shellers—giants Birdsong and Golden—shell nearly three-quarters of the American peanut crop between them.[12]

The number of factories turning these peanuts into peanut butter has also declined. "Fifteen years ago, there were twenty or more small peanut butter plants throughout the peanut-growing regions of the South," says Ben Houston, who used to manage the now-shuttered Sessions peanut butter plant in Enterprise, Alabama. "But they all closed down, because they were unable to compete with the big plants. For the most part, there aren't any small plants left."[13] The Sessions plant was where Sorrells Pickard (see chapter 16) was made and Lee Zalben's Peanut Butter & Co. (see later in this chapter) got its start.

Often, when small peanut butter plants disappear, the brands they make disappear with them. But others stubbornly hang in there. When I met him in August 2006, Ben Houston had a jar of Bully brand peanut butter on the desk of his Sessions plant office. Made for Mississippi State University, it had the university's bulldog mascot on its label. When I spoke with Houston two years later, after the plant had shut down, I asked him who would make Bully now.

"I don't know," he said. "It was in such small quantities that we did it as a favor. We had already told them before we closed the plant that we could not make any more for them, because the lady would call up and order a couple of pallets [a small wooden platform used for stacking goods] and then turn around and call up and cancel it. The caps, the labels—everything was special. It was just a pain in the neck," he laughs. "I doubt anyone will do it anymore."[14] But the Web site of Mississippi State University's Cheese Store reveals that Bulldog peanut butter is still growling away.

At the end of 2011, Georgia had four peanut butter plants: the Peter Pan plant in Sylvester, Kroger's Tara Foods plant in Albany, Sanfilippo and Son in Bainbridge, and American Blanching in Fitzgerald. In Kentucky, the Jif plant was in Lexington and the Algood Food Company in Louisville. In Arkansas, the Skippy plant was in Little Rock. There were still peanut butter plants in North Carolina (Hampton Farms in Severn and Edenton, and Peanut Processors in Dublin), Florida (Sunshine Peanut Company in Jacksonville), Oklahoma (Clements Foods in Oklahoma City), and Texas (Peanut Processors in Sherman).

Outside the South, Sunland, in Portales, New Mexico, specialized in peanut butter made from Valencia peanuts. Golden Boy Foods had a plant in Blaine, Washington. In Fredonia, New York, Carriage House of Fredonia was still making William F. Buckley Jr.'s beloved Red Wing peanut butter. There were also manufacturers of boutique peanut butters such as Krema in Columbus, Ohio, and Koeze in Grand Rapids, Michigan. But that was just about it. It was a long way down from 1919, when practically every city in the United States with 30,000 people or more had its own peanut butter factory.

As many peanut butter factories disappear, so do the brands they produce. Craig Sonksen owns the Krema Group, which makes Krema and Crazy Richard's. "When I bought Krema in 1988, my objective was to go around and purchase all the regional natural peanut butter brands," he says. "Crazy Richard's, in Philadelphia, was our first purchase. (But) all those brands are gone. There was a drought in 1990–1991, and a lot of those brands disappeared."[15] Among them was W. B. Roddenbery of Cairo, Georgia, which made the Happy Kids brand. Another victim of that year's drought was Long's Ox-Heart peanut butter, made by the Oswego Candy Works of Oswego, New York.

When I say the market share of the Big Three has been creeping up at the expense of smaller brands of peanut butter, Sonksen says the same is true of the food business in general. "The grocery industry has changed so much," he says. "It's so hard for a small brand today—it doesn't matter if you're peanut butter or anything else. Food brokers represent companies who want to sell to grocery stores. There used to be food brokers in every market, hundreds of regional food brokers all over the country. You could go to one of those guys and they'd help you get into the stores. Well, that has consolidated. Today there are about three major food brokers. And they don't have the time of day for the small guy. That's part of why the small brands disappear."[16]

Even when there appears to be a diversity of brands, there can still be concentrated ownership behind them:

- Adams peanut butter, popular in the Northwest, was founded around the time of World War I in Tacoma, Washington, by Rex F. Adams, a former high school football star who succumbed to the 1918 Spanish flu epidemic.[17]
- Laura Scudder's, which gets a lot of shelf space in Southern California, was founded in 1926 by its namesake in Monterey Park, a San Gabriel Valley suburb of Los Angeles. A feminist pioneer who couldn't get her lone delivery truck insured by male insurance agents during the Great Depression, she turned to a female insurance agent, who later wound up insuring her entire fleet. Scudder also pioneered the use of cellophane bags to keep her potato chips and other products fresh.[18]
- Santa Cruz Organic may never have had anything to do with Santa Cruz (at least no one I spoke with at the Chamber of Commerce or the

University of California Santa Cruz Department of Economics knew anything about them), but it has a business office in Chico, in the Central Valley of Northern California.

Despite their diverse geographical and business roots, all these brands are now made by Smuckers, along with its Smuckers Natural brand, in a place detached from their origins: Smuckers' natural peanut butter plant in New Bethlehem, Pennsylvania.[19]

One sector of the peanut and peanut butter industries that hasn't become concentrated is the system of buying points where farmers take peanuts to have their quality assessed and price established. There are about 415 buying points across the South and Southwest, according to Tyron Spearman, executive director of the National Peanut Buying Points Association. Shellers Birdsong and Golden own about twenty each, for a combined total of 10 percent. Beyond that, he says, some owners may have five or six each, but that's it. Usually a farmer with a lot of acreage will own one, joining forces with several smaller farmers.

How have buying points resisted the trend toward concentration? "It's the independence of the farmer," Spearman says. "If he's a big farmer that's got a thousand acres of peanuts and he's got a buying point, he don't want you messing with it. And he gets a $40 a ton commission."[20]

★★★

Perhaps the largest plant outside of the Big Three that's still making peanut butter is Kroger's Tara Foods plant in Albany, Georgia. In addition to making peanut butter, it also produces sauces, extracts, cooking vinegars, wines, coffee syrups, and reconstituted lemon juice. Just as it makes a wide variety of foods, Tara also produces a wide variety of peanut butters. It's a custom formulator, meaning it produces peanut butters for different brands and labels, using up to forty-five formulas for everything from peanut butter in a jar to peanut butter as an ingredient in cookies, confections, and snacks.

Walt Albritton is the technical services manager at Tara. Affable, portly, good-natured, and sporting a brushy mustache, he looks a bit like the actor Wilford Brimley. "Jif and the other majors have one formula and they run that every day, every day, every day," he says. "We might run four or five formulas a day, which requires a lot of changing over."[21]

Tara's peanut butter is ubiquitous. "Everyone in the United States who eats peanut butter or products containing peanut butter has probably had peanut butter out of Tara Foods," Albritton says. At his request, I don't mention any of the brands it makes, but they would be instantly familiar to readers. Tara is the sole supplier to some of the major bakers and confectioners in the United States and is probably the largest exporter of peanut butter into Mexico and the European Union. It produces about 80 million pounds of peanut butter a year. As impressive as that sounds, it pales before the 190 million or so pounds supposedly produced by Jif.

Other than the inability of smaller factories to compete with larger ones, why have so many peanut butter plants fallen by the wayside? "Aging and the expense of rebuilding a plant," Albritton says. "To build a first-class peanut butter plant takes millions and millions of dollars. Most everything, if you do it right, is stainless steel or acid brick tile or epoxy paints. We just put a new roaster in, and it was about a $1.6 million project. We just put a new filler in on the peanut butter line—$350,000. And we're looking at a new capper; it's going to be almost a million-dollar project, just to put the jar lids on."

Tara has hung in there because of the volume of peanut butter it generates. "The margins are low, so you gotta crank it out," Albritton says. "This plant runs twenty-four/seven [of course, it's not always making peanut butter]. It's a delicate balance between keeping it going twenty-four/seven and pushing our capacity too hard." Part of that balance, he says, is keeping the plant clean while you try to generate a high volume of high-quality product.

"You have a huge sanitation issue at a peanut butter plant," he notes. "You get back into the raw nut area and you've got peanut meal on the floor, in the air. The peanut is an allergen, so you have to keep that contained. There's an old saying in our business: 'If you lose control of your sanitation, you will lose control of your quality.' Your better producers adhere to a high level of discipline. You can violate that sanitation and production balance for a while, but it will come back to haunt you."[22]

★★★

Moving down the production scale from Jif to Tara to boutique, the Koeze Company of Grand Rapids, Michigan, uses World War II–vintage equipment (when available) to produce its peanut butter on an almost hand-crafted basis. "Making peanut butter this way is like driving a 1955 Buick," Koeze creative director Martin Andree says. "It's as artisanal as food making gets. The roasters are similar to coffee roasters."[23]

Fourth-generation company head Jeff Koeze is natty in a sport jacket and bow tie. The Koeze Company was founded in 1910 by his great-grandfather Sibbele, who settled in the Grand Rapids area, a hub for Dutch migration to the United States. It has been making peanut butter since 1925, although in the 1970s and 1980s, it moved away from making artisanal peanut butter, serving instead as a custom formulator for major grocery chains. For several years, it got out of peanut butter altogether. But that changed in 2000.

"For our ninetieth anniversary, we decided as part of the celebration and marketing to bring back some of our favorite products from the past," Koeze says. "Peanut butter was the primary one. We sort of did it as a publicity stunt, and it just kept getting bigger and bigger. When it got picked up by Zingerman's, a foodie mecca in Ann Arbor, we thought, 'Maybe we've got something here.' "[24]

Koeze's Cream Nut peanut butter is one of the few peanut butters, if not the only one, to still use Virginia peanuts. Until the early 1970s, a mixture of Spanish and Virginias was the standard for quality peanut butter in the United States, until it was dethroned by Florunners. Why has Koeze stuck with Virginias? "If you were buying peanuts in the 1920s, you were buying Virginias, for the most part" he says. "We just kept doing it, 'cause we like 'em." Koeze feels Virginias have the best peanut flavor, but acknowledges his verdict may be the product of custom. "So much of our taste is a question of expectations," he says. "If you're eating handfuls of Virginia peanuts, then eat peanut butter made from Virginias, you're going to go, 'Wow, that really tastes like peanuts!' "

Just as it's unique in its use of Virginias, Koeze Cream Nut is also unique in its texture, which is neither creamy nor crunchy, but coarse or grainy, a consistency midway between the two. Rather than grinding its peanuts several times with a high-powered grinder, Koeze gives its peanuts a single coarse grind. "My own judgment is that modern, high-speed mills create a soupy kind of liquid that separates really quickly," he says. "So it's kind of a matter of taste. I think it's nice to have it kind of sticky and crunchy."

The machinery at the Koeze plant is rare and semi-antique. It uses barrel-style roasters that are still used to make coffee, rather than the giant assembly-line-style belt roasters used by major manufacturers. Koeze has a three-bag roaster, meaning it can roast three 100-pound sacks of peanuts at a time. Since a three-bag roaster takes twenty minutes to roast a load of peanuts, it can roast 900 pounds an hour, although Koeze says that number goes down to 750 pounds by the time you account for water evaporating in the roasting process and removal of the peanut skins.[25]

"I couldn't estimate what Smucker's [Jif] could do with their roaster," he says. "It wouldn't surprise me to see 10,000 pounds an hour or even 20,000 pounds. It depends on whether they run one or multiple roasters, how wide the belt is, and how many pounds they can spread out on it." After roasting its peanuts, the Koeze Company grinds them in an eight-inch-wide Bauer mill, which, he estimates, dates to the 1930s or 1940s. It took Koeze three years to find one, and he's still looking for another. Larger operations use Urschel dicers, which are thirty inches wide, much more powerful, and noisier; he compares their sound to screaming rats.

Driving a 1955 Buick instead of a 2013 Ferrari, Koeze has nonetheless seen sales take off. He sold about 25,000 jars in 2006, 50,000 in 2007, and 100,000 in 2008. The Koeze Company isn't as much of a boutique as it used to be.

★★★

In the past few decades, peanut butter has taken turns neither George Bayle nor John Harvey Kellogg could have imagined. There's now creamy, crunchy, and coarse or grainy peanut butter. You can find peanut butter made from runner peanuts and, with a bit of looking, from Virginias, Spanish, and Valencias. There's stabilized and unstabilized and, as a subset of unstabilized, organic. There are honey-roasted, low-salt, low-fat, and low-sugar peanut butters, peanut butter with omega-3 oil added, and with jelly added in. There's a dehydrated peanut butter known as PB2. There are small packages to go, packages you can squeeze peanut butter out of, and other shapes and sizes of containers as well. There are small peanut butter and honey sandwiches wrapped in their own pie-like crust (called, ironically, crustless). There's also a rainbow of flavored varieties (chocolate, bananas, and chili pepper, to name a few) which, as far as the U.S. Food and Drug Administration is concerned, aren't peanut butter at all but peanut spreads.

Until the early 1990s, *Consumer Reports* acknowledged only the creamy and crunchy styles of peanut butter. But in 1995, it tested six kinds of Skippy alone: creamy, super chunk, roasted honey-nut creamy, roasted honey-nut super chunk, reduced-fat creamy, and reduced-fat super chunk.[26] Industry observers peg the late 1980s and early 1990s as the time when, motivated by consumer health concerns, low-salt, low-fat, and low-sugar varieties began to appear. Kraft's Koogle, in 1975, was the grandfather of today's flavored spreads, with Jif's Smooth Sensations in 1999 the father.

For most varieties of peanut butter, sales are climbing as the result of distressed economic conditions since the fall 2008 stock market crash. Industry observers are divided as to whether this will require expanded plant capacity.

Don Taylor worked in quality control at Jif from 1957 through 1991. "Since I left," he says, "the progress they've made there, the amount they're able to manufacture now with fewer people. . . . They can put out millions and millions of cases and supply the entire world with Jif peanut butter, if they're so inclined. They were progressing toward that when I left. Now it just boggles my mind."[27]

But another industry observer has said new factories will be needed. Richard Barnhill is president of Mazur & Hockman, a peanut broker in Albany, Georgia. It negotiates the sale of raw peanuts from shellers to peanut butter manufacturers. "Peanut butter has been growing very strongly and continues to do so," he says. "I think we're currently pushing the capacity of our peanut butter production in the United States. In 2009 production grew about 90 million pounds. You do that for several years and we will be getting to the limits of our capability. Somebody either needs to expand a plant or build a new one. There hasn't been a new peanut butter plant in several years."[28] Barnhill's observation has been borne out, as Golden Boy Foods opened a plant to make peanut and almond butter in Troy, Alabama, in early 2012.[29]

"The demand is mostly domestic and mostly related to the economy," he continues. "In hard times, one of the first things that goes is eating out. You can take a family of four to Outback and spend $100 or go to the grocery store and spend $100 and eat for a week. Peanut butter is a key component in stretching that food dollar."[30]

★★★

Even with growing sales of peanut butter in jars, the U.S. market is so saturated that experts expect industry growth to come in three other areas: candies and confections, flavored peanut spreads, and therapeutic peanut paste.

Asked about her favorite way to eat peanut butter, a poster on seriouseats.com named techgirl replied, "I like my peanut butter covered in chocolate, and sealed in an orange wrapper with the word Reese's on it."[31] She's not alone: Reese's has made peanut butter cups since 1923. More obscurely, the Flavor Candy Company of Chicago in 1927 started to make "chicken bones," inch-long butterscotch shells stuffed with peanut butter and rolled in coconut. Clark and Zagnut candy bars have long been popular with the American public.

In recent years, Reese's has added more than a dozen peanut butter–chocolate confections. In addition to the traditional milk chocolate peanut butter cup, it now offers dark chocolate peanut butter cups, white chocolate peanut butter cups, large peanut butter cups, miniature peanut butter cups, four peanut butter cups to a package, and, for Easter, peanut butter eggs. There are also Reese's Pieces and several peanut-butter-laden candy bars. Along with Hershey's, which owns Reese's, other companies are diving in. "Look at all the peanut butter candies Hershey's has now—Fast Break, variations on it, and variations on the Reese's Peanut Butter Cup," says Don Koehler, executive director of the Georgia Peanut Commission. "You've got Mars now with peanut butter M&Ms."[32]

Flavored peanut butter spreads, or what Walt Albritton calls exotics, are also a growth area. A leading producer is Peanut Butter & Co., in Manhattan's Greenwich Village, which makes peanut spreads with white chocolate, dark chocolate, cinnamon raisin, maple, honey, and hot spices, as well as both stabilized and unstabilized creamy and crunchy peanut butter. Owner Lee Zalben notes that as his business has grown, chocolate has replaced cinnamon raisin as his best seller. "We started off in the New York metro area, and I think cinnamon raisin is a flavor combination that is instantly recognizable to people here," he says. "But as we've expanded nationwide, the chocolate peanut butter flavor is a little more recognizable."[33]

Another leader in peanut spreads was P. B. Loco in the Minneapolis–St. Paul area, although it failed to ride the peanut-flavored-spread wave, closing in early 2010. Its spreads were flavored with bananas, chocolate chip cookie dough, dark chocolate, raspberry white chocolate, caramel apple,

The Simon and Garfunkel

A sandwich of the author's own devising.

1 whole wheat bagel
Peanut butter
Thin slab of mozzarella cheese
Olive oil
2–3 crimini or other small mushrooms
Pepper
Spinach
1 clove garlic, crushed
Parsley, sage, rosemary, and thyme
Slice of tomato
Slice of lemon

Cut bagel in half: spread peanut butter on one side, and put a slice of mozzarella on it.

Heat olive oil.

Cut up mushrooms, sauté in olive oil, and sprinkle with pepper.

Briefly add small amount of spinach to mushrooms while they're being sautéed, and sprinkle with pepper.

Drain excess oil from frying pan; put mushrooms and spinach on peanut butter–mozzarella side of bagel.

Spread crushed garlic on other half of bagel.

Sprinkle garlic side of bagel with parsley, sage, rosemary, and thyme.

Put tomato on peanut butter–mozzarella–vegetable side of bagel.

Squeeze lemon slice through strainer or colander onto both the spiced side and the peanut butter–mozzarella–vegetable side of bagel.*

Put sandwich together and cut in half.

★★★

Yield: 1 sandwich

* DEPENDING ON HOW MUCH LEMON JUICE YOU SQUEEZE ON IT, IT CAN GET A LITTLE MESSY, SO DON'T SERVE IT ON A FIRST DATE OR WHEN YOU HAVE THE BOSS OVER.

curry, and sun-dried tomato. Despite its distance from the Upper West Side, P. B. Loco also had a cinnamon raisin spread. Not everyone feels the love for flavored peanut spreads, however.

"I happen to be a big fan of both peanut butter and pickles and peanut butter and bacon. But I wouldn't ever buy peanut butter and pickle peanut butter," says Jeff Koeze. "If that's what I want, I'll just do it. Why do I need a whole jar of it? If I want cinnamon or bananas or whatever weird thing I want to add, like hot sauce or anchovies, I'm not going to buy a whole jar of it pre-mixed. Just at the concept level, I don't get it, but they must be doing okay, because they continue to sell them."[34] Similarly Marion Nestle, the Paulette Goddard Professor of Nutrition, Food Studies, and Public Health at New York University, says, "I'm a peanut butter purist. I want my peanut butter with precisely one ingredient: peanuts. I don't want added oils, hydrogenated or not, salt or sugar, let alone marshmallows or chocolate. The minute they start doing that, they turn a lovely food into a junk food."[35]

Plumpy'Nut and other therapeutic peanut pastes are another potential growth area for peanut butter, although that will depend on how successful Nutriset is in defending its patents against U.S. peanut processors eager to enter the market. UNICEF started buying Plumpy'Nut in small amounts in 2003; by 2008 it was buying 8,000 tons a year.[36] Nutriset's shipments of Plumpy'Nut tripled between 2007 and 2008 alone.[37] In 2009 its Plumpy'Nut sales were more than $70 million, most of it to UNICEF.[38] That's a lot of peanut butter.

★★★

Growth of the peanut butter industry will require a strong farm economy, but that may be in jeopardy in years to come.

As the South becomes increasingly urbanized, farming land disappears. Don Koehler points out that fewer and fewer congressional districts are rural, so Congress is less sensitive to the needs of farmers. "It's getting more and more difficult in Washington when you don't have the farm base anymore," he says. "In Georgia, we've got thirteen congressional districts. Four of them are rural and everything else touches Atlanta. Folks are going to get a shock as to the value that farm programs have been to consumers."[39]

When I first met retired farmer Stanley Pittman in the fall of 2006, he noted that as the price of land went up, farmers could make more money by selling it than by farming it. As this happened, he said, the United States would need to get more of its peanuts from abroad. But foreign farmers don't face the same restrictions American farmers do on noxious chemicals such as DDT. If this happens, peanut butter will contain chemicals that Americans haven't had to deal with in a long time.[40] Two years later, the southern real estate market had cooled off. But as population growth drives urbanization and farmland recedes, foreign peanuts may start looking increasingly good to peanut butter makers.

Another threat to the future of peanut butter comes from the current vogue for shrinking government, which has led to sharp funding and staff cuts to government agricultural research laboratories and the institutions of higher education they support. Wil Parker has fifty years of experience in the peanut and peanut butter industries in a variety of executive and technical posts.

"The creaminess, the spreadability, and the shelf life of [stabilized] peanut butter, the quality—all are probably superior to that of any time in the past," he says. "There really aren't many countries where the food quality compares with what we have in the United States. That goes directly back to government support through the Department of Agriculture to land-grant colleges and universities.

"In the old days, the Department of Agriculture was very active and had a lot of good science," he adds, pointing to USDA labs like the National Peanut Research Laboratory in Dawson, Georgia; the Southern Regional Research Center in New Orleans; and the National Agricultural Utilization Research Center in Peoria, Illinois. "It's not a priority like it was before, and that's a mistake," he says. "Because we are where we are because of the foresight of people who created that system."[41]

★★★

Also looming ahead is the brave new world of genetically modified peanut butter. Genetic modification takes place when scientists add genetic material from a different species to a plant or an animal, or overexpress or silence a gene already in it.

Of course, as retired plant breeder Dan Gorbet has pointed out, most stabilized peanut butter is already genetically modified.[42] The most common vegetable oils used to hydrogenate peanut butter are soy, cottonseed, and rapeseed or canola. As of 2001, 80 percent of soybeans and 68 percent of cotton grown in the United States were genetically modified.[43] But now the peanut industry is looking to genetically modify peanuts themselves.

In 2007 the peanut industry embarked on a $10 million, seven-year effort to complete the genetic mapping of peanuts.[44] The aim is to improve the resistance of peanuts to diseases and pests. "From a competitive standpoint alone, our industry needs genomics to compete within the agriculture industry," says Darleen Cowart, chairman of the Peanut Foundation, which is part of the American Peanut Council. "Other crops, like cotton, corn, and soybeans, are much further along in their genomic research."[45] But not everyone is sanguine about the prospect of peanut butter becoming more genetically modified than it already is.

Asked about a future that includes genetically modified peanut butter, Wil Parker pauses and says, "That's kind of an enigma. There's been a tremendous amount of progress in other crops. So it's almost inevitable it will happen." But, he adds, "There's really not much justification for it right now. They've done a lot of good work on peanut breeding without having to do that. High-oleic peanuts [which prolong peanut butter's shelf life by increasing the amount of slow-to-break-down oleic oil in peanuts] are a good example. That's been done through natural cross-breeding."[46] And Craig Sonksen, who sells the Krema Natural and Crazy Richard's brands, is even less enthusiastic. When asked how he'd feel about eating genetically modified peanut butter, he tersely says, "Don't want to do it."[47]

While peanut butter country looks forward to a brave new future, it still grapples with its past. In southwestern Georgia, there's both a Jefferson Davis Memorial Highway and a State Historic Site. There are signs for the Sons of the Confederacy and stores where you can buy Confederate regalia. The young black woman who gave me a tour of the Civil Rights Museum in Albany told me things are much better than they used to be, but they're not all the way there.

With all the changes in peanut butter's more than 100 years, one thing hasn't changed: Americans unfailingly turn to it for energy, flavor, and solace. "Peanut butter is the ultimate American comfort food," says Lee

Zalben. "We're introduced to it at a very young age. It's sort of a staple throughout our childhood, and as we grow up and get old, peanuts and peanut butter take us back to simpler, happier times. It's like a memory for your mouth."[48] And writer Norbert Blei assumes an almost mystical tone in describing peanut butter's primordial pull. "In days of distress, some men turn to martinis, other men to peanut butter," he says. "Some of the best times were peanut butter and jelly times. No other food, besides milk and cookies, brings back Mom, home, life in the kitchen in quite the same way. It goes beyond mere hunger and enters the realm of spiritual nourishment."[49]

Appendix One

AUTHOR'S RECOMMENDATIONS

Best-Tasting Overall
Arrowhead Mills Creamy Organic
Trader Joe's Crunchy Valencia with Roasted Flaxseeds

Best Crunchy
Krema Nut Company Natural Crunchy (Columbus, Ohio)
Trader Joe's Crunchy Valencia with Roasted Flaxseeds

Best Creamy
Arrowhead Mills Creamy Organic

Best Coarse/Grainy
Koeze Cream-Nut (Grand Rapids, Michigan)
Somis Nut House Natural Salted (Somis, California; production suspended at time of publication)

Best Using Spanish Peanuts
Krema Nut Company Natural Crunchy

Best Using Virginia Peanuts
Koeze Cream-Nut

Best Using Valencia Peanuts
Trader Joe's Crunchy Valencia with Roasted Flaxseeds
Arrowhead Mills Creamy Organic

Best Big Three Hydrogenated Creamy
Jif

Best Big Three Hydrogenated Crunchy
Peter Pan

Best Discount
Kirkland Natural Creamy (Costco house brand)

Best Alleged Natural (stabilized with fractionated palm oil)
Natural Directions Organic

Best International
Calve Pindakaas (Netherlands)
Mamba Encore (Haiti)

Most Intense Fresh-Peanut Aroma
Mamba Encore (Haiti)

Flavored (which makes it a peanut spread, not peanut butter)
No award given in this category, as the author is a peanut butter purist.

Peanut Butter and Jelly Combo
No award here, either: the one I tasted had an appallingly sludgy texture, and how much trouble is it really to open two different jars and spread the contents on a piece of bread?

Appendix Two

PEANUT BUTTER TIME LINE

1894	George Bayle allegedly begins to manufacture peanut butter in St. Louis.
1895 (November 4)	John Harvey Kellogg files the first patent on a peanut-butter-like substance.
1897 (April 13)	Kellogg's patent is granted.
1898	Joseph Lambert develops an early peanut butter mill.
1899	Two brands of peanut butter are being sold in New Haven, Connecticut.
1901	Joseph Lambert founds Lambert Food Company, selling both nut butters and the mills to make them.
1903	Ambrose Straub patents the second mill for grinding peanut butter.
1904	C. H. Sumner sells peanut butter from a booth at the St. Louis World's Fair, where many Americans taste it for the first time.

1904	Beech-Nut becomes the first national brand to sell peanut butter.
1908	Lambert Food Company is renamed Lambert Machine Company. It discontinues making nut butters and focuses exclusively on producing the machines that make it.
1909	Heinz becomes the second national brand to sell peanut butter.
1914	Twenty-one brands of peanut butter are being sold in Kansas.
1916–1919	The amount of peanut butter consumed in the United States during this period exceeds the total of all peanut butter previously consumed.
1921 (March 17)	Frank Stockton of Pittsburgh, Pennsylvania, files the first patent for hydrogenating peanut butter. His method calls for full hydrogenation.
1921 (April 5)	Joseph Rosenfield (later Rosefield) of Alameda, California, files the second patent for hydrogenating peanut butter. His method calls for partial hydrogenation.
1921 (November 1)	Stockton's patent is granted.
1923 (February 13)	Rosenfield's patent is granted.
1923	Heinz becomes the first major brand of peanut butter to be stabilized by hydrogenation, using the Frank Stockton patent for full hydrogenation.
1927 or 1928	Peter Pan is launched, becoming the second major brand of peanut butter to be stabilized by hydrogenation. It uses the Joseph Rosenfield (later Rosefield) patent for partial hydrogenation.
1932	As the result of a dispute with the Derby Foods Division of Swift, makers of Peter Pan, Joseph

	Rosefield stops licensing his patent for hydrogenating peanut butter to Derby and ends their business relationship.
1932	Leo Brown files a patent for a method of partially hydrogenating peanut butter. His method will be used by Peter Pan when it loses the right to license the Rosefield patent.
1933	Joseph Rosefield begins to produce Skippy peanut butter at the Rosefield Packing Company in Alameda, California. The date of first use is variously indicated as February 1, May 1, and August 8.
1933	Leo Brown's patent is granted; Peter Pan uses it after Joseph Rosefield withdraws his patent.
1935	Joseph Rosefield may have test-marketed the first crunchy peanut butter in Salt Lake City, Utah.
1942–1945	Peanut butter is included in the rations of American soldiers fighting overseas during World War II. GIs acquire a taste for it, return home, and feed it to their baby-boom children.
1946	William T. Young begins to manufacture Big Top peanut butter, the precursor of Jif, in Lexington, Kentucky.
1950	Heinz, which was the second national brand to sell peanut butter, stops doing so after forty-one years.
1955	Big Top peanut butter is purchased by Procter & Gamble.
1955	Best Foods buys the Rosefield Packing Company, makers of Skippy.
1956	Beech-Nut, the first national brand to sell peanut butter, stops doing so after fifty-two years.

1958	Procter & Gamble begins to make Jif, which has such a high concentration of hydrogenated vegetable oil (almost 25 percent) that the U.S. Food and Drug Administration says it has to be called a "peanut spread" rather than peanut butter.
1958	The Corn Products Company (later CPC) buys Skippy from Best Foods.
ca. 1958	Possibly as a result of Jif using vegetable oils other than peanut oil to stabilize peanut butter, other major brands stop using more-expensive peanut oil as a stabilizer. Soy, cottonseed, and canola or rapeseed oils become the three most common stabilizers for peanut butter.
1959	As a reaction to Jif's high percentage of hydrogenated vegetable oil, the U.S. Food and Drug Administration files a notice in the *Federal Register* stating its intent to establish a standard of identity under which peanut butter must contain a minimum of 95 percent peanuts.
1965 (November 1) – 1966 (March 15)	FDA hearings on a standard of identity for peanut butter last four and a half months and generate a record nearly 8,000 pages long.
1970	The Florunner, a runner peanut hybrid more prolific and tasty than previous runners, is released by the University of Florida, starting a shift from the use of mostly Spanish and Virginia peanuts in peanut butter to runners.
1970	Frank Ford brings Deaf Smith peanut butter to market, triggering a revival of natural or old-fashioned peanut butter and marking the first time Valencia peanuts are used in peanut butter.
1970 (December 14)	War between the FDA and the peanut butter industry, begun twelve years earlier, ends when

	the U.S. Supreme Court refuses to hear the peanut butter industry's appeal of the U.S. Court of Appeals for the Third Circuit's decision upholding a standard of identity under which peanut butter must contain at least 90 percent peanuts.
Early 1970s	First *Salmonella* contamination of Peter Pan, originating at Swift's Derby plant in Chicago. No casualty data available.
1974 (October 18)	The Corn Products Company, owner of Skippy, closes the original Skippy plant in Alameda, California.
1975	Kraft introduces Koogle, the first commercial flavored peanut spread, in four flavors: cinnamon, banana, chocolate, and vanilla. *Consumer Reports* turns thumbs down, saying, "Nutrition and taste argue against buying Koogle."
1976	Jimmy Carter is elected president, the first peanut farmer to hold the office since Thomas Jefferson.
1976 (February)	Elvis Presley and his retinue fly in his private jet from Memphis to Denver to dine on twenty-two orders of Fool's Gold Loaf, a monster sandwich made by a local restaurant consisting of hollowed-out bread spread thickly with peanut butter and blueberry jelly and filled with bacon. Plus drinks, of course. The order is delivered to them on the tarmac at Denver Airport. The price of an evening out: $16,000.
1980	Severe drought across the South decimates the peanut crop, precipitating a shortage of peanut butter.
1983	Swift sells Peter Pan to Esmark, a division of Hunt-Wesson Foods. Over the next seven years

	Peter Pan will change hands several times. In 1984 Hunt-Wesson sells it to Beatrice Foods; in 1986 Beatrice sells it to Kohlberg, Kravis, and Roberts; in 1990, Peter Pan is bought by ConAgra.
April 1987–August 1989	Jif becomes the first manufacturer of peanut butter to use plastic rather than glass jars.
1990	The Adult Peanut Butter Lovers Fan Club is formed by the Peanut Advisory Board, an industry trade group. The club will be disbanded by the board in 2002.
1995	CPC spins off Best Foods, makers of Skippy. Best Foods is now an autonomous company.
1996	The peanut industry responds to growing health concerns about peanut products by creating the Peanut Institute, dedicated to sponsoring research about and publicizing healthy aspects of peanuts and peanut butter. Within a few years, the decline in sales of peanut butter is reversed.
1999	Plumpy'Nut, a food based on peanut butter that proves useful in famine relief, is developed by French pediatric nutritionist Andre Briend and Michel Lescanne, the head of Nutriset.
2000	Anglo-Dutch conglomerate Unilever buys Best Foods, makers of Skippy.
2001 (October 10)	Procter & Gamble sells Jif to Smuckers in a sale that will be completed in early 2002.
2006 (August)	Cases of *Salmonella* poisoning from peanut butter appear around the country. They will be traced to the Peter Pan plant in Sylvester, Georgia.
2007 (February)	A second Peter Pan *Salmonella* contamination is confirmed; a recall is issued for it and Walmart's

	Great Value peanut butter. There are 714 confirmed cases of *Salmonella* connected with the outbreak, with four deaths believed to be connected to it.
2008 (September)	First cases of *Salmonella* that will later be traced to plants owned by the Peanut Corporation of America in Blakely, Georgia, and Plainview, Texas, begin appearing around the country.
2009 (February)	*Salmonella* contamination of peanut butter products made by the Peanut Corporation of America sparks the largest food recall in American history. There are 9 deaths and more than 700 cases. PCA owner Stewart Parnell pleads the Fifth Amendment when called upon to testify before Congress about the outbreak.
2010 (May)	Parkers Farm of Coon Rapids, Minnesota, recalls its peanut butter, salsa, and spreadable cheddar cheese because of contamination by virulent *Listeria monocytogenes.*
2010 (November 13)	The world's largest peanut butter and jelly sandwich, weighing 1,342 pounds, is made at the Great American Peanut Butter Festival in Grand Saline, Texas. It contains 292 pounds of peanut butter, 340 pounds of grape jelly, and 710 pounds of bread.
2011	Drought in the South leads to a peanut shortage and higher peanut butter prices in 2011–2012.

NOTES

1. PEANUTS 101

1. Much of the information in this paragraph comes from the articles "Fall Line" by Mack S. Duncan and "Coastal Plain Geologic Province" by William J. Frazier, *New Georgia Encyclopedia*, www.georgiaencyclopedia.org (accessed May 9, 2009).
2. "Peanut Butter," *Consumer Bulletin*, September 1962, 13.
3. Antonio Krapovickas, "The Origin, Variability, and Spread of the Groundnut (*Arachis hypogaea*)," in *The Domestication and Exploitation of Plants and Animals*, ed. Peter Ucko and G. W. Dimbledy (Chicago: Aldine-Atherton, 1969), 427.
4. Ibid., 429.
5. Ibid., 438.
6. David A. Knauft, Allan J. Norden, and Daniel W. Gorbet, "Peanut," in Walter R. Fehr, *Principles of Cultivar Development*, vol. 2, *Crop Species* (New York: Macmillan, 1987), 346.
7. Until the early 1970s, when they began to be supplanted by runners.
8. Krapovickas, "Origin, Variability, and Spread of the Groundnut," 438.
9. Ibid.; see also 440n62.
10. Ray O. Hammons, "Early History and Origin of the Peanut," in *Peanuts: Culture and Uses* (Roanoke, Va.: Stone, 1973), 31.
11. "Peanut" entry in the *Encyclopedia Americana* , vol. 21 (Danbury, Conn.: Grolier, 2003), 574.
12. Andrew F. Smith, *Peanuts: The Illustrious History of the Goober Pea* (Urbana: University of Illinois Press, 2002), 6.

13. Charles Micucci, *The Life and Times of the Peanut* (Boston: Houghton Mifflin, 1997), 20.
14. David Grunwald, "'Okay, Skippy,' Said Peter Pan. 'I'll Be Ready in a Jif'," *American Way*, April 1977, 33.
15. Jasper Guy Woodroof, *Peanuts: Production, Processing, Products* (Westport, Conn.: AVI, 1983), 181.
16. "Gold Filling," a brief history of peanut butter in the Peanut Butter Lovers' newsletter, distributed by the Peanut Advisory Board (now Southern Peanut Growers), ca. 1999, copy in possession of the author.
17. Krapovickas, "Origin, Variability, and Spread of the Groundnut," 437.
18. Ray O. Hammons, "Origin and Early History of the Peanut," in *Peanut Science and Technology*, ed. Harold E. Pattee and Clyde T. Young (Yoakum, Tex.: American Peanut Research and Education Society, 1982), 3.
19. Andrew F. Smith, interview with the author, August 7, 2006.
20. Krapovickas, "Origin, Variability, and Spread of the Groundnut," 437; Hammons, "Early History and Origin of the Peanut," 35.
21. Krapovickas, "Origin, Variability, and Spread of the Groundnut," 437.
22. "Peanut" entry in *Encyclopedia Americana*, vol. 21 (2003), 573.
23. *USA Peanuts* (Alexandria, Va.: American Peanut Council, n.d.), copy in possession of the author.
24. H. H. Mottern, "Peanuts and Human Nutrition," in *Peanuts: Culture and Uses* (Roanoke, Va.: Stone, 1973), 594.
25. The page "Nutrition Basics/Peanuts: Mother Nature's Whole Food" at www.peanut-institute.org (accessed April 16, 2008) indicates that one ounce of dry-roasted salted peanuts contains 7 grams of monounsaturated fat, 4.5 grams of polyunsaturated fat, and 2 grams of saturated fat.
26. Mottern, "Peanuts and Human Nutrition," 594.
27. Ibid.; William Cobb and Bobby Johnson, "Physicochemical Properties of Peanuts," in *Peanuts: Culture and Uses* (Roanoke, Va.: Stone, 1973), 235.
28. Tim Sanders, interview with the author, August 11, 2008.
29. "Peanuts," en.wikipedia.org (accessed February 15, 2010).
30. "Peanut" entry in the *Encyclopedia Britannica*, vol. 21 (1973), 502.
31. According to Dr. Scott Sicherer (e-mail to the author, July 2, 2010), six-tenths of 1 percent of Americans suffer from peanut allergies.
32. Andrew F. Smith, e-mail to the author, February 20, 2010.
33. Cobb and Johnson, "Physicochemical Properties of Peanuts," 242.
34. Entry on "Maillard reaction" from www.answers.com (accessed September 8, 2008).
35. Ben Houston, interview with the author, October 2, 2006.
36. Micucci, *Life and Times of the Peanut*, 17; "Peanut" entry in *Encyclopedia Americana*, vol. 21 (2003), 573.
37. Micucci, *Life and Times of the Peanut*, 24.
38. Krapovickas, "Origin, Variability, and Spread of the Groundnut," 436.

39. Hammons, "Early History and Origin of the Peanut," 37.
40. Smith, *Peanuts*, 5.
41. Hammons, "Early History and Origin of the Peanut," 21.
42. Information on percentages of the four U.S. market types of peanut within the U.S. crop as a whole is taken from an exhibit in "The Great American Peanut Tour" vehicle at the National Peanut Museum in Tifton, Ga., visited September 9, 2008.
43. "Peanuts" entry in *New Georgia Encyclopedia*, www.georgiaencyclopedia.org (accessed February 22, 2010).
44. Jeff Koeze, interview with the author, February 27, 2009.
45. "Peanut Butter: Sandwich Spread or Meat Substitute?," *Consumers' Research Bulletin*, March 1945, 12.
46. Brian Giunta, interview with the author, August 4, 2006.
47. Mike Kubicek, interview with the author, July 21, 2009.
48. Most if not all natural or old-fashioned peanut butters are sugar-free; calling a natural peanut butter sugar-free as a marketing device makes as much sense as calling it "pixie-dust free" or "plutonium-free."
49. Dan Gorbet, interviews with the author, December 4, 2007, and September 29, 2008.
50. Frank Delfino, interview with the author, July 23, 2008.
51. George Speck, interview with the author, January 23, 2009.
52. Kubicek, interview.
53. John Gretz, interview with the author, August 19, 2008.
54. John L. Hess and Karen Hess, *The Taste of America* (Urbana: University of Illinois Press, 2000), 18.
55. Stanley Pittman, interview with the author, July 8, 2008.

2. THE SOCIAL RISE OF THE PEANUT

1. Don Koehler, interview with the author, October 1, 2008.
2. A list of other peanut monuments throughout the peanut-growing regions of the South, such as the World's Largest Peanut in Ashburn, Georgia, and a statue and time capsule in Durant, Oklahoma, can be found in Andrew F. Smith, *Peanuts: The Illustrious History of the Goober Pea* (Urbana: University of Illinois Press, 2002), 125.
3. Shelley Brigman, "Monument Dedicated to an Insect," *Enterprise Ledger* (1919), on display in the Depot Museum in Enterprise, Alabama.
4. State percentages are from the chart "U.S. and All States Data: Peanuts for Nuts, 2005–2009," USDA National Agricultural Statistics Service. I used the 2009 figures for my computations.
5. J. Frank McGill, "Economic Importance of Peanuts," in *Peanuts: Culture and Uses* (Roanoke, Va.: Stone, 1973), 3.

6. "U.S. Peanut Supply," in *USA Peanuts* (Alexandria, Va.: American Peanut Council, n.d.), copy in possession of the author.
7. Ray O. Hammons, "Origin and Early History of the Peanut," in *Peanut Science and Technology*, ed. Harold E. Pattee and Clyde T. Young (Yoakum, Tex.: American Peanut Research and Education Society, 1982), 16.
8. "Jackson County, Florida," en.wikipedia.org (accessed February 15, 2011).
9. "Manhattan," en.wikipedia.org (accessed February 15, 2011).
10. Stanley Pittman, interview with the author, July 17, 2006.
11. Walt Albritton, interview with the author, October 3, 2008.
12. Stanley Pittman, interview with the author, September 27, 2008.
13. Ben Houston, interview with the author, October 2, 2006.
14. Wendell Williams, interview with the author, January 8, 2007.
15. Wendell Williams, interview with the author, September 29, 2008.
16. Information about Birdsong is from Gregg Grimsley, interview with the author, October 2, 2008.
17. Ibid.
18. "Georgia Peanut Processor Cited for 41 OSHA Violations," *Reliable Plant Magazine and Lean Manufacturing Journal*, www.reliableplant.com (accessed February 15, 2010).
19. "ERS USDA Briefing Room—Corn," http://www.ers.usda.gov/Briefing/Corn/ (accessed February 15, 2011); John Pocock, "80 Million Soybean Acres Possible for 2009," www.cornandsoybeandigest.com, December 18, 2008.
20. "USDA: 15.6 Million Acres of Cotton; Record Soybean Acreage," *Delta Farm Press*, March 30, 2001.
21. Barry Tillman, interview with the author, October 3, 2006.
22. Smith, *Peanuts*, 19.
23. J. Ernest Wrenn, *A History of Peanuts in Virginia* (self-published, 2006), 2 and 4, copy in possession of the author.
24. Smith, *Peanuts*, 20.
25. Ibid., 19.
26. Ibid., 28.
27. Ibid., 28–29.
28. "Social Rise of the Peanut," *Good Housekeeping*, December 1902, 468.

3. THE BIRTH OF PEANUT BUTTER

A very thorough discussion of the early days of peanut butter can be found in Andrew F. Smith, "Doctors and Vegetarians," in *Peanuts: The Illustrious History of the Goober Pea* (Urbana: University of Illinois Press, 2002), chap. 4.

1. See, for example, W. R. Beattie, *Peanut Butter*, Circular no. 98 (Washington, D.C.: U.S. Department of Agriculture, Bureau of Plant Industry, 1912), 4: "Peanut butter having the proper consistency contains about 41 or 42 percent

fat. . . . The Virginia, or Jumbo, type contains about the proper proportion of fat, but several manufacturers are adding some Spanish peanuts to give the product the desired smoothness." See also "Peanut Butter: Sandwich Spread or Meat Substitute?" in the March 1945 issue of *Consumers' Research Bulletin*, 12: "The best peanut butter is considered by the trade to be that made from No. 1 Virginia-type peanuts and No. 1 Spanish-type peanuts."

2. Jerome Rosefield, testimony before the FDA's 1965–1966 hearings on a standard of identity for peanut butter (FDC-76, 4099), January 5, 1966, Accession No. 088-74-0002, boxes 1–11, hearing transcripts, boxes 1–3, National Archives and Records Administration, College Park, Md.
3. Woodroof, Thompson, and Cecil, "Peanut Butter Improved by Changing Flavor and Texture," *Food Industries* magazine, April 1946, cited in testimony of Prince Harrill, chemist for the U.S. Food and Drug Administration, November 1, 1965, before the FDA's 1965–1966 hearings on a standard of identity for peanut butter (FDC-76, 345).
4. Bill Brown, procurement manager for the J. M. Smucker Company, speaking at the Southern Peanut Growers Conference in Panama City Beach, Florida, July 19, 2005, said creamy was 80 percent of the market, crunchy 20 percent. According to an e-mail sent to me by Leslie Wagner of the Southern Peanut Growers on June 17, 2011, Brown has revised crunchy's percentage of the market downward to 17 percent. His assessments are probably authoritative, but here are some other figures: according to an article from *Weight Watchers* magazine cited in the Winter 1997 issue of "Spread the News," distributed by the Peanut Advisory Board (now Southern Peanut Growers), 60 percent of peanut butter eaten in the United States was creamy and 40 percent crunchy. Going back farther in time, Larry and Honey Zisman said that creamy was 70 percent of the market and crunchy 30 percent in their *Great American Peanut Butter Cookbook* (New York: St. Martin's Press, 1985), 46.
5. Jerome Rosefield, when he testified on January 5, 1966, before the FDA hearings on a standard of identity for peanut butter (FDC-76, 4208), said Skippy introduced chunky in 1936 or 1937. But he admitted his memory for dates was faulty. I peg it at 1935 because that year a plaintiff suing Skippy for trademark infringement had his lawyer write to the L. O. Taft Company of Salt Lake City, asking the company to cease and desist from handling Skippy peanut butter. Skippy test-marketed chunky in Salt Lake City; it's my theory that publicity from the test-marketing brought Taft's distribution of Skippy to the attention of the plaintiff.
6. A. P. Grohens, "Manufacturers of Peanut Butter," *The Peanut Promoter*, vol. 2, no. 7 (1919), 43.
7. "Peanut Butter," *Consumer Reports*, June 1957, 276.
8. Jeff Koeze, interview with the author, February 27, 2009.
9. Michael Mullen, director of global corporate affairs for the H. J. Heinz Company, e-mail to the author, February 26, 2007.

10. Lavina C. Wilson, *Bartlett Arkell's Beech-Nut Packing Company* (Palatine Bridge, N.Y.: Desktop Publications, 2007), 37.
11. Smith, *Peanuts*, 30.
12. Andrew F. Smith, interview with the author, August 7, 2006.
13. Ibid.
14. All the information in this paragraph is from Smith, *Peanuts*, 34.
15. Patricia Harris, David Lyon, and Sue McLaughlin, *The Meaning of Food* (Guilford, Conn.: Globe Pequot, 2005), 6.
16. Suman Bandrapalli, "How a PB&J Came to Be," *Christian Science Monitor*, March 3, 1998.
17. George Jones, *My First Book of How Things Are Made* (New York: Scholastic, 1995), 20.
18. *About the Seventh-Day Adventists* (pamphlet) (South Deerfield, Mass.: Channing Bete, 2004), 4.
19. Fundamental Belief No. 21 on the list of twenty-eight fundamental beliefs on the Web site of the Seventh-Day Adventist Church, www.adventist.org (accessed September 16, 2008).
20. Smith, interview with the author, August 7, 2006.
21. Ellen G. White, *Counsels on Diet and Foods* (Hagerstown, Md.: Review and Herald, 2001), 363.
22. "Ellen G. White," en.wikipedia.org (accessed March 20, 2009).
23. "Battle Creek Sanitarium," en.wikipedia.org (accessed February 27, 2010).
24. Ibid.
25. "Ellen G. White."
26. Barbara Kramer, *The Founders of Famous Food Companies* (Berkeley Heights, N.J.: Enslow, 2002), 21.
27. Richard Allin, "Still Made in the U.S.," *Arkansas Democrat-Gazette* (Little Rock, Ark.), September 19, 2002.
28. Richard W. Schwarz, *John Harvey Kellogg, M.D.* (Nashville: Southern Publishing, 1970), 120.
29. John H. Kellogg, Food compound, US Patent 567,901, filed on November 4, 1895.
30. John H. Kellogg, Process of preparing nutmeal, US Patent 580,787, filed in 1897; John H. Kellogg, Process of producing alimentary products, US Patent 604,493, filed in 1898.
31. Smith, *Peanuts*, 32.
32. Heidi M. Steinhauer, review of *The Road to Wellville*, by T. Coraghessan Boyle, *School Library Journal*, October 1993, 166.
33. Michael Pollan, *The Omnivore's Dilemma* (New York: Penguin, 2006), 299.
34. "Battle Creek Sanitarium."
35. Pollan, *Omnivore's Dilemma*, 299.
36. "Battle Creek Sanitarium."
37. *The Golden Interlude, 1900–1910* (Alexandria, Va.: Time-Life Books, 1992), 146.

38. "Peanut Business Sold," *Washington Post,* August 14, 1921.
39. Prince Harrill, citing unnamed article in *Food Packer* magazine of March 1958, in testimony before the FDA's 1965–1966 hearings (FDC-76, 342).
40. Dr. Bernice B. Elkin, interview with the author, March 26, 2010.
41. Matthew Gilmore of the District of Columbia Department of Consumer and Regulatory Affairs, e-mails to the author, November 30, 2009, and December 2, 2009, citing Dr. Schindler's entries from 1919 and 1921 Washington, D.C., city directories.
42. "Willard Scott," muppet.wikia.com/wiki/Muppet_Wiki (accessed June 13, 2008).
43. John L. Hess and Karen Hess, *The Taste of America* (Urbana: University of Illinois Press, 2000), 7.
44. "The First Peanut Butter," *The Peanut Promoter,* April 1920, 84.
45. "Necrology: Death of Geo. A. Bayle, Sr., Well-Known Peanut Products Man," *The Peanut Promoter,* February 1922, 48.
46. See, for example, George A. Bayle Company display ad in *The Peanut Promoter,* November 1921, 63.
47. At www.peanutbutterlovers.com, click on "PB Lovers" then "PB 101," then "History": "1890: A St. Louis physician developed the idea of packaging peanut paste for people with bad teeth" (accessed April 11, 2012). A previous version of this, accessed on July 19, 2006, read, "In 1890, an unknown St. Louis physician supposedly encouraged the owner of a food products company, George A. Bayle Jr., to process and package ground peanut paste as a nutritious protein substitute for people with poor teeth who couldn't chew meat."
48. "The First Peanut Butter," 84.
49. C. A. A. Utt, "Some Data About Peanut Butter," *Journal of Industrial and Engineering Chemistry* 6, no. 9 (1914): 746.
50. *St. Louis Spectator: Representative Professional, Banking, Manufacturing and Wholesale Interests of St. Louis,* 1891. On file at the Missouri Historical Society in St. Louis.
51. "Necrology," *The Peanut Promoter,* February 1922, 48.
52. "The First Peanut Butter," 84.
53. Smith, *Peanuts,* 33; Andrew F. Smith, e-mail to the author, July 31, 2009.
54. Ray O. Hammons, "Early History and Origin of the Peanut," in *Peanuts: Culture and Uses* (Roanoke, Va.: Stone, 1973), 36.
55. "Who Really Invented Peanut Butter?," *Battle Creek Enquirer & News,* March 29, 1990.
56. Jasper Guy Woodroof, *Peanuts: Production, Processing, Products* (Westport, Conn.: AVI, 1983), 182.
57. "Who Really Invented Peanut Butter?"
58. Suzanne Corbett, interview with the author, March 1, 2007.
59. Smith, *Peanuts,* 38.
60. Ibid., 37.

61. Display ad for Quaker City peanut butter mills, *The Peanut Promoter*, July 1921, 11.
62. *The Golden Interlude, 1900–1910*, 198.
63. Smith, *Peanuts*, 37.
64. Pamela J. Vaccaro, *Beyond the Ice Cream Cone: The Whole Scoop About Food at the 1904 World's Fair* (St. Louis: Enid Press, 2004), 119.
65. Smith, *Peanuts*, 35; "Sliced Bread," en.wikipedia.org. (accessed May 17, 2008).
66. Don Koehler, interview with the author, October 1, 2008.
67. Beech-Nut Centennial Committee, *Beech-Nut: 100 Years of Quality* (Canajoharie, N.Y.: Jostens, 1991), 67.
68. "Bessie Beech-Nut" display ad in Wilson, *Bartlett Arkell's Beech-Nut Packing Company*, 40.
69. Mullen, e-mail to the author.
70. Starting in 1923, some Heinz butter labels noted they were stabilized using a patent issued on November 1, 1921, the date Frank Stockton of Pittsburgh was awarded Patent No. 1,395,934, Food product, for stabilizing peanut butter by means of full hydrogenation. Some Heinz peanut butter labels that year bear the date of the Stockton patent, while others don't, suggesting that Heinz sold both stabilized and unstabilized peanut butter that year. By 1924, though, all of its peanut butters were stabilized. Labels are in the collection of the library and archives division of the Historical Society of Western Pennsylvania in Pittsburgh.
71. Mullen, e-mail to the author.
72. Brian Giunta, interview with the author, August 23, 2006.
73. "The History of Peanut Butter," http://www.kitchenproject.com/history/PBJ/peanutbutter.htm (accessed March 8, 2010).
74. Tom Charlier, "Bedeviling Bug's Legacy Still Haunts the South," *Memphis Commercial-Appeal*, November 11, 2007.
75. Ibid.
76. Ibid.
77. "Science Raises the Lowly Peanut to Eminence," *Current Opinion*, July 1923, 92.
78. "Goober Wizard: Negro Scientist Turns Peanuts into Vital Crop for Dixie Farmers," *Literary Digest*, June 12, 1937, 20.
79. George W. Carver, *How to Grow the Peanut and 105 Ways of Preparing It for Human Consumption*, 7th ed. (Tuskegee, Ala.: Tuskegee Institute, 1940), 3.
80. Ibid., 4.
81. John Beasley, e-mail to the author, March 12, 2010.
82. Smith, *Peanuts*, 94.
83. William F. Buckley Jr., "In the Thrall of an Addiction," *National Review*, May 1, 1981, 509.
84. Barry Mackintosh, "George Washington Carver and the Peanut: New Light on a Much-Loved Myth," *American Heritage*, August 1977, 66.
85. Ibid.

86. Ibid.
87. Shelley Brigman, "Monument Dedicated to an Insect," *Enterprise Ledger* (1919), on display in the Depot Museum in Enterprise, Alabama.
88. Mackintosh, "George Washington Carver and the Peanut," 66.
89. Ibid.
90. "Goober Wizard," *Literary Digest*, June 12, 1937, 20.
91. Mackintosh, "George Washington Carver and the Peanut," 66.
92. Ibid.
93. John D. Garwood, "In Praise of Peanut Butter," *U.S. News & World Report*, June 30, 1986, 69.
94. Ibid.
95. Lester B. Colby, "20 'Peter Pans' Put Showmanship into Selling for Derby Foods," *Sales Management*, May 20, 1944, 26.
96. "Fed Peanut Diet Forcibly, So She Seeks Divorce," *The Peanut Promoter*, October 1921, 59.
97. Smith, *Peanuts*, 38.
98. I took 34 million pounds as the mid-range of 29 to 38 million pounds, which corresponds to the 1.2 to 1.6 million bushels of peanuts used in peanut butter that year as indicated by H. C. Thompson in *The Manufacture and Use of Peanut Butter*, Circular no. 128 (Washington, D.C.: U.S. Department of Agriculture, 1920). I multiplied the bushels by 30, as suggested in D. L. Wright, B. Tillman, and E. B. Whitty's article "Producing Peanuts for the Fresh (Green/Boiling) Market," http://edis.ifas.ufl.edu/ag194 (accessed December 31, 2008), which indicates that a bushel of Valencias weighs 30 to 35 pounds (a bushel of Spanish and Virginias, which were mostly used in making peanut butter then, weighs a bit less than Valencias); I multiplied that figure by eight-tenths to discard the shells, which aren't used in making peanut butter and which constitute about 20 percent of the peanut's weight.
99. Woodroof, *Peanuts*, 182.
100. Smith, *Peanuts*, 54.
101. Display ad, "A Hundred and One Recipes with Beech-Nut Peanut Butter," Wilson, *Bartlett Arkell's Beech-Nut Packing Company*, 41.
102. Smith, *Peanuts*, 89.
103. Ibid.
104. I took 158 million pounds as the mid-range of 6 to 8 million bushels used in peanut butter that year, as indicated by Thompson's *The Manufacture and Use of Peanut Butter*. The formula I used to compute this appears in note 98.
105. Grohens, "Manufacturers of Peanut Butter," 43.
106. J. L. Rosefield, "How Can We Increase the Consumption of Peanut Butter?," *The Peanut Journal*, December 7, 1923, 23.

4. PETER PAN

1. *Report of the Federal Trade Commission on the Meat-Packing Industry* (Washington, D.C.: Government Printing Office, 1919), 244–245.
2. C. A. A. Utt, "Some Data About Peanut Butter," *Journal of Industrial and Engineering Chemistry* 6, no. 9 (1914): 746.
3. "Frequently Asked Questions" page, www.peterpanpb.com/index.jsp (accessed December 21, 2007).
4. Deb Hermann, ConAgra spokeswoman, e-mail to the author, January 25, 2007. See also Joseph Nathan Kane, Steven Anzovin, and Janet Podell, *Famous First Facts: A Record of First Happenings, Discoveries, and Inventions in American History*, 5th ed. (New York: H. W. Wilson, 1997), 260, entry No. 3950; Jerome Rosefield, deposition, May 20, 1980, in *Skippy Inc. v. CPC International Inc.*, 15–16, copy of the deposition in possession of the author.
5. Marvin Rosefield, deposition, May 19, 1980, in *Skippy Inc. v. CPC International Inc.*, 8–9; Jerome Rosefield, deposition, May 20, 1980, in *Skippy Inc. v. CPC International Inc.*, 15–16; copies of both depositions in possession of the author.
6. On page 8 of his 1980 *Skippy v. CPC* deposition, Marvin Rosefield identified it as Dainty. But in Jerome Rosefield's testimony before the FDA's 1965–1966 hearings on a standard of identity for peanut butter (FDC-76, 4103–4104), January 5, 1966, he called it Delicia. Accession No. 088-74-0002, boxes 1–11, hearing transcripts, boxes 1–3, National Archives and Records Administration, College Park, Md.
7. A. P. Grohens, "Manufacturers of Peanut Butter," *The Peanut Promoter*, vol. 2, no. 7 (1919).
8. M. Sebrell, "Prohibition and Peanuts," *The Peanut Promoter*, December 1921.
9. "Professor Richard Burton Has Pronounced . . . ," *The Peanut Promoter*, April 1924, 7.
10. Lee Avera, testimony before the FDA's 1965–1966 hearings on a standard of identity for peanut butter (FDC-76, 4266).
11. "History" section of "Refrigerator" article, en.wikipedia.org (accessed August 21, 2009).
12. "Peanut Butter: Definitions and Standards of Identity," 32 *Federal Register* 17482, December 6, 1967.
13. See, for example, "Peanut Butter as We Know It," "History of Peanut Butter," www.peanutbutterlovers.com (accessed February 1, 2011).
14. Joseph Rosenfield, Peanut butter and process of manufacturing the same, US Patent 1,445,174, filed April 5, 1921, and issued February 13, 1923.
15. Jerome Rosefield, testimony before the FDA's 1965–1966 hearings (FDC-76, 4102).
16. Frank Stockton, Food product, US Patent 1,395,934, filed March 17, 1921, and issued November 1, 1921.

17. Ibid.
18. Frank Delfino, interview with the author, January 3, 2008.
19. Tim Gaus, e-mail to the author, June 26, 2009.
20. Michael Mullen, e-mail to the author, September 26, 2007.
21. Labels are in the collection of the library and archives division of the Historical Society of Western Pennsylvania in Pittsburgh. For 1923, some Heinz peanut butter labels bear the date of the Stockton patent, while others don't, suggesting that Heinz sold both stabilized and unstabilized peanut butter that year.
22. He went to work for the Rosefield Packing Company in 1926, originally in marketing, and moved to the technical side in about 1941. Avera held an executive research position for Rosefield Packing Company, Best Foods, and the Corn Products Company and was still professionally active in 1966.
23. Avera, testimony before the FDA's 1965–1966 hearings (FDC-76, 4264).
24. Frank Delfino, interview with the author, June 16, 2009.
25. Ibid.
26. Robert R. Allen, "Hydrogenation," in *Bailey's Industrial Oil and Fat Products*, vol. 2, 4th ed. (New York: John Wiley, 1982), 19, 66.
27. Chris Craney, interview with the author, July 10, 2009.
28. For a brief history of peanut butter, see Peanut Advisory Board (now the Southern Peanut Growers), "Gold Filling," *Peanut Butter Lovers* (newsletter), ca. 1999. Provided to the author by Leslie Wagner of the Southern Peanut Growers.
29. "History" section of "Hydrogenation" article, en.wikipedia.org (accessed July 7, 2009).
30. Allen, "Hydrogenation," 2.
31. "Peanut Butter: Sandwich Spread or Meat Substitute?," *Consumers' Research Bulletin*, March 1945, 12.
32. "Peanut Butter," *Consumer Bulletin*, September 1962, 13.
33. "Peanut Butter," *Consumer Reports*, August 1987, 475.
34. Dan Gorbet, interview with the author, December 4, 2007.
35. Dan Gorbet, interview with the author, September 29, 2008.
36. "Genetically Modified Food," www.answers.com (accessed November 8, 2010).
37. Ibid.
38. Angela Eward-Mangione, "Toss Timidity When Considering Trans Fats," *New Times Naturally*, May 2007, 20.
39. "USDA Study Says: Trans Fat Levels Are Not Detectable in Commercial Peanut Butter," *Food for Thought*, vol. 10, no. 2 (n.d.), published by the Peanut Institute, www.peanut-institute.org.
40. Ibid.
41. Delfino, interview, January 3, 2008.
42. List retired as lead scientist from the U.S. Department of Agriculture's Northern Laboratory in Peoria, Illinois, and has a personal library of 500 books on fats and oils.

43. Gary List, interview with the author, June 1, 2009.
44. Michael Jacobson, interview with the author, June 3, 2009.
45. "Skippy Peanut Butter Tested Again," *Consumers' Research Bulletin*, October 1945, 12.
46. Frank Delfino, interview with the author, July 23, 2008.
47. "Palm Oil in Peanut Butter," *Tufts Health & Nutrition Letter*, October 2009, 1. The article cites a response from the American Palm Oil Council saying that the primary saturated fat in palm oil, palmitic acid, is different from other saturated fats and may actually improve blood cholesterol levels. Nonetheless, the Tufts article continues, the American Heart Association recommends only sparing use of palm oil. The article adds that palm kernel oil, which is produced from the seeds rather than the fruit of the palm tree, has an astonishing 86 percent saturated fat, mostly lauric acid.
48. Bill Brown, procurement manager for the J. M. Smucker Co., at the Southern Peanut Growers Conference, Panama City Beach, Fla., July 19, 2005.
49. Avera, testimony before the FDA's 1965–1966 hearings (FDC-76, 4307).
50. George Case obituary, *Chicago Daily Tribune*, July 25, 1931. Case died on July 24.
51. Jerome Rosefield, deposition, May 20, 1980, in *Skippy Inc. v. CPC International Inc.*
52. According to Jerome Rosefield's testimony before the FDA's 1965–1966 hearings, the last name of Case's successor was Beilfuss (FDC-76, 4169).
53. Jerome Rosefield, testimony before the FDA's 1965–1966 hearings (FDC-76, 4102).
54. Ibid., 4103; Rosefield is quoted as saying "January 31, 1932," but in light of the dates listed for when Rosefield stopped licensing his patent to Swift and when Rosefield Packing Company started to make its own hydrogenated peanut butter, 1933 seems more logical.
55. Ibid.
56. Leo Brown, Peanut butter, US Patent 1,926,369, filed June 17, 1932, and issued September 12, 1933.
57. "Lays Siege to Peanut Butter Market," *Printers Ink*, March 1940, 21.
58. "Famous Peter Pan Statue Is Desecrated in London," *New York Times*, August 23, 1928, 1.
59. Christine De Poortere, e-mail to the author, March 17, 2009.

5. HOW PETER PAN LOST ITS GROOVE

1. In addition to the examples cited in the text, see Janice Jorgensen, ed., *The Encyclopedia of Consumer Brands*, vol. 1, *Consumable Products* (Detroit: St. James Press, 1994). It has extensive entries on Jif and Skippy but not a word on Peter Pan.

2. Swift & Company annual reports are held in the collection of the Los Angeles Public Library, but some years are missing.
3. Gordon Winkler, "Making Peanut Butter Is Slick Work, Folks Say," *Chicago Tribune,* November 9, 1950.
4. Louis Franklin Swift biographical essay in *Dictionary of American Biography,* supplements 1–2, *To 1940* (New York: Charles Scribner's Sons, under the auspices of the American Council of Learned Societies, 1944–1958), reproduced in *Biography Resource Center* (Farmington Hills, Mich.: Gale, 2008).
5. "Packers and Stockyards Act," en.wikipedia.org (accessed August 1, 2009).
6. "Frequently Asked Questions," www.peterpanpb.com/index.jsp (accessed December 21, 2007).
7. Janie Ingalls, e-mails to the author, May 17, 2011, and May 19, 2011, citing the 1920 consent decree, *United States v. Swift and Others,* no. 37623, 967.
8. Lester B. Colby, "20 'Peter Pans' Put Showmanship into Selling for Derby Foods," *Sales Management,* May 20, 1944.
9. "Say When" article, www.oldtvtickets.com (accessed March 3, 2009). The commercial can be viewed on YouTube under the heading "Peter Pan Peanut Butter commercial blooper (early 60s)."
10. Terry Galanoy, "The Bald-Headed Girl and Other TV Commercials You'll Never See," *Chicago Tribune,* November 29, 1970.
11. Ibid.
12. "Peanut Butter," *Consumer Reports,* May 1972, 287.
13. Frank Delfino, interview with the author, October 24, 2007; Larry Shearon, interview with the author, November 7, 2008.
14. "Earlier Peanut Butter Contamination Kept Quiet," www.consumeraffairs .com, March 5, 2007 (accessed January 6, 2009).
15. "Multistate Outbreak of *Salmonella* Serotype Tennessee Infections Associated with Peanut Butter—United States, 2006–2007," June 1, 2007, 56(21); 521–524, Centers for Disease Control and Prevention, www.cdc.gov/mmwr /preview/mmwrhtml/mm5621a1.htm (accessed July 24, 2009).
16. The deed for the property was referenced and filed in the Office of the Tax Commissioner for Worth County, Georgia, on October 16, 1984. Thanks to Worth County Tax Commissioner (and former Peter Pan employee) Tabetha DuPriest.
17. The plant had opened just over twenty-one years earlier, according to Susan McCord, "ConAgra Plant Re-Opens," *Times-Herald* (Albany, Ga.), October 20, 2007.
18. Susan McCord, "Gentle New Plant Manager at Peter Pan," *Sylvester Local News,* February 2, 2005.
19. Elliott Minor, "Town Still Backs Plant," *Times-Herald,* March 8, 2007.
20. William Marler, interview with the author, August 20, 2008.
21. Marian Burros, "Who's Watching What We Eat?," *New York Times,* May 10, 2007.

22. Paul Krugman, "Fear of Eating," *New York Times*, May 21, 2007.
23. Sherry J. Walls, "Erin Brockovich Involved in ConAgra Lawsuit," *Sylvester Local News*, June 6, 2007. See also "Multistate Outbreak of *Salmonella* Serotype."
24. Burros, "Who's Watching What We Eat?"
25. Marler, interview.
26. Sherry J. Walls, "ConAgra Lawsuits in Settlement Process," *Sylvester Local News*, June 4, 2008.
27. William Marler, e-mail to the author, February 6, 2011; Josh Funk, "Peanut Butter *Salmonella* Cases Top 600," Associated Press, June 1, 2007.
28. "Residents Loyal to Local Peter Pan Plant," *New York Times*, March 8, 2007.
29. Walls, "ConAgra Lawsuits in Settlement Process."
30. "In Brief: Peanut Butter Bacteria Tied to Leaks at Plant," *Wall Street Journal*, April 6, 2007.
31. Walls, "Erin Brockovich Involved in ConAgra Lawsuit."
32. Michael Jacobson, interview with the author, June 3, 2009.
33. Krugman, "Fear of Eating."
34. "ConAgra Wants to Win Back Patrons," *Times-Herald*, August 7, 2007.
35. "It's Official Now. We Can't Go Back," *Sylvester Local News*, October 24, 2007.
36. Marler, interview.
37. "July 2002 ConAgra E. coli O157: H7 Recall and Outbreak," www.marlerblog.com (accessed August 21, 2009).
38. "Pot Pie Recall," www.firstcoastnews.com (accessed July 25, 2009).
39. Michele Morrone, *Poisons on Our Plates* (Westport, Conn.: Praeger, 2008), 59.
40. "Third Body Found in N.C. Slim Jim Plant Blast," *USA Today*, June 9, 2009.
41. Tina Neer, interview with the author, February 26, 2007. Despite her telling me this, she graciously responded to several subsequent e-mails from me.
42. Sherry Walls, interview with the author, October 2, 2008.
43. Ibid.
44. McCord, "ConAgra Plant Re-Opens."
45. "Nuts," *Modern Marvels*, History Channel, DVD (August 2, 2006), AAE-7687.
46. Susan Bond, interview with the author, January 19, 2009.
47. Jim Kirk and John Schmeltzer, "Old Enduring Brands Fight for Their Slice of the Market," *Chicago Tribune*, October 3, 2004.
48. George Lazarus, "Peter Pan Gets Taste of Jam Mart," *Chicago Tribune*, September 4, 1975.
49. "Top Individual Brands: Peanut Butter—Total U.S. F/D/MX, Latest 52 Weeks Ending August 13, 2006" (Chicago: Information Resources Inc. [IRI], 2006), copy in possession of the author.

6. SKIPPY

1. National Publishers Association ad, *National Nut News,* February 1932, 17.
2. William F. Buckley Jr., "In the Thrall of an Addiction," *National Review,* May 1, 1981, 509.
3. Brian Williams, "WFB," MSNBC's "Daily Nightly" blog, http://dailynightly.msnbc.msn.com, February 27, 2008 (accessed February 27, 2008).
4. Buckley, "In the Thrall of an Addiction," 509.
5. "Paper Tower," *Authors Guild Bulletin,* Summer 2008, 20.
6. "Skippy Grows Apace When Company Abandons 'Better Mousetrap' Theory," *Sales Management,* April 1, 1945, 60.
7. 1880 Census record for Manuel Rosenfield, Louisville, Ky.
8. We know this from newspaper accounts of the shooting of blacksmith Thomas Kendrick by John Rosenfield, Joseph Rosenfield's older brother. See, for example, "A Bad Man Gets His Just Desserts," *Morning Times* (Cripple Creek, Colo.), November 12, 1898.
9. "A Bad Man Gets His Just Desserts"; "Justified," *Victor (Colo.) Daily Times,* November 12, 1898; "Rosenfield Exonerated," *Morning Times,* November 13, 1898.
10. The notice in the *Daily Camera* (Boulder, Colo.), May 15, 1903, reads in full: "Rev. J. A. Davis on Wednesday, May 13, united in marriage here Joseph L. Rosenfield, of Pueblo, and Mary I. Call, of Cheyenne."
11. 1920 Census record for Joseph Rosefield, Alameda, Calif.
12. Suzanne T. Storar, "Nuts Over Skippy," *Alameda Magazine,* September–October 2003, 54.
13. Rick Rosefield, interview with the author, January 3, 2008.
14. Rick Rosefield, interview with the author, July 23, 2008.
15. Rosefield, interview, January 3, 2008.
16. According to Joseph Rosefield's November 9, 1958, obituary in the *San Francisco Chronicle,* he founded it in 1914; according to Jerome Rosefield's testimony before the FDA's 1965–1966 hearings on a standard of identity for peanut butter (FDC-76, 4100), January 5, 1966, it was 1915. Accession No. 088-74-0002, boxes 1–11, hearing transcripts, boxes 1–3, National Archives and Records Administration, College Park, Md.
17. George Mackin, interview with the author, December 11, 2007.
18. "Skippy Grows Apace."
19. Rick Rosefield, interview with the author, August 25, 2008.
20. Thomas Fuller, interview with the author, October 25, 2007.
21. Lee Avera, testimony before the FDA's 1965–1966 hearings on a standard of identity for peanut butter (FDC-76, 4333).
22. Mackin, interview.
23. Rick Rosefield, interview with the author, September 11, 2007.

24. Jerome Rosefield, testimony before the FDA's 1965–1966 hearings (FDC-76, 4097).
25. Frank Stockton, Food product, US Patent 1,395,934, filed March 17, 1921, and issued November 1, 1921.
26. Frank Delfino, interview with the author, October 24, 2007.
27. Jerome Rosefield, testimony before the FDA's 1965–1966 hearings (FDC-76, 4103–4104).
28. Marvin Rosefield, deposition, May 19, 1980, in *Skippy Inc. v. CPC International Inc.*, 8–9; Jerome Rosefield, deposition, May 20, 1980, in *Skippy Inc. v. CPC International Inc.*, 15–16; copies of both depositions in possession of the author.
29. Marvin Rosefield, deposition, May 19, 1980, in *Skippy Inc. v. CPC International Inc.*, 19–20.
30. Joseph L. Rosefield's (then Rosenfield) first patent, which was the basis for both Peter Pan and Skippy, was Peanut butter and process of manufacturing the same, US Patent 1,445,174, filed April 5, 1921, and issued February 13, 1923. The other nine patents are:

    Joseph Lewis [*sic*] Rosenfield, Peanut butter and process of manufacturing the same (reissue of previous), US Patent Re. 15,918, reissued September 23, 1924.

    Joseph L. Rosenfield, Peanut butter, US Patent 1,528,077, filed October 26, 1922, and issued March 3, 1925.

    Joseph L. Rosenfield, Nut-meat product and process of manufacturing the same, US Patent 1,716,152, filed November 10, 1924, and issued June 4, 1929.

    Joseph L. Rosenfield, Nut-meat product and process of producing same, US Patent 1,756,702, filed March 30, 1925, and issued April 29, 1930.

    J. L. Rosefield, Peanut butter package, US Patent 2,141,725, filed September 25, 1935, and issued December 27, 1938. (First patent with name spelled "Rosefield.")

    Joseph L. Rosefield and Fitzhugh L. Avera, Method of rendering flavors accessible in nut butters and the product obtained thereby, US Patent 2,402,915, filed November 6, 1944, and issued June 25, 1946.

    Joseph L. Rosefield, Jerome M. Rosefield, and Marvin Rosefield, Peanut butter and process of manufacturing the same, US Patent 2,397,564, filed October 7, 1942, and issued April 2, 1946.

    Fitzhugh L. Avera, assignor to Rosefield Packing Company, Stabilized peanut butter, US Patent 2,552,925, filed March 11, 1949, and issued May 15, 1951.

    Fitzhugh L. Avera, Process of preparing stabilized peanut butter, US Patent 2,688,554, filed December 23, 1950, and issued September 7, 1954.
31. Jerome Rosefield, testimony before the FDA's 1965–1966 hearings (FDC-76, 4159).
32. A plaintiff's attorney involved in a trademark infringement case against Skippy wrote to the L. O. Taft Company in August 1935 telling the company to desist from distributing Skippy peanut butter on the grounds that it was infringing

on his client's trademark. A copy of the letter is in the possession of the author.

33. Skippy introduced crunchy or chunk-style peanut butter at about this time, and Jerome Rosefield told the FDA hearings on a standard of identity for peanut butter in 1966 (FDC-76, 4208) that the test-marketing was done in Salt Lake City. It's my theory that the Taft Company came to the attention of the plaintiff and his lawyer because of publicity over the test-marketing of crunchy.
34. "Builders of Oakland: Skippy Peanut Butter" (advertisement by the Central Bank of Oakland), *Oakland Tribune,* October 25, 1948.
35. Jerome Rosefield, testimony before the FDA's 1965–1966 hearings (FDC-76, 4207–4208).
36. Jerome Rosefield's testimony before the FDA's 1965–1966 hearings (FDC-76, 4209): "The public liked it. I don't like it, it is not as spreadable, not as creamy, but Mrs. Housewife likes it."
37. *The Magic of Peanut Butter: 100 New & Favorite Recipes by Skippy* (New York: Sterling, 2005), 12.
38. Jerome Rosefield, testimony before the FDA's 1965–1966 hearings (FDC-76, 4208).
39. http://www.peanutbutter.com/history.asp (accessed December 11, 2006); *Magic of Peanut Butter,* 12.
40. Fred Keller, interview with the author, March 13, 2007.
41. Truman Capote, *Breakfast at Tiffany's* (New York: Signet/New American Library, 1958), 46.
42. Frank Delfino, interview with the author, January 3, 2008.
43. Jerome Rosefield, digest of deposition, May 20, 1980, in *Skippy Inc. v. CPC International Inc.* (210 USPQ 589, E. District, Alexandria, Va., 1980), 5.
44. "Skippy Grows Apace."
45. Jerome Rosefield, testimony before the FDA's 1965–1966 hearings (FDC-76, 4131–4132).
46. "Canners and Packers," in *Food Products Directory, the Blue Book of Food Packers* (1937–1938) (San Francisco: W. J. McCamman, 1937), 33.
47. "Canners and Packers," in *Food Products Directory, the Blue Book of Food Packers* (1942–1943) (San Francisco: W. J. McCamman, 1942), 37.
48. Bert Gannon, interview with the author, January 21, 2008.

7. SKIPPY ON TOP

1. Rosefield Packing Company Statement of Profit and Loss for the Three Years Ended December 31, 1949, copy in possession of the author.
2. "Builders of Oakland: Skippy Peanut Butter" (advertisement by the Central Bank of Oakland)," *Oakland Tribune,* October 25, 1948.

3. "New Whispering Sweepstakes to Push Skippy Peanut Butter," *Advertising Age*, May 27, 1963, 10.
4. Frank Delfino, interview with the author, October 24, 2007.
5. Rick Rosefield, interview with the author, January 3, 2008.
6. Suzanne T. Storar, "Nuts Over Skippy," *Alameda Magazine*, September–October 2003, 54.
7. "Rosefield Packing Co. Expanding Plant Facilities Here," *Alameda Times-Star*, November 28, 1949.
8. Jerome Rosefield, testimony before the FDA's 1965–1966 hearings on a standard of identity for peanut butter (FDC-76, 4131), January 5, 1966, Accession No. 088-74-0002, boxes 1–11, hearing transcripts, boxes 1–3, National Archives and Records Administration, College Park, Md.
9. Rosefield, interview.
10. Thomas Fuller, interview with the author, October 25, 2007.
11. Paul Kiely, interview with the author, July 31, 2008.
12. Rick Rosefield, interview with the author, September 11, 2007.
13. Delfino, interview.
14. "Rosefield Sold to Best Foods for $6 Million," *Alameda Times-Star*, December 21, 1954.
15. Rosefield, interview, September 11, 2007.
16. Jerome Rosefield, testimony before the FDA's 1965–1966 hearings (FDC-76, 4120–4121).
17. Delfino, interview.
18. Ibid.
19. "Skippy," in *Encyclopedia of Consumer Brands*, ed. Janice Jorgensen, vol. 1, *Consumable Products* (Detroit: St. James Press, 1994), 530.
20. "Hellman's and Best Foods," en.wikipedia.org (accessed January 17, 2011).
21. "Joseph L. Rosefield Dies at 75," *San Francisco Chronicle*, November 9, 1958.
22. Carl Bleier, interview with the author, September 30, 2008.
23. Frank Delfino, interview with the author, January 3, 2008.
24. Frank Delfino, interview with the author, July 23, 2008.
25. Paul G. Vigness, *Alameda Community Book* (Alameda, Calif.: A. H. Cawston, 1952), 115.
26. "Rosefield Packing Co. Expanding Plant Facilities Here."
27. Marc Albert, "Peanut Butter Jam Hits the West End," *Alameda Sun*, September 14, 2007.
28. "Plant Shuts Oct. 18," *Alameda Times-Star*, September 14, 1974.
29. Storar, "Nuts Over Skippy," 54.
30. Larry Shearon, interview with the author, November 7, 2008.
31. Bleier, interview.
32. Ibid.
33. Shearon, interview.
34. Bleier, interview.

35. Shearon, interview.
36. Ibid.
37. James Hirchak, interview with the author, August 18, 2008.
38. "In Our Own Back Yard," *Arkansas Democrat-Gazette* (Little Rock, Ark.), November 24, 2007.
39. Shearon, interview.
40. "Skippy," 530.
41. Hirchak, interview.
42. Delfino, interview, October 24, 2007.
43. "Hellman's and Best Foods."
44. Ibid.
45. Delfino, interview, January 3, 2008.
46. "Peanut Butter Plant Damaged," *Arkansas Democrat-Gazette*, December 5, 2003.
47. Richard Allin, "Still Made in the U.S.," *Arkansas Democrat-Gazette*, September 19, 2002.
48. The sequence of events in the last three paragraphs of this chapter played out over three months between early December 2006 and the end of February 2007.

8. JIF

1. Most of the information in this paragraph is from William T. Young Jr., interview with the author, July 9, 2008, and Young's e-mail to the author, November 16, 2009.
2. "Timeline: Major Events in the Life of W. T. Young," sidebar to "W. T. Young Dies," *Lexington Herald-Leader*, January 13, 2004.
3. W. D. Kenney and J. L. Shepherd, "Developing a Peanut Combine Harvester," *Proceedings of the Association of Southern Agricultural Workers*, Forty-seventh Annual Convention, Biloxi, Miss., February 9–11, 1950.
4. Stanley Pittman, interview with the author, September 28, 2008.
5. Bill Diehl, "Machine Promises Peanut Revolution," *Atlanta Constitution*, November 2, 1950.
6. John Johnson, interview with the author, November 16, 2010.
7. Vicki Myron, *Dewey: The Small-Town Library Cat Who Touched the World* (New York: Grand Central Publishing, 2008), 54.
8. Brenda Arlene Butler, *Are You Hungry Tonight? Elvis' Favorite Recipes* (New York: Gramercy Books, 1992), 7.
9. Jenna Milly, "A Hunka-Hunka Fried Peanut Butter," August 26, 2002, www.cnn.com/travel (accessed March 16, 2008).
10. "Elvis Presley's Grilled Peanut Butter and Banana Sandwich," www.splendidtable.publicradio.org (American Public Media) (accessed March 16, 2008).
11. "A Hunka-Hunka Fried Peanut Butter."

12. Karen Weis, research librarian at the National Agricultural Library in Beltsville, Md., e-mail to the author, October 9, 2009.
13. J. Frank McGill, "Economic Importance of Peanuts," in *Peanuts: Culture and Uses* (Roanoke, Va.: Stone, 1973), 10.
14. Al Silverman, "Everybody's Nuts About Peanut Butter," *Coronet*, September 1960, 145.
15. Karen Weis, research librarian at the National Agricultural Library in Beltsville, Md., e-mail to the author, December 14, 2009.
16. Diane Wagner, Procter & Gamble corporate archives, e-mail to the author, November 23, 2009.
17. Young, interview.
18. "W. T. Young Foods Acquired by P&G in Stock-Swap Deal," *Lexington Herald*, August 23, 1955.
19. Young, interview.
20. "W. T. Young Foods Acquired by P&G in Stock-Swap Deal."
21. Ted Woehrle, interview with the author, January 28, 2009.
22. Diane Wagner, Procter & Gamble corporate archives, e-mail to the author, December 2, 2009; includes the attachment "Procter & Gamble Stock Split History."
23. John Gretz, interview with the author, August 19, 2008.
24. Paul Kiely, interview with the author, July 31, 2008.
25. Andy Mead, "W. T. Young Dies," *Lexington Herald-Leader*, January 13, 2004.
26. Ibid.
27. Billy Reed, "At Age 76, W. T. Young Still a Master at Winning," *Lexington Herald-Leader*, October 11, 1994.
28. Mead, "W. T. Young Dies."
29. "Our Commitment" on "About Jif" page of www.jif.com (accessed January 25, 2012).
30. Lucile V. Bailey, "Procter-Gamble's Portsmouth-Made Peanut Butter Goes to Test Markets," *Norfolk Ledger-Dispatch*, March 5, 1957.
31. Frank Delfino, interview with the author, July 2, 2010.
32. William Covington, interview with the author, July 23, 2008.
33. David Guin, interview with the author, August 18, 2008.
34. Nicole Laflamme, archives coordinator for the J. M. Smucker Company, e-mail to Diane Wagner, Procter & Gamble corporate archives, January 20, 2010; forwarded to the author by Wagner.
35. Don Taylor, interview with the author, August 13, 2008.
36. Jerome Rosefield, testimony before the FDA's 1965–1966 hearings on a standard of identity for peanut butter (FDC-76, 4183), January 5, 1966, Accession No. 088-74-0002, boxes 1–11, hearing transcripts, boxes 1–3, National Archives and Records Administration, College Park, Md.
37. Taylor, interview.
38. "Peanut (?) Butter," *Consumer Reports*, October 1959, 511.

39. Bailey, "Procter-Gamble's Portsmouth-Made Peanut Butter Goes to Test Markets."
40. "Peanut (?) Butter," 511.
41. Ibid.
42. "Real Old-Fashioned Peanut Butter—It's Better for You," *Consumer Bulletin*, September 1959, 30.
43. Ibid.
44. Ibid.
45. "Jif," in *Encyclopedia of Consumer Brands*, vol. 1, *Consumable Products* (Detroit: St. James Press, 1994).
46. Department of Health, Education, and Welfare/Food and Drug Administration, "Peanut Butter; Notice of Proposal to Establish Definition and Standard of Identity," 24 *Federal Register* 5391, July 2, 1959.
47. Suzanne White Junod, "Food Standards in the United States: The Case of the Peanut Butter and Jelly Sandwich," in *Food, Science, Policy and Regulation in the Twentieth Century: International and Comparative Perspectives*, ed. David F. Smith and Jim Phillips (London: Routledge, 2000), 184.
48. Department of Health, Education, and Welfare/Food and Drug Administration, "Peanut Butter," 26 *Federal Register* 11209, November 28, 1961.
49. Department of Health, Education, and Welfare/Food and Drug Administration, "Peanut Butter: Stay of Order Establishing Identity Standard," 27 *Federal Register* 943, February 1, 1962.
50. Joseph C. Goulden, *The Super-Lawyers* (New York: Weybright and Talley, 1971), 186.
51. Department of Health, Education, and Welfare/Food and Drug Administration, "Peanut Butter: Stay of Order."
52. "Peanut Butter," *Consumer Bulletin*, September 1962, 13.
53. Department of Health, Education, and Welfare/Food and Drug Administration, "Peanut Butter; Definitions and Standard of Identity," 29 *Federal Register* 15173, November 10, 1964.
54. Department of Health, Education, and Welfare/Food and Drug Administration, "Peanut Butter; Definition and Standard of Identity," 30 *Federal Register* 8626, July 8, 1965.
55. Goulden, *The Super-Lawyers*, 187.
56. "A Sticky Issue," *Newsweek*, November 1, 1965, 70.
57. Carole Sugarman, "Veteran of the Peanut-Butter War," *Washington Post*, January 13, 1985.
58. Ernest A. Lotito, "Peanut Butter Hearing Has Nutty Start," *Washington Post*, November 2, 1965.
59. "Wives Win Point on Increasing the Peanuts in Peanut Butter," *New York Times*, November 2, 1965.
60. "Cancer Specialist Asks Rules on Peanut Butter," *New York Times*, February 8, 1966.

61. Lee Avera, testimony before the FDA's 1965–1966 hearings on a standard of identity for peanut butter (FDC-76, 4387).
62. Ibid.
63. Sugarman, "Veteran of the Peanut-Butter War."
64. Ibid.
65. Department of Health, Education, and Welfare/Food and Drug Administration, "Peanut Butter; Definition and Standard of Identity; Findings of Fact, Conclusions and Final Order," 33 *Federal Register* 10506, July 24, 1968.
66. Goulden, *The Super-Lawyers*, 187.
67. Ibid.
68. Ibid.
69. Jerome Rosefield, testimony before the FDA's 1965–1966 hearings (FDC-76, 4149).

9. "CHOOSY MOTHERS CHOOSE . . ."

1. Billie Jean Gibbons, interview with the author, August 14, 2008.
2. Rita Keys, interview with the author, July 20, 2008.
3. John Gretz, interview with the author, August 19, 2008.
4. Paul Kiely, interview with the author, July 31, 2008.
5. "Peanut Butter," *Consumer Reports*, October 1982, 522.
6. "Peanut Butter," *Consumer Reports*, August 1987, 475.
7. "The Nuttiest Peanut Butter," *Consumer Reports*, September 1990, 588.
8. "Peanut Butter: It's Not Just for Kids Anymore," *Consumer Reports*, September 1995, 576.
9. "A Better Butter?," *Consumer Reports*, May 2002, 24.
10. Dottie Bean, "American Favorite Made in Lexington," *Lexington Herald-Leader*, March 21, 1993.
11. Paul Prather, "Lexington Plant Makes It in a Jiff," *Lexington Herald-Leader*, September 25, 1989.
12. Kiely, interview.
13. Prather, "Lexington Plant Makes It in a Jiff."
14. Kiely, interview.
15. David Guin, interview with the author, August 18, 2008.
16. Cheryl Truman, "That Nutty Neighbor," *Lexington Herald-Leader*, September 29, 1999.
17. Siona Carpenter, "Two Injured in Fire at P&G East Third Plant," *Lexington Herald-Leader*, October 6, 1990.
18. Gretz, interview.
19. William Covington, interview with the author, July 23, 2008.
20. Kiely, interview.

21. Neil Kreisberg, interview with the author, February 16, 2009.
22. Hunter Yager, interview with the author, March 7, 2009.
23. Ted Woehrle, interview with the author, January 28, 2009.
24. Ibid.
25. Kreisberg, interview.
26. Yager, interview.
27. Edward Meyer, interview with the author, March 7, 2009.
28. Woehrle, interview.
29. Kreisberg, interview.
30. Woehrle, interview.
31. Amy Baldwin, "Jif Spreads Its Three New Blends in Direction of Choosy Moms," *Lexington Herald-Leader*, September 8, 1999.
32. Keys, interview.
33. "Koogle: Does It Pass the Peanut Butter Test?," *Consumer Reports*, June 1975, 338.
34. Jim Jordan, "P&G Might Shed Its Jif Plant," *Lexington Herald-Leader*, April 26, 2001.
35. Ibid.
36. Janet Patton, "Jelly Buys Peanut Butter for $1 Billion," *Lexington Herald-Leader*, October 11, 2001. A tip of the hat to the headline writer for this article, whose subhead included the phrase "breadfellows unite," inspiring me to purloin it.
37. "A Match Made in Lunchbox Heaven," *Fortune*, October 29, 2001.
38. Robert Barker, "No Suckers, Those Smuckers," *Business Week*, March 4, 2002.
39. "Tyco International," en.wikipedia.org (accessed December 17, 2009).
40. "Dennis Kozlowski," en.wikipedia.org (accessed December 17, 2009).
41. Janet Patton, "Spread the News," *Lexington Herald-Leader*, December 30, 2003.
42. Don Taylor, interview with the author, August 13, 2008.
43. Don Koehler, interview with the author, October 1, 2008.
44. Ibid.
45. Bob Batz Jr., "Tale of Peanut Butter Festival Is Spread Thin," *Pittsburgh Post-Gazette*, September 14, 2006.
46. Max Brantley, "Ubiquitous Lunch Box Item Starts as Serious Business at LR Peanut Butter Plant," *Arkansas Gazette* (Little Rock, Ark.), August 16, 1982.
47. Larry Shearon, e-mail to the author, January 21, 2009.
48. Gibbons, interview.
49. Leslie Wagner (executive director of the Peanut Advisory Board, now the Southern Peanut Growers), e-mail to the author, June 4, 2011.
50. Statistics in this paragraph are from "Top Individual Brands: Peanut Butter—Total U.S. F/D/MX, Latest 52 Weeks Ending August 13, 2006" (Chicago: Information Resources Inc. [IRI], 2006), copy in possession of the author.

51. www.wackyuses.com/jif.html (accessed October 15, 2009).
52. "2000 Uses for Peanut Butter . . . and Then Some!," members.kconline.com /kerr/pb.htm (accessed December 27, 2009).

10. PEANUT BUTTER GOES INTERNATIONAL

1. "United States Export Statistics: Peanut Butter, Annual Series 2004–2009," chart compiled by Global Trade Information Services, Inc., and provided to the author by the American Peanut Council.
2. P. R. Ruparel (Rupa Foods, India), e-mail to the author, February 27, 2009.
3. Patricia Harris, David Lyon, and Sue McLaughlin, *The Meaning of Food* (Guilford, Conn.: Globe Pequot, 2005), 13.
4. Jasper Guy Woodroof, *Peanuts: Production, Processing, Products* (Westport, Conn.: AVI, 1983), 184.
5. Brian Sternthal, "Jif Peanut Butter," http://www.kellogg.northwestern.edu /faculty/sterntha/htm/module3/8.html (accessed June 15, 2008).
6. Norbert Blei, "There's Peanut Butter on My Finger (and a Warm Glow in My Heart)," *Chicago Tribune,* September 22, 1974.
7. All the statistics in this paragraph are from "United States Export Statistics: Peanut Butter, Annual Series 2004–2009." Thanks to Louise McKerchar in the London office of the American Peanut Council for checking my math.
8. Walt Albritton, interview with the author, October 3, 2008.
9. Patrick Archer, interview with the author, October 9, 2007.
10. Margaret Atwood, "Death by Landscape," in *The Norton Anthology of Short Fiction,* 7th ed., ed. Richard Bausch and R. V. Cassill (New York: Norton, 2006), 31.
11. "Squirrel (peanut butter)," en.wikipedia.org (accessed May 7, 2009).
12. "Peanut Butter/About Us," www.sanitarium.com.au (accessed March 26, 2008).
13. Melissa Norris, customer relations consultant for Sanitarium, e-mail to the author, March 26, 2008.
14. Charles Perry, "E Pluribus Chunky," *Los Angeles Times,* March 10, 1994.
15. Woodroof, *Peanuts,* 181.
16. Regine Zamor, e-mail to the author, April 21, 2010.
17. "Peanut Butter to Arrive in Haiti This Friday," www.alpeanuts.com (accessed January 31, 2010).
18. Regine Zamor, e-mail to the author, January 31, 2010.
19. Archer, interview.
20. "German Zoo Uses Peanut Butter to Catch Runaway Kangaroo," *Der Spiegel Online International,* May 20, 2008.
21. Leslie Wagner, interview with the author, July 20, 2008.

22. Rita Keys, interview with the author, July 20, 2008.
23. "Tour de France Team Finally Gets Their Peanut Butter," July 19, 1999, PR Newswire, www.highbeam.com (accessed January 3, 2009).
24. Arthur P. Henderson, "Portsmouth's Peanut Butter Firm Took Hosiery Plant," *Norfolk Ledger-Star*, March 14, 1964.
25. Don Koehler, interview with the author, October 1, 2008.
26. "Peanut Butter Urged for Famine Relief," *The Peanut Promoter*, February 1922, 13.
27. Celestine Bohlen, "All Russia Needs Now Is a Lot of Jelly," *New York Times*, June 7, 1992.
28. Archer, interview.
29. John H. Wilson and Rosemary Shenouda, "Saudi Arabia Offers Enticing Niche Markets, Too," *AgExporter*, December 1999, www.findarticles.com (accessed May 22, 2008).
30. "Middle East Combinations: Spread," *New York Times*, September 7, 1980.
31. Woodroof, *Peanuts*, 184.
32. Marc Prou, professor of Africana Studies at the University of Massachusetts at Boston, e-mail to the author, May 3, 2010.
33. William I. Lengeman III, "Beyond Jelly: Reinventing the Peanut Butter Sandwich," www.epicurean.com (accessed April 26, 2010).
34. Charles Perry, "Our Daily Spread," *Los Angeles Times*, March 10, 1994.
35. "Americans Buying More Peanut Butter," *Spread the News* (newsletter of the Adult Peanut Butter Lovers' Fan Club, published by the Peanut Advisory Board, now the Southern Peanut Growers), Summer 1997.
36. Jim Jordan, "P&G Might Shed Its Jif Plant," *Lexington Herald-Leader*, April 26, 2001.
37. David Guin, interview with the author, August 18, 2008.
38. Ray O. Hammons, "Origin and Early History of the Peanut," in *Peanut Science and Technology*, ed. Harold E. Pattee and Clyde T. Young (Yoakum, Tex.: American Peanut Research and Education Society, 1982), 16.
39. Andrew F. Smith, interview with the author, August 7, 2006.
40. Archer, interview.
41. Don Taylor, interview with the author, August 13, 2008.
42. John Powell, interview with the author, October 3, 2008.
43. In 1911 the amount of peanut butter produced in the United States was 22 million pounds, based on the figure of 1 million bushels used in W. R. Beattie, *Peanut Butter*, Circular no. 99 (Washington, D.C.: U.S. Department of Agriculture, Bureau of Plant Industry, 1912) and assuming 22 pounds per bushel of Virginia peanuts. By 1919 U.S. peanut butter production had grown to 6 to 8 million bushels (H. C. Thompson, *The Manufacture and Use of Peanut Butter*, Circular no. 128 [Washington, D.C.: U.S. Department of Agriculture, 1920]) or between 132 and 176 million pounds. More recently, the USDA's

National Agricultural Statistics Service indicated U.S. peanut butter consumption in 2007 and 2008 was 1 billion pounds (Peanut Institute, "Total U.S. Peanut Butter Consumption" chart, 1987/88–2007/08).

44. Woodroof, *Peanuts*, 183.
45. Dan Gorbet, interview with the author, December 4, 2007.
46. Leslie Wagner, interview with the author, November 5, 2008.
47. Leslie Wagner, interview with the author, January 10, 2007.

11. THE MUSIC OF PEANUT BUTTER

1. In Andrew Hamilton's biographical entry for the Marathons on www.allmusic.com (accessed January 28, 2011), he explains, "The five singers who sang on 'Peanut Butter,' a popular R&B novelty tune, were really the Vibrations masquerading as the Marathons." And a profile of the Olympics by Bryan Thomas on the same Web site, which is also cross-posted to www.emusic.com, notes, "Several members of the Olympics . . . recorded a cover of the Marathons' hit 'Peanut Butter.' . . . The song was essentially a rewrite of the Olympics' '(Baby) Hully Gully.' Arvee sued and acquired the 'Peanut Butter' master through contract-infringement litigation. They then rounded up some more singers (including a few Olympics) to record the successor to 'Peanut Butter' and other album tracks. What makes this more confusing is the fact that the Marathons had some, if not total, personnel overlap with the Vibrations on [the] Checker [label] (who had in 1956 been known as the Jayhawks). The same group also performed onstage as the Marathons. This initially has caused confusion as to whether the two groups shared the same lineup and who did which song and who was in which group at what time" (http://www.emusic.com/listen/#/artist/-/10555923/).

12. DEAF SMITH

1. Frank Ford, interview with the author, September 11, 2008.
2. Phil Rogers, posted on March 27, 2008, to "Deaf Smith County Peanut Butter" thread, started July 31, 2004, at citycomfortsblog.typepad.com (accessed January 21, 2009).
3. Boyd Foster, interview with the author, February 21, 2009.
4. Ibid.
5. Frank Ford, interview with the author, November 4, 2008.
6. Foster, interview.
7. Ford, interview, September 11, 2008.
8. Ibid.
9. George Speck, interview with the author, January 23, 2009.

10. Information about Deaf Smith (the man) comes from "Deaf Smith," en.wikipedia.org (accessed March 13, 2009).
11. "A Better Butter?," *Consumer Reports*, May 2002, 24.
12. Ford, interview, September 11, 2008.
13. Herb Marchman, interview with the author, March 4, 2009.
14. Natalie Johnson, "Nuts About Peanuts," on the College of Agricultural, Consumer and Environmental Sciences page of the Web site of New Mexico State University, http://aces.nmsu.edu/pubs/resourcesmag/fall98/peanuts.htm (accessed January 27, 2009).
15. Jimmie Shearer, interview with the author, January 21, 2009.
16. Johnson, "Nuts About Peanuts."
17. "Peanut Butter," *Consumer Reports*, August 1978, 435.
18. Leslie Wagner, executive director of the Peanut Advisory Board, now the Southern Peanut Growers, e-mail to the author, June 7, 2011.
19. Ford, interview, September 11, 2008.
20. Speck, interview.
21. Marchman, interview.
22. Norbert Blei, "There's Peanut Butter on My Finger (and a Warm Glow in My Heart)," *Chicago Tribune*, September 22, 1974.
23. "Peanut Butter," *Consumer Reports*, August 1987, 477.
24. Foster, interview.
25. When I accessed the "Our History" page of www.arrowheadmills.com on September 8, 2008, it stated that Arrowhead Mills had been purchased by Hain Celestial in 1999. But the 2001 annual report of the Hain Celestial Group lists 1998 as the purchase date, as does the article "Pact Is Reached to Acquire Natural Foods Businesses," *Wall Street Journal*, April 27, 1998.
26. Speck, interview.
27. Ford, interview, November 4, 2008.
28. David Sucher, posted April 22, 2008, to "I Am Still Getting Visits and Comments About Deaf Smith County Peanut Butter" thread on citycomfortsblog.typepad.com (accessed January 21, 2009).
29. Jim Fleischman, posted on April 29, 2008, to "I Am Still Getting Visits and Comments About Deaf Smith County Peanut Butter" thread started April 22, 2008, on citycomfortsblog.typepad.com (accessed January 21, 2009).
30. Diana Allen, posted on January 17, 2009, to "Deaf Smith County Peanut Butter" thread on citycomfortsblog.typepad.com (accessed January 21, 2009).
31. "The Captain," posted on January 11, 2006 to "Deaf Smith County Peanut Butter" thread on citycomfortsblog.typepad.com (accessed January 21, 2009).

13. THE RISE AND FALL OF THE FLORUNNER

1. "Peanut Butter," *Consumer Bulletin*, November 1970, 4.
2. "Real Old-Fashioned Peanut Butter—It's Better for You," *Consumer Bulletin*, September 1959, 2.
3. Dan Gorbet, interview with the author, August 28, 2008.
4. Dan Gorbet, interview with the author, September 29, 2008.
5. Stanley Pittman, interview with the author, July 8, 2008.
6. Frank Delfino, interview with the author, January 3, 2008.
7. Pittman, interview.
8. Gorbet, interview, September 29, 2008.
9. Dan Gorbet, interview with the author, June 23, 2010.
10. Don Koehler, interview with the author, October 1, 2008.
11. Gorbet, interview, September 29, 2008.
12. Koehler, interview.
13. Gorbet, interview, June 23, 2010.
14. Pittman, interview.
15. Gorbet, interview, June 23, 2010.
16. Ernest Hemingway, *Islands in the Stream* (New York: Scribner, 1970), 376.
17. Ibid.
18. William I. Lengeman III, "Beyond Jelly: Reinventing the Peanut Butter Sandwich," www.epicurean.com (accessed November 7, 2008).
19. Steven Rattner, "Peanuts: From Carver to Carter," *New York Times*, August 24, 1976.
20. Ibid.

14. THE PEANUT BUTTER CRISIS OF 1980

1. "Purchaser at Best Foods Faces Peanut Shortfall," *New York Times*, December 5, 1980.
2. "Summer Drought: A Grim Harvest," *Newsweek*, December 22, 1980, 6.
3. Ibid.
4. Clyde H. Farnsworth, "Peanut Prices: A Tug of War," *New York Times*, October 13, 1980.
5. David Pauly, "The Great Goober Gap," *Newsweek*, December 22, 1980, 69.
6. Ibid.
7. Farnsworth, "Peanut Prices."
8. Albert Nason, interview with the author, April 16, 2009.
9. "Purchaser at Best Foods Faces Peanut Shortfall."
10. Florence Fabricant, "Stores Face a Shortage of Peanut Butter," *New York Times*, January 28, 1981.

11. "Purchaser at Best Foods Faces Peanut Shortfall."
12. Charles Madigan, "More Than $500 a Ton? That's Just Peanuts," *Chicago Tribune*, January 4, 1981.
13. "Peanut Cost Soars After Poor Crop," *New York Times*, December 4, 1980.
14. "Peanut Import Quota Lifted," *New York Times*, December 6, 1980.
15. "Zookeepers Concerned About Shortage of Peanuts," *New York Times*, December 14, 1980.
16. "Quota for Imports of Peanuts Raised," *New York Times*, January 7, 1981.
17. Pauly, "The Great Goober Gap," 69.
18. "Purchaser at Best Foods Faces Peanut Shortfall."
19. Pauly, "The Great Goober Gap," 69.
20. "The Peanut-Butter Crunch," *Newsweek*, January 19, 1981, 76.
21. Pauly, "The Great Goober Gap," 69.
22. Fabricant, "Stores Face a Shortage of Peanut Butter."
23. "Peanut-Butter Crunch," 76.
24. Fabricant, "Stores Face a Shortage of Peanut Butter."
25. "Peanut Envy," *Time*, March 30, 1981.
26. "Doug Rauch Has Built a Better Mouth Trap—If the U.S. Is Bolled Over by Cotton Peanut Butter," *People*, May 4, 1981, 106.
27. Seth S. King, "Roasted Peanuts: Toll of the Drought," *New York Times*, February 1, 1981.
28. John Gretz, interview with the author, August 19, 2008.
29. Carl Bleier, interview with the author, September 30, 2008.
30. Seth S. King, "Peanut Crisis Eases, But It's Not Over Yet," *New York Times*, June 10, 1981.
31. Larry Shearon, interview with the author, November 7, 2008.
32. Rita Keys, interview with the author, July 20, 2008.
33. King, "Roasted Peanuts."
34. King, "Peanut Crisis Eases."
35. "Goobergate: The Maker of Peter Pan Peanut Butter Is Being Roasted by Texas Peanut Farmers," *Texas Monthly*, July 1983, 84.
36. Seth S. King, "Big Crops Forecast for Corn, Wheat," *New York Times*, August 13, 1981.
37. "Goobergate," 84.
38. "Swift Sued by Peanut Farmers," *Chicago Tribune*, July 17, 1982.
39. Clayton Lacy, interview with the author, April 15, 2009.
40. Web site of the Economic Research Service of the U.S. Department of Agriculture, http://ers.usda.gov/data/foodconsumption/FoodAvailIndex.htm.
41. Gretz, interview.

15. "YOU MEAN IT'S NOT GOOD FOR ME?"

1. "Aflatoxin Cited in Peanut Butter Recall," *Consumer Reports,* September 1976, 493.
2. "PB&J, Hold the Peanut Butter," *FDA Consumer,* November 1980, 30.
3. John Gretz, interview with the author, 19, 2008.
4. "Peanut Butter," *Consumer Reports,* May 1972, 288.
5. "Aflatoxin in Peanut Butter: A Tough Question," *Consumer Reports,* August 1978, 437.
6. Walt Albritton, interview with the author, October 3, 2008.
7. Ned Groth, interview with the author, July 7, 2010.
8. "Aflatoxins: Occurrence and Health Risks," on the "Plants Poisonous to Livestock" page of the Web site of the Cornell University Department of Animal Science, www.ansci.cornell.edu (accessed May 7, 2008).
9. Tim Sanders, interview with the author, August 11, 2008.
10. Groth, interview.
11. Ibid.
12. Ibid.
13. Roger O. Hirson, interview with the author, September 2, 2006.
14. Dr. Henry J. Heimlich, "'Dangerous' Peanut Butter," *New York Times Magazine,* January 18, 1981.
15. Christopher Weiss, interview with the author, July 8, 2010.
16. All statistics in this paragraph are from Dr. Scott Sicherer, e-mail to the author, July 2, 2010.
17. Scott H. Sicherer and Hugh A. Sampson, "Peanut Allergy: Emerging Concepts and Approaches for an Apparent Epidemic," *Journal of Allergy and Clinical Immunology* 120, no. 3 (2007): 492.
18. J. O. Hourihane et al., "The Impact of Government Advice to Pregnant Mothers Regarding Peanut Avoidance on the Prevalence of Peanut Allergy in United Kingdom Children at School Entry," *Journal of Allergy and Clinical Immunology* 19 (2007): 1197–1202.
19. Sicherer, e-mail to the author.
20. Amy M. Branum and Susan L. Lukacs, *Food Allergy Among U.S. Children: Trends in Prevalence and Hospitalizations,* NCHS Data Brief no. 10 (Hyattsville, Md.: National Center for Health Statistics, 2008).
21. Christopher Weiss, FAAN vice president for advocacy and government relations, e-mail to the author, April 4, 2011.
22. Although this theory intuitively makes sense to me—massive degradation of the environment contributes to health problems—Christopher Weiss, vice president of advocacy and government relations for the Food Allergy & Anaphylaxis Network, is dubious. "I don't think allergists would buy into this theory," he told me during a July 8, 2010, interview. "I would question whether this woman has true food allergies as opposed to intolerances."

23. See, for example, Jerome Groopman, "The Peanut Puzzle," *New Yorker*, July 7, 2011.
24. Don Koehler, interview with the author, October 1, 2008.
25. Manav Tanneeru, "Kids and Allergies: When PB&J Turns Dangerous," www.cnn.com, March 26, 2007.
26. Dr. Scott Sicherer, interview with the author, July 7, 2010.
27. Sicherer and Sampson, "Peanut Allergy," 492.
28. Greg Kocher, "Food Allergy Afflicted Families Form Support Group," *Lexington Herald-Leader*, July 30, 2006.
29. "Answers from Dr. Greene: Fatal Nut Allergy," A.D.A.M. Health Solutions Web site, www.adam.com; also on www.drgreene.com (accessed July 3, 2006).
30. Dan Brown, *The Da Vinci Code: Special Illustrated Edition* (New York: Doubleday, 2004), 414. Another example from contemporary fiction: Wyatt, a supporting character in Jon Michaud's *When Tito Loved Clara* (Chapel Hill, N.C.: Algonquin, 2011), suffers from a severe peanut allergy.
31. "Reactions and Stories: In Memory: Remembering Those Who've Had Fatal Food Reactions" on the discussion boards at www.foodallergysupport.com (accessed February 14, 2011).
32. Andrew F. Smith, e-mail to the author, February 20, 2010.
33. Sicherer, interview.
34. Weiss, interview.
35. Melissa Kossler Dutton, "Schools' Peanut Ban Sparks Backlash," *Orange County Register* (Santa Ana, Calif.), August 14, 2008.
36. Weiss, interview.
37. Ibid.
38. James Barron, "Dear Mr. Carver: This Is a Cease and Desist Order," *New York Times*, September 27, 1998.
39. Russ Bynum, "Ban Peanuts on Planes? It's Not Nutty to Those with an Allergy," *Deseret News*, March 13, 2010.
40. Jeff Brucculeri, "Salted Peanuts Are Under Attack at Baseball Stadiums," *Tulsa Beacon*, August 7, 2008.
41. Ibid.
42. "Can Your Peanut-Allergic Child be Treated by Simply Wearing a Patch?," *Science Transforming Life* (National Jewish Health newsletter, Denver, Colo.), vol. 2, no. 6 (June 2011), 2.
43. Dr. Scott Sicherer, "Note to Parents and Teachers," in *The Peanut-Free Café*, by Gloria Koster (Morton Grove, Ill.: Albert Whitman, 2006).
44. Gary List, interview with the author, June 16, 2009. For a more thorough discussion of peanut butter and trans fats, see chapter 4.
45. "USDA Study Says: Trans Fat Levels Are Not Detectable in Commercial Peanut Butter," *Food for Thought*, vol. 10, no. 2, n.d. Published by the Peanut Institute, www.peanut-institute.org.
46. Koehler, interview.

47. "Peanut Butter: Health Food or Diet Disaster?," *Glamour*, November 1988, 280.
48. *The Peanut Institute: A Snapshot* (Albany, Ga.: Peanut Institute, n.d.), 5, copy in possession of the author.
49. Ibid.
50. National Agricultural Statistics Service, U.S. Department of Agriculture, "Peanuts Disappearance: Availability by Type of Product" chart, http://www.ers.usda.gov/Data/FoodConsumption/FoodAvailSpreadsheets.htm. Scroll down to "Data Set: Peanuts" and click on "peanuts and tree nuts," then click on "peanut use" at the bottom of the screen. Information about peanut butter is in the third column from the left.
51. Pat Kearney, interview with the author, July 9, 2010.
52. *The Peanut Institute*, 14.
53. Marion Nestle, *What to Eat* (New York: North Point Press, 2006), 392.
54. *The Peanut Institute*, 6.
55. Ibid.
56. Peanut Institute, "Total U.S. Peanut Butter Consumption" bar graph on the Web site of the American Peanut Shellers Association, http://www.peanut-shellers.org/pdf/2009ConsumptionCharts.pdf, citing figures provided by the National Agricultural Statistics Service of the U.S. Department of Agriculture; there are four graphs: total peanut consumption, snack peanuts, peanut candy, and (the one you're looking for) peanut butter (accessed January 23, 2012).

16. THE SHORT, HAPPY LIFE OF SORRELLS PICKARD

1. Herb Dow, interview with the author, February 11, 2006.
2. Stanley Pittman, interview with the author, July 17, 2006.
3. Dan Gorbet, interview with the author, December 16, 2008.
4. First annual report of Sorrells Pickard Gourmet Peanut Butter, February 1998, copy in possession of the author.
5. Dave Hovet, interview with the author, October 2, 2006.
6. H. C. Thompson, *The Manufacture and Use of Peanut Butter*, Circular no. 128 (Washington, D.C.: U.S. Department of Agriculture, 1920).
7. Herb Dow, interview with the author, February 21, 2006.
8. Susan Schaben, "Sorrells Pickard Takes on Peanut Butter Giants," *Orange County Business Journal*, June 19, 2000.
9. Ibid.
10. Dow, interview, February 21, 2006.
11. First annual report of Sorrells Pickard Gourmet Peanut Butter, February 1998.
12. Dow, interview, February 11, 2006.
13. Hovet, interview.
14. Dow, interview, February 21, 2006.

17. PEANUT CORPORATION OF AMERICA

1. Louis Hoglund, "Death Linked to *Salmonella*, Family to Sue," *Enterprise-Bulletin* (Perham, Minn.), January 20, 2009, reprinted at www.foodhaccp.com (Food Safety Daily News) (accessed October 20, 2010).
2. Jeffrey Almer, testimony before the Subcommittee on Oversight and Investigations of the House Energy and Commerce Committee, February 10, 2009. Video of the subcommittee's hearing, "Peanut Butter *Salmonella* Outbreak" (http://www.c-spanvideo.org/program/283983-1), is available in the video library at www.c-span.org.
3. Hoglund, "Death Linked to *Salmonella*."
4. David Schardt, "Caution! On the Menu: Russian Roulette," *Nutrition Action Healthletter*, March 2010, 6.
5. Almer, testimony before the Subcommittee on Oversight and Investigations.
6. "Clifford Tousignant—One Family's Story," www.about-salmonella.com (accessed October 20, 2010).
7. Ibid.
8. "Clifford Frederick Tousignant," *Duluth News Tribune*, January 14, 2009.
9. Centers for Disease Control and Prevention, "Multistate Outbreak of *Salmonella* Infections Associated with Peanut Butter and Peanut Butter-Containing Products—United States, 2008–2009," Morbidity and Mortality Weekly Report, vol. 58, no. 4, February 6, 2009, 85–90, http://www.ncbi.nlm.nih.gov/pubmed/19194370 (accessed October 27, 2010).
10. Ibid.
11. William Marler, e-mail to the author, October 18, 2010.
12. "Officials Probe Peanut Butter as *Salmonella* Culprit," www.foxnews.com, January 10, 2009 (accessed January 10, 2009).
13. Chairman Bart Stupak (D-Mich.), opening statement at Subcommittee on Oversight and Investigations of the House Energy and Commerce Committee hearing on the PCA *Salmonella* outbreak, February 10, 2009.
14. "Kellogg to Recall Products Over *Salmonella* Concerns," www.cnn.com, January 16, 2009 (accessed February 3, 2009).
15. Susie Madrak, "FDA Announces New Product Recalls in Peanut Contamination," www.crooksandliars.com, February 3, 2009 (accessed February 3, 2009).
16. Dahleen Glanton, "Inside 'Nasty' Nut Processor," *Chicago Tribune*, February 6, 2009.
17. "First Animal Injured in *Salmonella* Outbreak," *USA Today*, February 7, 2009.
18. "Welcome to Peanut Corporation of America" page, www.peanutcorp.com (accessed January 6, 2009). Later that year, anyone accessing the site would only see instructions on how to file a claim for death or injury resulting from *Salmonella*. The Web site no longer exists.

19. Glanton, "Inside 'Nasty' Nut Processor."
20. Ibid.
21. Gardiner Harris, "Peanut Product Recall Grows in *Salmonella* Scare," *New York Times*, January 28, 2009.
22. Ibid.
23. Glanton, "Inside 'Nasty' Nut Processor"; "Inspection Findings: Georgia" section of "Peanut Corporation of America" article, en.wikipedia.org (accessed October 13, 2010).
24. Harris, "Peanut Product Recall Grows."
25. Ibid.
26. "Key Whistleblowers: Kenneth Kendrick" page at www.foodwhistleblower.org (accessed February 19, 2011).
27. Stewart Parnell, e-mail to Sammy Lightsey, August 21, 2008, cited in "The *Salmonella* Outbreak: The Continued Failure to Protect the Food Supply" page for the Democrats on the U.S. House Energy and Commerce Committee/Hearings: Subcommittee on Oversight and Investigations, http://democrats.energycommerce.house.gov/index.php?q=hearing/the-salmonella-outbreak-the-continued-failure-to-protect-the-food-supply (accessed November 1, 2010).
28. Stewart Parnell, e-mail to Sammy Lightsey, October 6, 2008, cited in "The *Salmonella* Outbreak" (accessed November 1, 2010).
29. Much of the information in this paragraph comes from Dan Chapman and Margaret Newkirk, "Blakely Plant Part of Firm with Humble Start," *Atlanta Journal-Constitution*, February 8, 2009.
30. "King Nut Issues Peanut Butter Recall," news release, www.kingnut.com, January 10, 2009 (accessed January 10, 2009).
31. Bob Keefe, "Troubled Peanut Firm's Chief Also an Industry Quality Adviser," *Atlanta Journal-Constitution*, January 31, 2009.
32. "Peanut Supplier Banned from Federal Business," *New York Times*, February 5, 2009.
33. Marler, e-mail, October 18, 2010.
34. Andrew Martin and Liz Robbins, "Fallout Widens as Buyers Shun Peanut Butter," *New York Times*, February 6, 2009.
35. Bo Emerson, "Peanut Fear Overtakes Its Comfort," *Atlanta Journal-Constitution*, February 17, 2009.
36. "Parker's Farm *Listeria* Recall Involves Cheese, Salsa, Peanut Butter," www.recalllawsuit.com (accessed May 6, 2010); "Parkers Farm Inc. Recalls Several Products Because of Possible Health Risk," January 8, 2010, www.fda.gov/Safety/Recalls/ (accessed February 21, 2011).
37. Brian Palmer, "Why Do Americans Love Peanut Butter?," www.slate.com, February 9, 2009 (accessed March 1, 2009).
38. "Georgia Plant Blamed for Peanut Butter Recall Lays Off Almost All Workers," www.wsbtv.com, January 22, 2009 (accessed January 23, 2009).

39. Harris, "Peanut Product Recall Grows."
40. Glanton, "Inside 'Nasty' Nut Processor."
41. "Texas Peanut Plant Shuts After Tests," *New York Times*, February 10, 2009.
42. Ilan Brat and Julie Jargon, "Career in Peanuts Began as Detour from Oceanography," online.wsj.com, February 18, 2009 (accessed March 17, 2009).
43. Christy Hardin Smith, "This Is Just Nuts!," www.firedoglake.com, February 4, 2009 (accessed February 7, 2009).
44. Schardt, "Caution! On the Menu: Russian Roulette."
45. "Death by Peanut Butter," *Providence Journal*, February 28, 2009.
46. "FDA Approves *Salmonella*," *The Onion*, March 12, 2009.
47. Hearing of the Subcommittee on Oversight and Investigations of the House Energy and Commerce Committee on peanut butter *Salmonella* outbreak, February 10, 2009. Video of the subcommittee's hearing, "Peanut Butter *Salmonella* Outbreak" (http://www.c-spanvideo.org/program/283983-1), is available in the video library at www.c-span.org.
48. "Peanut Corp. Owner Refuses to Testify to Congress," www.oregonlive.com, February 11, 2009 (accessed March 18, 2009).
49. William Marler, e-mail to the author, June 1, 2011.
50. Craig Schneider and Bob Keefe, "Blakely Peanut Illness: Little Has Changed Since Scare," *Atlanta Journal-Constitution*, January 31, 2010.
51. Marler, e-mail, October 18, 2010.
52. Schneider and Keefe, "Blakely Peanut Illness."
53. "Government Launches Criminal Probe in Peanut Recall," www.foxnews.com, January 31, 2009 (accessed October 27, 2010).
54. In a phone call during the week of October 18, 2010.
55. I spoke with both Stewart Parnell and his daughter, Katie, on October 27, 2010. She called me back the next day, telling me she had proof there had been no *Salmonella* in the Blakely plant. I asked her to send it to me but haven't received anything yet.
56. Brat and Jargon, "Career in Peanuts Began as Detour."
57. Much of the information in this paragraph comes from Chapman and Newkirk, "Blakely Plant Part of Firm with Humble Start."
58. Mary Clare Jalonick, "Ex-Peanut Exec Back to Work After *Salmonella* Case," *Atlanta Journal-Constitution*, September 8, 2010.
59. "Friends of Peanut Executive Laud Him," *Richmond Times-Dispatch*, February 17, 2009.
60. Marler, e-mail, October 18, 2010.

18. PEANUT BUTTER SAVES THE WORLD

1. Anderson Cooper, "A Life Saver Called "Plumpy'nut," www.cbsnews.com, October 21, 2007 (accessed October 30, 2007).

2. Ibid.
3. Ibid.
4. Ibid.
5. Mardi Manary, e-mail to the author, December 6, 2010.
6. Martin Enserink, "The Peanut Butter Debate," *Science*, October 3, 2008, 36.
7. Andrew Rice, "The Peanut Solution," *New York Times Magazine*, September 2, 2010.
8. Ibid.
9. Ibid.; Pooja Bhatia, "A Tremor for Haiti's Aid Industry," www.foreignpolicy.com, June 30, 2010 (accessed July 1, 2010).
10. Bhatia, "Tremor for Haiti's Aid Industry."
11. Enserink, "Peanut Butter Debate."
12. Rice, "Peanut Solution."
13. Ibid.
14. Ibid.
15. "Take Action" page, www.projectpeanutbutter.org (accessed November 8, 2010).
16. Mardi Manary, e-mail to the author, November 24, 2010.
17. "About" page, www.peanutbutterhouse.org (accessed October 7, 2010).
18. Rice, "Peanut Solution."
19. Marie Wisecup, e-mail to the author, December 10, 2010.
20. Enserink, "Peanut Butter Debate."
21. Rice, "Peanut Solution."
22. Ibid.
23. Manary, e-mail, November 24, 2010.
24. Ibid.
25. Rice, "Peanut Solution."
26. Ibid.
27. Ibid.
28. Bhatia, "Tremor for Haiti's Aid Industry."
29. Ibid.
30. Ibid.
31. Frank Delfino, interview with the author, October 24, 2007.
32. Ibid.

19. WHERE ARE THE PEANUT BUTTERS OF YESTERYEAR?

1. Kim Severson, "Who's Sticking with Us?," *New York Times*, February 4, 2009.
2. "Total U.S. Peanut Butter Consumption," chart prepared by the Peanut Institute, based on data released by the National Agricultural Statistics Association (NASS) on August 28, 2008, for 1988–2007, http://peanut-shellers.org/pdf/2009ConsumptionCharts.pdf (accessed January 7, 2011).

3. Michael Whitney, "Louisiana Fisherman: Oil 'Is a Total Disaster'," http://seminal.firedoglake.com/diary/53375 (accessed June 2, 2010).
4. Paul Bedard, "Washington Whispers," www.usnews.com, June 1, 2003, cited in Patricia B. Mitchell, "Choosy Moms and Others Choose: Jif," www.foodhistory.com (accessed November 20, 2010).
5. Maureen Dowd, "The Oval Intervention," *New York Times*, December 9, 2006.
6. Erik Dohlman, agricultural economist with the Economic Research Service of the U.S. Department of Agriculture, interview with the author, April 17, 2009.
7. Habiba Alcindor, "Black Farms, Black Markets," *The Nation*, September 11, 2006.
8. "Discrimination by USDA Against Black Farmers Gets Presidential," *The Daily Yonder* (Austin, Tex.), March 4, 2008.
9. Tadlock Cowen and Jody Feder, Congressional Research Service, "The Pigford Case: USDA Settlement of a Discrimination Suit by Black Farmers," January 13, 2009, www.wikileaks.org (accessed May 4, 2012). Also listed as "The Pigford Cases," www.nationalaglawcenter.org/assets/crs/RS20430.pdf, June 14, 2011 (accessed May 4, 2012).
10. Wendell Williams, interview with the author, September 29, 2008.
11. John Powell, interview with the author, October 3, 2008.
12. Richard Barnhill, president of Mazur & Hockman, Albany, Ga., interview with the author, November 30, 2010.
13. Ben Houston, interview with the author, August 6, 2008.
14. Ibid.
15. Craig Sonksen, interview with the author, November 12, 2010.
16. Ibid.
17. "Factory Takes Over Building Just Finished," *Tacoma Daily Ledger*, April 16, 1922.
18. "Laura Scudder," en.wikipedia.org (accessed March 12, 2007).
19. Bob Batz Jr., "Tale of Peanut Butter Festival Is Spread Thin," *Pittsburgh Post-Gazette*, September 14, 2006.
20. Tyron Spearman, interview with the author, November 23, 2010.
21. Walt Albritton, interview with the author, October 3, 2008.
22. Ibid.
23. Martin Andree, interview with the author, January 26, 2009.
24. Jeff Koeze, interview with the author, February 27, 2009.
25. Ibid.
26. "Peanut Butter: It's Not Just for Kids Anymore," *Consumer Reports*, September 1995, 576.
27. Don Taylor, interview with the author, August 13, 2008.
28. Barnhill, interview.
29. Robbyn Brooks, "Ready to Run," *Troy (Ala.) Messenger*, December 22, 2011.
30. Barnhill, interview.

31. techgirl, post to www.seriouseats.com thread "What's Your Favorite Way to Eat Peanut Butter?," started December 11, 2010 (accessed December 12, 2010).
32. Don Koehler, interview with the author, October 1, 2008. Other new peanut butter candies and confections include Snickers's Peanut Butter Squares and Trader Joe's Peanut Butter Goodies, which are vanilla cookies topped with peanut butter mousse and covered with milk chocolate and chopped peanuts.
33. Lee Zalben, interview with the author, May 4, 2006.
34. Koeze, interview.
35. Marion Nestle, e-mail to the author, May 8, 2011.
36. Martin Enserink, "The Peanut Butter Debate," *Science*, October 3, 2008, 36.
37. Poojah Bhatia, "A Tremor for Haiti's Aid Industry," *Foreign Policy*, June 30, 2010.
38. Ibid.
39. Koehler, interview.
40. Stanley Pittman, interview with the author, October 1, 2006.
41. Wil Parker, interview with the author, November 10, 2010.
42. Dan Gorbet, interview with the author, September 29, 2008.
43. "Genetically Modified Foods," www.answers.com (accessed November 8, 2010).
44. "Grower's Corner: Genomics Update," www.nationalpeanutboard.org/growers (accessed June 28, 2010).
45. Ibid.
46. Parker, interview.
47. Sonksen, interview.
48. Zalben, interview.
49. Norbert Blei, "There's Peanut Butter on My Finger (and a Warm Glow in My Heart)," *Chicago Tribune*, September 22, 1974.

INDEX

Page numbers in *italics* indicate illustrations.

ARTS AND TRADITIONS OF THE TABLE

PERSPECTIVES ON CULINARY HISTORY

ALBERT SONNENFELD, SERIES EDITOR

Salt: Grain of Life, Pierre Laszlo, translated by Mary Beth Mader

Culture of the Fork, Giovanni Rebora, translated by Albert Sonnenfeld

French Gastronomy: The History and Geography of a Passion, Jean-Robert Pitte, translated by Jody Gladding

Pasta: The Story of a Universal Food, Silvano Serventi and Françoise Sabban, translated by Antony Shugar

Slow Food: The Case for Taste, Carlo Petrini, translated by William McCuaig

Italian Cuisine: A Cultural History, Alberto Capatti and Massimo Montanari, translated by Áine O'Healy

British Food: An Extraordinary Thousand Years of History, Colin Spencer

A Revolution in Eating: How the Quest for Food Shaped America, James E. McWilliams

Sacred Cow, Mad Cow: A History of Food Fears, Madeleine Ferrières, translated by Jody Gladding

Molecular Gastronomy: Exploring the Science of Flavor, Hervé This, translated by M. B. DeBevoise

Food Is Culture, Massimo Montanari, translated by Albert Sonnenfeld

Kitchen Mysteries: Revealing the Science of Cooking, Hervé This, translated by Jody Gladding

Hog and Hominy: Soul Food from Africa to America, Frederick Douglass Opie

Gastropolis: Food and New York City, edited by Annie Hauck-Lawson and Jonathan Deutsch

Building a Meal: From Molecular Gastronomy to Culinary Constructivism, Hervé This, translated by M. B. DeBevoise

Eating History: Thirty Turning Points in the Making of American Cuisine, Andrew F. Smith

The Science of the Oven, Hervé This, translated by Jody Gladding

Pomodoro! A History of the Tomato in Italy, David Gentilcore

Cheese, Pears, and History in a Proverb, Massimo Montanari, translated by Beth Archer Brombert

Food and Faith in Christian Culture, edited by Ken Albala and Trudy Eden

The Kitchen as Laboratory: Reflections on the Science of Food and Cooking, edited by César Vega, Job Ubbink, and Erik van der Linden

Let the Meatballs Rest: And Other Stories About Food and Culture, Massimo Montanari, translated by Beth Brombert

The Secret Financial Life of Food: From Commodities Markets to Supermarkets, Kara Newman

Drinking History: Fifteen Turning Points in the Making of American Beverages, Andrew Smith